Complete the American Revolution!

What 9-11, Corporate Scandal and the 2000 Presidential Election Have in Common and What We Can Do about It

Albert Piacente

Hamilton Books
an imprint of
University Press of America,® Inc.
Dallas · Lanham · Boulder · New York · Oxford

Copyright © 2004 by
Hamilton Books
4501 Forbes Boulevard
Suite 200
Lanham, Maryland 20706
UPA Acquisitions Department (301) 459-3366

PO Box 317
Oxford
OX2 9RU, UK

Library of Congress Control Number: 2004102913
ISBN 0-7618-2901-6 (paperback : alk. ppr.)

I am not an advocate for frequent changes in laws and [institutions], but laws and institutions must go hand in hand with the progress of the human mind. As that becomes more developed, more enlightened, as new discoveries are made, new truths discovered and manners and opinions change, with the change of circumstances, institutions must advance also to keep pace with the times. We might as well require a man to wear still the coat which fitted him when a boy as civilized society to remain ever under the regimen of their...ancestors.

Thomas Jefferson
(bracketed passage and edit are mine.)

Contents

Preface

Feeling safe on that airplane? Sure you are. Someone with two weeks training lead a bomb-sniffing dog past your bag. Job and retirement secure? No sweat. Corporate executives and Wall Street brokers told you not to worry. Excited to vote again? Aren't we all? This time around I'm positive our votes won't be ignored either before they are cast or afterwards. .

Let's face it, something is rotten in more than the state of Denmark, something is rotten all over the world. So what are we going to do about it? Get tattoos or tongue studs, give $25 to Greenpeace and join a march supporting the oppressed group *du jour*? There's a solution to our ills; it's done so much good so far. Maybe we should give to charity or do some volunteer work; helping humanity one person at a time should only take forever. Better still, how about reading another self-help book written by some new-age, psychobabble guru that shows how to obtain spiritual contentment and financial success? That'll do the trick; there's nothing quite like putting our heads in the sand.

For decades we Americans, and people all over the world, have tried to ensure our security and happiness by fine-tuning the systems under which we live, or by retreating into our private, consumption-driven worlds. Neither path has proven successful. Deep down we know each is little more than a cosmetic covering something troubling: our governments are the captives of special interests, our businesses have grown inexorably in size yet not responsibility and our schools have become ineffective and corrupt. If we want to deal with all this, and gain security and opportunity as a result, we must rid ourselves of cosmetic concealments and do something difficult and courageous. We must turn to politics, *genuine* politics. Politics not mired in the worn out theories of past generations. Politics beyond the provenance of "activists" on the left or right. Politics that isn't played out in 30-second-TV commercials or on musical stages, in 3-minute-pop songs, by self-deluded rock stars who think they are making a difference.

Try this: think locally and act globally—just the opposite of the famed lefty bumper sticker. *Focus* on your most personal hopes, dreams and fears, those things closest to your heart, those things about which you lay awake at night worrying—not the problems and potential of "humanity," the "environment," "women," "African-Americans," etc. *Notice* most of your worries stem from your distrust of unfair political, economic and educational systems, systems that are unfair because they can limit your security and success, the security and success of your loved ones, and the security and success of people all over the world, without ever really considering us as individuals. *Think* about what will make those systems genuinely more fair, what will make them substantially more responsive to you, the people you love and people around world. *Act* to make them more fair and responsive, to change those systems no matter how global in nature. *Focus. Notice. Think. Act.* That is what I am trying to do. Join me. If you have ducked aircraft, been ignored at the polls, downsized by a company, mysteriously passed over for promotion, lost your retirement savings, inexplicably turned down by a school or denied any opportunity for security or success, join me. Reject the conservative/liberal divide. Reject current "identity" and single-issue politics. Reject the flight into gilded isolation. Reject the cynical belief that this is as good as things get. Accept the need for a *genuine* politics and public life. Accept that the only real security for yourself, your loved ones and the world at large requires system-wide political, economic and social reform.

* * *

As should be evident, I intend this book to produce action in the face of the concrete problems confronting each one of us. Read and judge it accordingly. Read it as a plan of action. Do not read it as you might read most other contemporary social/political commentary, looking for either a great deal of abstract scholarship or heated partisanship. We have had enough of both. It is time for "We, the people," in the many institutions we inhabit, to take sensible action. Read this book as an American colonist from the 18th Century might have read Thomas Paine's *Common Sense*; that is the style in which it is written.

I have abandoned, as much as possible, the style of "professional" intellectuals who do social/political commentary—and professional intellectuals in general—because such style does not serve the end of producing action. In-depth scholarly analysis laced with the minutiae of "scholarly" style, as well as the divisive rhetoric of most contemporary social/political journalism, produce feelings of division and alienation not unity and motivation. That is why I turned to the style of the 18th Century American pamphlet. At once direct and accessible to any literate person, I believe this style is better suited to appeal to a large cross section of our population, and to do so in a way that moves us to action. Almost all that you will find contained within this book then is a plan of action, and why I believe it to be the best plan of action given we face certain problems. There is very little appeal to "studies," statistics, scholarly works of various sorts or jargon. This is not a complete treatment of all the topics contained within therefore, meaning one that considers everything that anyone has ever said. Nor is this an attempt to address every political, economic, educational or social issue people believe is important and promote one side in the contemporary social/political spectrum. It is simply an attempt to use common sense to unify people behind a program of broad, system-wide change—change each individual in this country, and around the world, really needs and I believe most want.

I am not writing to "professional" intellectuals in other words. I am not writing to professors, journalists or pundits. I am writing to anyone who fears they or their loved ones could be the next victim of a terrorist attack. To employees at all levels—even executives—who feel trapped and insecure in their jobs, looking over their shoulders for pink slips every time their company's next quarterly report is issued. To workers who want full-time work but get only part-time offers. To small investors worrying about the security of their retirement. To citizens who feel ignored, bored and disaffected by politics, but who believe politics could be so much more. To students who can't get the classes they need, in the university they want, in a field that excites them. To mothers and fathers who work 50 to 60 hours a week, at home *and* at their job, and still feel they are failing themselves and their families. I am writing to anyone who believes the very institutions in which they are governed, work and learn cause most of their problems, most of the hardship and injustice they experience. Anyone who wants more security and opportunity through greater control of their destiny, regardless of whether they are old or young; male or female; well off, middle class or poor; black, brown, red, yellow or white; Christian, Muslim or Jew; straight, bi or gay. I write to these people, in a style I hope they find at once direct and to the point.

* * *

In structure, this book has two distinct parts. Chapters 1 and 5 constitute one part. It is here that I explain exactly what I mean by the seemingly outrageous claim that the American Revolution is incomplete, and then present reasons why I believe it should be completed. Chapters 2, 3, and 4 constitute the second part. It is in these chapters where I set out in detail what it might mean to complete the American Revolution. These three Chapters are intended to give a real vision of what America and the world could be if America remains loyal to its most fundamental creed. Both parts are to work together, but they can be separated. In fact, all of the ideas contained in this book are up for re-arrangement and revision as times and other people dictate. There is nothing final about what is said here. This is one person speaking to others, hoping to encourage deliberation and action, nothing more. Use what is contained within accordingly.

I must acknowledge a number of people who influenced me greatly. First and foremost are the Founders of the American nation and their intellectual ancestors. Chief among them Thomas Jefferson, John Adams, James Madison and most of all, Thomas Paine. Within a period of 30 years they made more political/social progress than the world has made in the intervening 200 years plus. They provide a model of what the socially committed, citizen intellectual should be, a model that I hope to emulate but will surely never match. In a more contemporary vein, John Dewey has been a constant inspiration for me as an action-oriented citizen intellectual, as well as a source of ideas about topics in philosophy, democratic theory and education. Frithjof Bergmann made it possible for me to get through the opening throes of graduate school without losing my soul, and to start down the road of connecting intellect and action. Richard Rorty allowed me to question the assumptions on which much contemporary intellectual debate is based, and showed me that it is possible to cut through the pretension of that debate like a warm knife through butter. Robert Dahl, Michael Walzer, Seyla Benhabib and Charles Derber removed my feelings of intellectual isolation simply by writing about concrete institutional change in a way I always wanted to, but never believed I could—or more importantly should.

I also must thank those who have given me personal support and encouragement, particularly Bob Gurland and my parents. As well, those who discussed with me or read one or all of the many incarnations of this essay: James Alvarez, Chien-Ju Chang, Tamara Davydova, Erich Deise, Baron Gera, Ian Gilchrest, Mark Goebel, Thomas Gundling, Ali Hashemi-Nejad, Tetsu Horikawa, Jennifer Jorczak, Natela Lolaev, Arthur Lothstein, David Park, Marjorie Piacente, Richard Rorty and Ariela Tubert, just to name a few. I can say in all honesty, much of what is good in this book, and none of what is bad, came from them.

Albert Piacente
New York, NY
December 14th, 2003

Chapter 1
Why Complete the American Revolution?
Part I:
A Common Sense Justification

I'm angry about 9-11. Not just that a lot of people died in the international version of a sucker-punch, but that now we've traded in the Cold War for yet another war that seemingly has no end: the "War on Terrorism." Somehow our peace and security keeps getting pushed off into the far distant future. This disappoints me. More so, it angers me.

I'm also angry about the never-ending slate of corporate scandals. I haven't lost my job or retirement savings but many have, and I'm subject to the same forces they were subject to. The employees and small stockholders of Enron, WorldCom, Tyco, Arthur Andersen, etc., not to mention countless customers of various Wall Street firms, were the powerless dupes of the ultra-rich and powerful, those in contemporary America who can manipulate the stock market and elections, by-pass the law and make themselves wealthy, all while impoverishing a lot of others. I know I could be next. This frightens me. It also makes me angry.

I'm angry about the 2000 presidential election as well. Not necessarily about who won—there wasn't a single candidate I favored to be honest. I'm angry about how they won. The will of the majority was overturned by some vestige of anti-democratic elitism left over from centuries ago, one of many in the Constitution intended to protect "We, the people" from ourselves,[1] though as we all know even the expression of that will has itself become blocked by a system polluted by wealth and insider influence.

I'm angry about these things and I'm guessing you are too, otherwise you wouldn't still be reading this. But we are focusing on only the tip of the iceberg. There is so much more to be angry about. An endless parade of lackluster candidates from whom we can choose with no more enthusiasm than if we were picking cherry or lime Jell-O from a hospital bed. Arrogant Democrats and Republicans who have a monopoly unseen in any area of American life since John D. Rockefeller, Andrew Carnagie and J.P. Morgan roamed the world. Media that is open to anyone as long as they can ensure a large enough revenue stream for the big-money interests by which the media is owned. Schools that don't work no matter how much support they are given. Businesses that don't care about anything beyond their executive's compensation and the short-term, bottom line. Families under stress due to overworked parents and under-cared-for children. The list goes on and on with each item a further reason for anger. But I am not here to tell you what you already know. I am here to suggest a reason why there are all these things to be angry about, and how we might be able to change them. Let me start by telling you a story.

As a teenager I worked in the shipping department of a sporting goods manufacturer; on the loading dock to be precise. My job was to pack tennis rackets and accessories into boxes and load those boxes onto trucks. It was hard work, as is most manual labor, but camaraderie among the guys on the loading dock made the time pass. The only real problem was our boss. Call him Mr. Jones.

Mr. Jones had gotten his first job with the company through a family connection when the company was small. As the company grew he ascended the corporate ladder to ever-higher levels of management and responsibility and for some reason had been put in charge of the entire shipping department; a position for which he had only the most limited training as far as any of us, his employees, could tell. The result was his leadership lacked direction, efficiency and hence, authority. This situation was exacerbated by the expanding number of people working in the shipping department, expanding almost weekly due to a rapid growth in business, so his negligible management skills were taxed to their fullest.

One day the situation came to a head. A batch of tennis racket covers— vinyl things that protect tennis rackets from damage—were to be shipped, but they had a defect. The defect could be righted by simply wiping the covers with furniture polish, a trick I had stumbled upon, so I suggested to my co-workers on the loading dock that we begin cleaning the covers and shipping them out. They agreed. We got to work. Upon getting word of this, Mr. Jones charged out of his office and, without asking anyone anything, proceeded to yell at all of us on the loading dock in front of the entire shipping department. When I say yelling, I mean yelling, yelling at a volume I had not heard since my mother saw me approaching a hot oven when I was a toddler. He claimed we had no authority to do what we were doing and in fact, for reasons never explained and left unknown, we were to ship the covers defect and all.

Considering our need for money, everyone at whom Mr. Jones had yelled took the calmest, legally allowed response to his action: we swallowed our pride and accepted the abuse—the least calm would have been quitting though some of us felt like abandoning legality altogether and slashing his car tires. We continued working on the loading dock until business slowed down and we were either laid off or quit.

That's how the story actually went, but let's say it went worse. Let's say Mr. Jones hadn't just yelled at us, demeaning as that was, but that he fired us on the spot. Fired us from these jobs that were not simply a means of making money but were our chosen careers. Not only were they our chosen careers but they were jobs we loved, completely identified ourselves with, and served as the sole source of income for the only other things that mattered to us, our spouses and children. Or, let's say we're fired not due to any incident involving Mr. Jones but due to some decision made by Mr. Jones' boss', boss', boss; some person none of us knew or had even heard of before, in a corporate office three thousand miles away, a decision that causes the need for "downsizing".[2] Or, let's completely change the situation and say it has nothing to do with our getting fired but rather with an idea we employees have for improving the loading dock, an idea Mr. Jones shoots down for reasons known only to him.

Extrapolating from what actually happened it is easy to see things could have gone worse on the loading dock, worse than they in fact went, but that's not really the important point of my story. What is the important point? What connection does any of this have with 9-11, corporate scandals, the 2000 Presidential Election or the other issues mentioned before? Well, the point is plain and simple. Many of our worst experiences, those seemingly isolated, personal experiences that make us feel insecure and humiliated, that breed so much of our fear, cynicism, anger and stress, connect with the larger events of the world, and they connect because they stem from the same problem.

Take the corporate scandals. What my co-workers and I experienced on that loading dock, and could have experienced had things gone worse, is exactly what the employees and small stockholders of Enron, WorldCom, Tyco, Arthur Andersen, etc. experienced: power wielded by those in charge, according to their own agenda, over employees and small stockholders who had no legally recognized control over how power was used and who used it—sure the small stockholders had a vote, but due to the rules surrounding stockholder voting they were subject to the corporate equivalent of Jim Crow (for more on this see "Reason 2" in this chapter). Our boss on the loading dock made his decisions in private and as he liked without his employees having any legally recognized say over who was boss or what the boss did, and so Enron's, WorldCom's Tyco's and Arthur Andersen's employees and small stockholders were equally powerless. What happened at Enron and the rest is what people placed above the employees and small stockholders in these corporations dictated, and that was that. End of story.

The same goes for the 2000 election. Here the connection with my loading-dock story might not be so obvious at first, but is probably more so given what we have just said about the recent, big corporate scandals. Though in the case of the 2000 election the citizenry was allowed to express its will—there was an election after all even if it was one corrupted by wealth and influence—that will was nonetheless ignored. Those over whom the power of the President was to be wielded, we citizens, did have a say in who should wield that power, but not a crucial say. Power in this case, as in the case of corporations or the loading dock, was exercised by those in control while they ignored the input of those they controlled. And they ignored them because they were allowed to ignore them.

9-11 is yet another example. At first the connection with my loading-dock story, as well as with corporate scandals and the 2000 Presidential Election for that matter, might seem even more tenuous than some of the other connections just made. It might seem that way until you realize that many people around the world view America as I view my former boss on the loading dock, as the former employees and small stockholders of Enron, WorldCom, Tyco and Arthur Andersen now view their former executives and board members, and as many American voters view the Electoral College, the Supreme Court and the American political system in general. America represents to many across the globe power used with little input by, or consideration for, the various peoples that will be affected by that power—an image which has only gotten worse since the advent of George W. Bush's unilateralism. Not to excuse the violence of 9-11, but this is the way America is viewed, and when you look at the American presence around the world you can see instances where this viewpoint is warranted. Please read this carefully. The viewpoint is warranted in certain instances, and more importantly, I DID NOT say the violent response is warranted. What response is warranted? That will come out in the course of this book, but the important point now is that this connection between 9-11 and these other events is there when you think about it.

My simple story from the loading dock and a million other similar stories from around the world, some of which you can tell I bet, are connected with 9-11, corporate scandals, the 2000 Presidential Election and a whole host of other issues. They are connected by the fact that power is used in American society, and throughout the world, in such a way that the voices of those over whom power is to be wielded are ignored, and they are ignored because by law they can be ignored. In each case there is a system in place, a set of institutions in which most of those inside the institutions lack ultimate control, or even a legally recognized voice that must be heeded. In some cases these institutions are political, in others economic, in still others educational. At times these institutions are inside one nation, in some cases a few nations, in others many. But regardless of the specific circumstances, in all cases the problem is the same. And this problem is not one problem among many. This is the central problem we face in American society and throughout the world today. It is why we have so many things to be angry about. It is why there are so many things wrong. It is the problem which, when dragged into the light, will show us how things can be different.

Of course, this runs counter to popular opinion. Most politicians, pundits, activists and social critics tell us we face other problems. Security concerns, recession worries, tax problems, welfare reform, growing poverty, racism and sexism, drug abuse, gun control, abortion strife, environmental disaster, declining family "values"; these are what typically come in for scrutiny when people start discussing the ills of America and the world. These are what get debated when campaigns turn to the "issues." These are what get covered on many news stations and TV and radio talk shows. But all their attention is undeserved. Not to say these aren't important issues, they're just not what we need to focus on. What we need to focus on is the problem behind the problems. We need to focus on the fact that to a limited extent in politics, and to a much less limited extent in the economy and educational system, we Americans, as well as people throughout the world, are given no controlling voice by law in the institutions of which we are a part. We are given no controlling voice, and this means a lack of power resulting in our having limited control over our security and limited opportunity for success. If we cannot choose *by law* who runs the political, economic and educational institutions we need, and in which all of us take part to one extent or another, then these institutions will not serve our interests and those of our loved ones. They will serve the interests of someone besides ourselves and our loved ones, often at the expense of ourselves and our loved ones. We must keep focused on the fact that it is this lack of a controlling voice by law, and the limited security and opportunity that ultimately results, which is behind such problems as our security concerns—what is terrorism besides the lashing out of the powerless in a symbolic and deadly way against those who they see as powerful? It is the problem behind poverty—what is poverty but a lack of economic security and opportunity? It is the problem behind racism and sexism—what are racism and sexism but a lack of equal political, economic and educational power and opportunity. It is the problem behind almost every problem we face both individually and socially; a problem that impacts everyone—though it certainly affects some more than others.

What I am saying is that 9-11, corporate scandals and the 2000 presidential election are just a few of the more well-known examples of a much larger problem, a problem for which we need an explanation if we are to find a solution. Why do we lack control by law in so many institutions? Is it the result of our natures, some facet of the human condition that cannot be changed as we need to be governed for our own good? Is it a conspiracy, something the rich and powerful have foisted upon us all? Maybe it is just a result of "white-male" dominated Western culture—the most popular whipping boy for everyone on the radical left these days? The answer is that it is none of these things. The cause is much more simple: the American Revolution has yet to be completed. We Americans, and people throughout the world, suffer to a more or less limited degree in politics and to a much greater degree in the economy and educational system with the same cronyist, insider, closed, uncompetitive, paternalist, inherited, aristocratic power structure that Americans suffered with throughout every part of society prior to the American Revolution. It is this paternalist, aristocratic power structure that caused 18th Century Americans to have no control by law over their political, economic and educational institutions. It is this paternalist, aristocratic power structure that still causes contemporary Americans and others around the world to have no control by law over certain political institutions—and *de facto* no control over almost every political institution—and across the board in our economic and educational institutions. This is why the 2000 Presidential Election happened the way it did. This is why Enron, WorldCom, Tyco, Arthur Andersen, etc. happened the way they did. And NOT to excuse the heinous criminality of the terrorists, I believe it is the ultimate cause of the events of 9-11. It is also the cause of much more exponentially greater in importance than just these events. Not to say that 9-11, corporate scandal and the 2000 election are unimportant, but we are talking about a problem that impacts every aspect of our lives every day of our lives, not something that happens only in the headlines of newspapers. However, more needs to be said about all this. Much more. For starters, what exactly do I mean when I claim the American Revolution is incomplete? More importantly, why is it incomplete? I turn to these questions now.

The American Revolution Isn't Complete?!

Whatever it was initially, the American Revolution became an experiment in democracy. It became an attempt to see if a better society could be created, and hence a better life for the individual, by giving the individual a legally recognized say in how society functions and control over the powers that be. It became an attempt to see if power could be non-violently transferred other than by inheritance. It became an attempt to challenge the-long standing aristocratic idea that rank, and the privileges associated with rank, should be transferred based on blood.

To be a bit more precise, the American Revolution became a test of the following principle, the principle at the heart of the most famous rallying cry of the Revolution "No taxation without representation": *No one should hold power over us without our permission*. And who is the "us"? Anyone over whom power is to be wielded. As John Adams put the point:

> ...Metaphysicians and politicians may dispute forever, but they will never find any other moral principle or foundation of rule or obedience, than the consent of governors and governed.[3]

The Revolution became a test of this "Consent Principle," as we can term it for obvious reasons, as well as a test of the optimism that underlies it. The optimism that people can control their own destinies by ruling themselves. The optimism that people are capable of changing things for the better including themselves. The optimism that blames "badness" not on "human nature" but on a lack of freedom and opportunity. The optimism that adults could be treated as adults, that they do not need a surrogate parent in the person of a monarch or other leader.

I say the American Revolution *became* an experiment in democracy, *became* a challenge to the notion of paternalistic, aristocratic, inherited power, because in its beginnings the goal of the Revolution, as well as the means to achieve it, was different to different people. It is not even clear that the many diverse actors of the period shared any ideological or programmatic unity making them a single Revolutionary movement. About the only thing that tied them together was their love of freedom.[4] This ultimately provided very little ideological or programmatic unity however, because it was unclear then, as it often is now, just what a love of freedom commits one to either as an individual or a society. It was certainly unclear, particularly to the citizen intellectuals and politicians of the time, that a love of freedom committed one to democracy. People in the 18th Century did not share our present confidence that democracy is the best way to guarantee freedom. Many people of the period feared democracy in fact, believing a democratic society would be lawless and anarchic, yielding terror not freedom.

This anti-democratic sentiment found many different expressions. Some claimed we must maintain a monarch and install a hereditary "nobility" as a check on popular "excess":

> A number of writers came to the conclusion that the only solution [to the problems facing the Colonies prior to the Revolution] was the creation of a privileged social order.... Ideally, Governer Bernard [Govenor of Massachusets] wrote, an hereditary nobility should be created in the colonies. And though he acknowledged that America was not yet "(and probably will not be for many years to come) ripe enough for an hereditary *nobility*," he saw no reason why "a *nobility* for life could not be established at once.[5]

Others believed that the American government should be a constitutional monarchy:

> Madison's arguments for a national government and Mason's in opposition demarcated the broad outlines of "debate" over the Constitution.... Opinion ranged from extreme antifederalists whose

views verged on "Switzering anarchy"...to extreme nationalists who
seemed to favor a constitutional monarchy rather than a republic....[6]

And regardless of how the government itself was to be organized, the
opinions of many about "the people" and "democracy" were very low:

> To them it did not seem reasonable to "collect and assemble
> together the tailors and the cobblers and the ploughsmen and the
> shepherds" of a vast domain and expect them to "treat and resolve
> about matters of the highest importance of state."* They would not
> know enough in government, they would not be suffcently
> disinterested or independent of pressures to manage a government
> properly. Surely tradition and the lessons of history indicated that
> without an economically independent, educated, leisured order of
> society standing securely and permanently above the petty selfisness
> of the multitudes of ordinary men scattered through half a continent,
> nothing could be expressed in government but the "infinite diversity
> of particular interests [and] dissonant opinions"; and the result
> might well be chaos."[7]

No less a figure than John Adams, in response to radical democrats
such as Thomas Paine in *Common Sense* or the much more radical anonymous
author of the pamphlet *The People the Best Governers*, feared a government
based on the idea that: "The people know best their own wants and necessities,
and therefore are best able to rule themselves." Adams feared it because:

> ...government so democratical, without any restraint or even an
> attempt at any equilibrium or counterpoise...must produce confusion
> and every evil work.[8]

Even the arch-patriot George Washington was still toasting the King's
health with his officers in the early years of his leadership of the Revolutionary
Army, and colleagues felt comfortable making the following claim to him as late
as 1787:

> And however absurd the idea, you will agree with me the men must
> be treated as men and not machines, much less as philosophers, and
> least of all things as reasonable creatures; seeing in effect they
> reason not to direct but to excuse their conduct.[9]

Despite these fears, and in the face of opposition, a level of
programmatic unity was ultimately achieved between various competing parties,

and a democratic system was central to that program. The leaders of this nation drafted a democratic Constitution, a Constitution then accepted by the people's representatives in the thirteen states. However, these first steps taken towards making American society democratic, towards basing it on the Consent Principle and the optimism underlying it, were taken with hesitation. That is why I call democracy a "test" and "experiment". They were taken with hesitation because the effect of doing this was thought to be *very* uncertain. As we have seen, many 18th Century American leaders, and 18th Century Americans in general, were unconvinced a society based on the Consent Principle could work. They took the chance nonetheless, and the experiment in democracy was begun.

It was only a limited experiment however. The democratic system adopted was a compromise meant to appease constituencies with various views on the extent and type of democracy to be enacted. We can see this in terms of the spectrum in Figure 1:

| Constitutional Monarchist | Mixed System U S Constitution of 1789 | Extreme Democrat |
| Alexander Hamilton | John Adams | Thomas Paine |

Figure 1

On the extreme left hand side is the most conservative ideological slant, one represented well by Alexander Hamilton. The main concern of those on the left was to safeguard America against the "baser" parts of society, and to make sure that those who were "natural betters" were given a dominant role in the governance of this country.[10] These people wanted to limit democracy in the extreme, to ensure that the government still functioned much like a surrogate parent to the citizens of this country. To put this in more cynical terms, their paramount desire was to maintain the existing status quo in terms of who had wealth and power and who did not, maintain it under the guise of providing a leisured class that was better suited to rule. On the extreme right hand side is the most radical ideological slant, one represented well by Thomas Paine. The main concern here was to eliminate the existence of absolute power, particularly as a privilege given by birth.[11] They were concerned to maximize individual liberty by minimizing government's control over the individual. To them, the system should be as democratic as possible. In the center is the actual system adopted, as we all know, and it was a system meant to capture ideas from both the extremes. This centrist position is well represented by John Adams, though ultimately most of the pantheon of American Revolutionary heroes would fit here as well, including Thomas Jefferson, Benjamin Franklin and George Washington. This compromise position removed the ability of anyone to obtain absolute power by basing all law on the Consent Principle, yet it assured that consent was not always directly given. It was a system based on a watered down Consent Principle, one where very little direct control was had by the people over those in power, but a great degree of indirect and limited control was had.

That the American system, as captured in the United States Constitution of 1789, was a compromise between these two extremes might come as a surprise to some of you. Our national myth suggests that everyone at the Constitutional Convention, and everyone involved on the American side in the Revolution for that matter, was committed to an absolute, unlimited democracy. The whole Revolution is romantically viewed by many to be a contest between British monarchists and American democrats. That there was anti-democratic sentiment among even our most famous Founders can be a shock. Nonetheless, the sentiment was there, and the evidence that our system was a compromise meant to appease some of this sentiment shines through, particularly in the Constitution itself.

Overall, the Constitution's tone is quite democratic. The document is established in the name of "We, the people...", showing support for the basic democratic idea that the only legitimate base for authority is the consent of the governed. The fundamental structure of the government it outlines is democratic as well. Power in the United States was ultimately to rest in the hands of those either directly chosen by the people, or indirectly through a number of complex mechanisms involving their representatives at various levels of government.

Beyond this though, much of the Constitution is very anti-democratic. Many of the subtleties of the Constitution were worked out to ensure those in power were not directly impacted by "the people" to any great extent. The model of relatively direct democracy outlined in Thomas Paine's *Common Sense* was rejected. It was rejected in favor of a bicameral, representative legislature, a balance of power among branches of government, and other complex pieces of governmental organization limiting control of the government by the direct voice of the people.[12] John Adams' model of democracy, whose fears regarding a thorough going democracy we have already seen, won out over Paine's.

Anti-democratic fears were assuaged in more direct and obvious ways. For instance, extreme limitations were placed on suffrage. Not only was a substantial minority of the population held as property until the Civil War and the passage of the 15th Amendment in 1870, and hence could not vote, but fully half the population was not eligible to vote until 1920 with the passage of the 19th Amendment. Beyond these and other limitations on suffrage the United States Senate was established as a group not beholden to any direct democratic process, on the model of the Roman Senate, and the chief executive was chosen by an unelected "college of electors" not simply through direct general election—as we are now painfully aware.

However, limitations on the democratic experiment in America went well beyond just these more or less subtle, formal strictures in the Constitution.

Democracy was tried in government, with the limitations we have just discussed, but no other arenas of power were democratized in any way. Probably a sensible policy as the more limited the experiment the more limited the damage if it fails—though I doubt the founders of this country saw it this way—no one involved in creating American democracy ever really discussed extending the democratic experiment outside the political arena. The thought never seemed to enter their minds in fact.   The leaders of the American Revolution were definitely of the 18th Century, seeing power as primarily vested in government. They had not experienced the industrial revolution, which showed that extreme amounts of power could be concentrated in non-political institutions, institutions that could then threaten freedom as much as, and in similar ways to, the government itself.

In 18th Century America the only centralized, organized power that existed across large geographic areas was political power.   Economic, educational and other potential centers of power were not organized sufficiently to create the problems that political power had created. As such, they were not seen as a threat to freedom. It would not have dawned on an 18th Century American to fear concentrated economic or educational power because there was no such thing. In America at the time, the vast majority of the population was economically and educationally self-supporting on small independent farms and in small school houses—in the rare cases where these small school houses were available—spread across the countryside. It was this class of self-sufficient, free, "yeomen" farmers that Jefferson envisioned as the basis of the American democratic order in fact.   There was only the barest hint, in some of the interchange between Hamilton the urban conservative and Jefferson the agrarian liberal, that concentrations of wealth might ultimately present problems for "the people".   But this never brought any discussion about experimenting with democracy to control this power, as democracy was being experimented with to control political power.   Had most 18th Century American Revolutionaries foreseen the potential for the concentration of economic and educational power, a concentration like the one we now experience, they would most likely have feared it as well. The American Constitution may even have ended up a very different document.   However, they did not see this, and could not have I believe, and thus the experiment took the shape that we all know.

This is the experiment that was tried. It was a limited test of the Consent Principle.   It ended *by law*, but not *in fact*, most paternalistic, aristocratic, permanent, inherited, blood-based power in politics. It did not touch such power anywhere else. It made the citizenry adults in some ways, but left our political institutions our parents at times, and almost all other institutions of which we were members our parents at all times.   Because of these limitations, the test of this principle is not yet complete. Given the American Revolution is ultimately a test of this principle, the Revolution is incomplete. Not that our system is that bad—the world has been, and is now, filled with systems far worse. In pointing out the limited nature of the democratic experiment in America I do not mean to criticize what was done in the past. The Constitution is a great document, and this experiment in limited democracy, in a limited application of the Consent Principle, has been a rousing success. My only point here has been that the American Revolution, as the historical embodiment of the Consent Principle, is not yet complete.

6 Reasons to Complete the American Revolution

You now know what I mean when I say the American Revolution is incomplete, and why I believe it is incomplete. Given this, we need to confront another question: Why should we complete the American Revolution as I suggest in the title of this book? Why should we extend democracy throughout politics as well as business and education? It is a very natural tendency not to want to rock the boat needlessly and that might seem what I am suggesting. Why change the way things work right now?

Reason 1: No More 9-11's
The most basic cause of 9-11 is the powerlessness, the exclusion from the world power structure, felt by so many in the face of the dominance of the United States, the West and its allies in general. Not that such powerlessness justifies blowing up buildings, as I said before and as I am saying again now, because **blowing up buildings is unjust, stupid and worst of all not a solution to this problem of powerlessness even for those who are powerless**. Many throughout the United States have suffered greatly as a result of terrorist attacks, but many throughout the world will suffer far worse in the face of the United States' and the world's response, many who these attacks were intended to "help". The terrorists are really hurting those they claim they are trying to champion. To which some of you might respond, particularly if you live in places targeted by terrorists: who cares? But this is foolhardy if we are out to prevent something like 9-11 from happening again, as we all ought to be. 9-11 is a disaster for the United States, for the people those who committed the attacks were trying to help, and for everyone on the planet as it has destabilized the world. Therefore, we must ask what we can do about the powerless, the well-spring of terrorism, from whom could issue forth another 9-11 or something even worse?

What we can and must do, of course, is cap this well-spring. The problem is that the way we cap this well-spring must be different than the way we have dealt before with other sources of violent international conflict. In the past when violent international conflict has arisen, the most common method for eliminating the cause of the conflict has been to attack the nation from which the problem emanated. For instance, WWII had its genesis in the United States at Pearl Harbor—the event most closely akin to 9-11—and the American response to eliminating the cause of the conflict was to attack Japan and its allies. Traditionally, violent international conflicts have been understood as conflicts between *nations* and they were dealt with accordingly. The offending nation, or more accurately the offending regime in the other nation, was attacked thereby getting at the root problem that caused the attack in the first place. *However, the violent international conflict with which we are now involved cannot be understood in this way.*

The powerless are diffused around the world throughout nations of all sorts, including even the U.S., with various religious, cultural, ethnic and other axes to grind. Some of them have taken up terrorism, but most have taken no action of any sort but simply form the raw material for future attacks not yet imagined. The powerless are on every continent, in every geographic clime. As a result, our response to this conflict must be different than it has been to past conflicts. We cannot understand this as a military conflict between *nations*. That is why the current policy of the United States and its allies is the wrong policy. They are trying to fight a war, and to do so on the traditional model. There is little doubt that this will result in justice being brought to some who have before, or are now, engaging it acts of terrorism, but it will do little to get at the root problem, powerlessness, and it will most likely create many more terrorists than it eliminates. The "War on Terrorism" does not work to include those who feel excluded from the world's power structure, it might even make them feel more excluded, thus exacerbating the problem. The policy of the Untied States and its allies not only fails to get to the root problem but simply is not one that can be sustained for very long. What are the U.S., Great Britain, etc., supposed to do, attack every country where there are terrorists or potential terrorists? They cannot afford this economically, politically or socially, not to mention that they would end up attacking many who had nothing to do with terrorism and again, only make matters worse. This conflict is fundamentally different and therefore if it is to be fought well, meaning by well that the cause of the conflict gets removed without creating more of a problem in the process, then it must be fought differently than violent conflicts in the past have been fought, with wars between nations. It must be fought by institutions other than nation states and the organizations that revolve around the nation-state system, organizations like the UN. This conflict is truly international in that every nation is involved with no one nation or even group of nations easily identifiable as the guilty party in every, or even most, cases—there is no "axis of evil". What is needed to fight this conflict then is an organization, or some set of organizations, that is truly international in a way unlike all other organizations on earth, a type of international organization that can get to the powerless all over the world *and make them empowered.* We need organizations that transcend traditional national boundaries and are capable of including not excluding people from the world power structure. Are there such organizations? There are, and they are called multi-national corporations. I believe the solution to this conflict lies in global, multi-national corporations. *Globalization can be the basis of a just "new world order" that empowers the unempowered and thereby eliminates the cause of terrorism.*

Economic globalization has been over the past 100 years or more, though increasingly in the past 30, one of the most important events occurring internationally. The advent of hundreds of truly multi-national corporations, with holdings and employees across the globe, has altered the human landscape as much as any event in history. And almost without exception this alteration has been viewed with hostility by anyone not part of the power elite. To workers in the United States it is a way of stealing their jobs and giving them to under-paid, exploited workers in the Third World. To people in the Third World it is the latest and arguably greatest variety of imperialism yet experienced, a variety of imperialism possibly worthy of committing 9-11—years of political imperialism overthrown only to be replaced by a *deep* economic *and* cultural imperialism euphemistically called globalization. To supporters of democracy and human rights it is a way for corporations to become more powerful than governments and hence undermine constitutional guarantees of rights and democratic process. To environmentalists it is a way of turning the entire world's resources over to their merciless grim reaper: international big business. To these groups and others, globalization is not only a threat it is *the* threat. And the way these groups have chosen to confront this threat? End, or at least control and weaken, globalization. That is a large part of what 9-11 was an attempt to do. Why else make the focal point of the attack the *World Trade* Center? That is what the 1999 Seattle protests, as well as a number of other protests throughout the world against the International Monetary Fund, World Trade Organization and World Economic Forum have been an attempt to do. That is why many speak about putting trade tariffs and environmental treaties in place. That is the issue that has hung up a number of major labor contracts in the manufacturing sector throughout the world economy and ultimately resulted in strikes. Globalization is viewed by almost every group on the planet that takes itself to be seeking justice as its enemy. They are all wrong.

Rather than fighting globalization, a futile battle for terrorist, labor union, protestor and national government alike, it should be fostered, fostered *as long as* the multi-national corporations in question are governed democratically.[13] If these corporations are made democratic, globalization will promote democracy and justice around the world, not inhibit it. It will give corporate employees in the Third World voting power in the institutions for which they work, and hence a chance to end their own exploitation and the rape of their natural resources, while being imbued with the virtues of democracy for, most likely, the first time. It will give corporate employees in the United States a way of working out, in a fashion acceptable to all, differences with their corporate executives—whom they would elect as Americans now elect Congress and the President—and their fellow corporate employees in other parts of the U.S. and the globe—all of whom get to vote. It will aid in the spread of democratic government, not undermine it, by setting up a working democratic model in many countries that have no such model, thus aiding the spread of democracy to an extent unimagined by national governments acting under the constraints of nation-state driven foreign policy—democracy cannot be imposed from without through "nation building" but might grow from within. It will provide the United States and its allies with its first consistent foreign policy in the post-Cold War era, as the spread of democracy and the spread of commerce will go hand in hand. Most importantly, it will aid, in a way no action has yet, the elimination of the powerlessness that caused 9-11 and that forms the fertile ground for so much future terrorism worldwide. It will aid this by giving peoples around the world, whether employees of IBM, Microsoft, Nike, Burger King, GM, Coke, Banana Republic or the host of other corporations that run all over the face of the globe, direct impact in the policies of these corporations thereby making them an effective, potent force. Globalization, if multi-national corporations are made to run democratically, means gradual worldwide inclusion and empowerment and hence the slow but sure removal of the cause of past and future 9-11's. Globalization can become, simply by *altering the mechanism of corporate governance*, the greatest boon to democracy yet seen worldwide. In fact, it would become the opening step in what has been only a dream to many: the creation of an international democratic order. If we are out to prevent another 9-11 and to see democracy spread around the world, this *will not* happen through political or military means such as treaties, coalitions, smart bombs or the United Nations. It can and *will* happen through inclusionary economic means, if we create a global web of democratically governed multi-national corporations.

Alter the mechanism of corporate governance and globalization becomes the best gradual, non-coercive means of fostering an inclusionary, just world order. Fail to alter the mechanism of corporate governance, leave the world economic power structure as it is now, and globalization remains what it is now: the means of establishing the hegemony of corporations and their ilk over peoples of every culture, ethnicity, race, and religion, including the very nation states that have long been taken to be the check on these corporations, with injustice and violence as the result. We all know that the true international order is now economic. The nation-state has been replaced by the multi-national corporation as the genuine seat of power internationally, with no other organization of a religious or cultural variety even coming close to replacing the nation state as a check on this economic order. As such, the policies of multi-national corporations, if corporations are left undemocratic, will be set by their corporate leadership, with the complicity of the world's political leaders whom that corporate leadership controls in ways both direct and indirect, policies that will undoubtedly benefit mostly that leadership and the large shareholders who put them in power. This means a world order dominated by policies that serve only a small fraction of the world's population, hence creating injustice and ultimately violence. There is no way to stop this, there is no way to stop a continuous series of 9-11's emanating from peoples across the globe who feel their spiritual, cultural and ultimately material livelihoods are threatened, because no existing institution can regulate globalization. Either we alter the mechanism of corporate governance or globalization runs unregulated and unchecked, with all the injustice and violence that engenders. There is no middle ground. Governments, treaties, unions, protestors and terrorists have all tried to stop globalization, or at least slow it down and make it more just. They have all failed. The international order has passed by such essentially nation-state-based efforts. The dominance of corporations is here. Either they are made just by being made democratic, or unchecked injustice and violence continues to be the order of the day.

We have now come to our first reason for completing the American Revolution. Completing the American Revolution means extending democracy into the realm of business, particularly the large multi-national corporation, thereby creating the best chance for establishing a more just international order and hence a more peaceful world. By not completing the American Revolution, we almost certainly guarantee an increasingly rapid slide into terrorist and other violence caused by an unjust international order. Why complete the American Revolution? To bring the virtues of democracy all over the world through a non-coercive, gradual method that will undermine the causes of terrorism and forward the prospects for peace. Otherwise, prepare for more 9-11's.

Reason 2: No More Corporate Scandals

We have been talking about powerlessness around the world, but now we need to talk more directly about powerlessness at home. As was suggested above, it is not just the individual in the Third World that feels the sting of insecurity as a result of having little control over their destiny, especially their economic destiny. Employees and small investors throughout America have this same feeling, especially employees and investors in big business, and the recent slate of corporate scandals have shown to many the source of much of that feeling: a power elite controlling their economic destiny. That is why corporate scandal has become more than simply a business story, more than just corporate bankruptcy and corruption playing itself out in the financial pages. Enron, WorldCom, Tyco, Arthur Andersen and the host of Wall Street scandals have hit a raw nerve in the United States. Many realize, as they had apparently forgotten during the heady days of the NASDAQ bubble, dotcoms and the "surging" economy, that economic security, and that means our most basic security, is easily lost. It is easily lost in the face of forces currently outside our control. It easily lost in the face of institutions over which we have no control. The secure job of today is downsized tomorrow. The full-time employee becomes the outsourced part timer. Ample retirement savings worked for over years are turned worthless by a few bad weeks on the stock market. So what can we do about it?

The answer here is the same as in the international case because the problem is the same: powerlessness. We must extend democracy into the economic realm.[14] We must make sure that businesses, at least of a certain size, are democratically governed. We must make sure that *all* employees of big business, management *and* labor, have direct, *legally* recognized, input into who runs where they work and hence controls their economic lives—as for the role of investors in this, see Chapter 3. We must place our economic institutions of all sorts on the consent basis that our political institutions were partially placed on hundreds of years ago.

Short of doing this, we are left with the few mechanisms for controlling our economic lives which have all proven themselves inadequate. The first and foremost of these has been the exercise of our essential free-market right: the right to leave by quitting or selling. The problem is that though we always have a legal right to leave any economic institution we dislike, this makes no *real* difference in the control we have over our economic lives. The economy is dominated by institutions such as large corporations, banks, insurance companies and the like, and the ability to leave one of these institutions gives us no control over that, or any other, institution. Leaving provides no real control at all.[15] Leaving may alter the characters in the drama but it doesn't alter the basic relationship between ourselves and whoever is controlling the economic institutions making the judgments impacting our security and opportunity[16]. No matter how many times we move on, if we are not given any direct control over those in charge *by law*, then we are not *really* in control. Who cares that we are free to move from one economic institution to another, from one job or investment to another to put it simply, if we may find ourselves in the exact same situation we are trying to flee, or one even worse? When we make bowing out the only way we can control *by law* those making the judgments impacting our economic security and success, we have condemned ourselves to having almost no control whatsoever—not to mention the harrowing experience of throwing our economic lives into upheaval.

It is strange that so many people suggest the ability to leave a situation means you have control over that situation. It is strange because we do not accept that leaving is control when it comes to many aspects of the government, the Congress for instance. If I said to Americans we should not be allowed to vote for members of Congress as long as we are free to leave the country whenever we choose, they would recoil in horror. In this case we think voting is the only real control. We think control through consent given *by law* is the only way to have power. To say we need no more control than the ability to flee, that the freedom to leave is all the freedom we need, that there are plenty of other nice countries out there so why not move elsewhere, would seem completely inadequate to most Americans, almost ridiculous. So why is it any better as a response to what I am saying about those running our businesses and the economy in general? It isn't a better response. Therefore, why don't we be honest and admit that if we cannot vote for those in charge of the economic institutions of which we are a part, then we are not in control?

It is this point that makes the current economic "programs" of both conservatives and liberals, Republicans and Democrats, off the point. To listen to either side debate economic "issues" is to listen to a debate primarily about how best to grow the economy. On the conservative side talk is of tax cuts and the spur such cuts will give to the GNP; on the liberal it is of "targeted" tax cuts—which means less cuts though they are loathe to admit this—and the importance of government programs to increased growth. It both cases growth is the issue, ultimately translating, as I heard one 2004 Presidential candidate describe his entire campaign slogan, into more "jobs, jobs, jobs." But growth is not *at all* the important economic issue as a larger economy with more jobs does not mean you and I have any more control over our economic lives—witness the aftereffects of the 90's boom on the jobs and investments of many Americans and others around the world. To put this simply, *bigger does not mean better*. When it comes to the issue of security and ultimately opportunity, *size doesn't matter*!

Let's use the analogy so often made when growth is discussed to see how growth is off the point. "A rising tide lifts all boats." So most conservatives and liberals proclaim, and with this they intend to show that even if your boat is small its economic level is raised when the economy grows. The problem missed by this image is that some boats are capable of sinking others and in a higher tide this just means those in the sinking boats merely have more water in which to drown! Simply because we have *more of something* doesn't imply we have *more control of that something*. If the King of England said in 1774 that he was going to double the territory of the American Colonies—100% growth, much greater growth than anyone talks about in a one year period in the U.S. economy—should the Founders have stopped grumbling about his authoritarian, paternalistic control? Of course not, because this new land, even if it gave colonists the ability to move frequently and work more land, was still controlled by the King. So why should we see the situation any differently in a growing economy? No matter how many percent a year the GNP increases, and no matter how many jobs are created, this does not mean we have more say over our economic lives and security. Just because I have five jobs available to me instead of two, or none at all for that matter, doesn't mean any one of the five allows me more control over my work environment and hence control over my security and success. This is particularly so as we never seem to get away from the rollercoaster ride of growth and recession, so the one job I choose out of the five available this year is downsized the following year and I am right back where I started. The issue here is not quantity of options but quality of input. To repeat, *a bigger economy does not necessarily mean a better economy*—as a bigger country doesn't mean a better one!

To be absolutely clear, what I am arguing is that our current economic situation resembles the political situation of American colonists in the 18th Century.[17] In the 18th Century an American colonist could move from county to county, from colony to colony, maybe even from English to French to Spanish territory. But anywhere they went they were ultimately under the control of some Monarch and/or Parliament they did not appoint, and over whom they had no control *by law*. This lack of control and the abuse of the individual that such a system engendered, either actually or potentially, produced powerlessness and fear. And it produced anger, as political authorities expected to be viewed much like parents, those who you must love and not question, and who in return will love and care for you—which includes the occasional spanking for your own good, right? The American Revolutionaries responded to this situation by making government consent-based, at least partially, not by saying leave for new territory if you are unhappy. We should respond in the same fashion when the economy is discussed, thereby continuing the work they started. Our situation may be more complex and more difficult to see—though now with all the corporate scandals that have occurred and continue to occur, not quite as difficult to see—but it is still analogous. There are people in positions of power who directly impact the success and security of thousands of us, sometimes millions, and these people obtained this power simply by birthright, or by appointment without any direct, fair, legally sanctioned input from the people they control. This is as pernicious in our time as it was in the 18th Century, whether our economy is growing or not, and I think we must use the same solution in our time as was used in the 18th Century: democracy. We must extend the democratic experiment further. After all, if we accept this solution in the political case, why not accept it in others? Only in this way can we get the control over our lives and our destinies that we want and deserve.

Of course, other ways besides exercising our free market right to leave, or my suggestion of extending democracy, have been offered for gaining more control over our economic lives. Some, mostly liberals—when they take off their growth hats—see this as the task of the government. That is one of the reasons that many, again mostly liberals, have responded to the rash of corporate scandals by calling for more government regulation. Corporate scandals are not viewed as an example of a deep crisis in economic structure but instead as merely a flaw in accounting practices combined with a few at the top who got too greedy. The answer then, according to them, is to regulate those accounting practices so that excesses of greed are checked. Unfortunately, this response is inadequate.

Government regulation has proven extremely difficult to design so that it works as intended and does not undermine the efficiency of our society. What government regulation often does is create a large bureaucracy, one that is expensive, difficult to run and does not accomplish what it was designed to accomplish—with successful regulation also depending upon the government not being controlled by the very corporate forces it is supposed to regulate, something we all know, and we will discuss in greater detail shortly, is open to great doubt. The experience of government in the United States from the 1950's to the present, particularly Federal Government, should be enough evidence of the inadequacies of government regulation. Rather than helping problems like poverty, housing shortages, failing schools, crime, drugs, pernicious concentrations of corporate power, etc., the government has often made them worse. For instance, laws regulating business practice number in the 1000's and there are many government regulatory agencies whose sole task it is to watch over businesses, i.e., the SEC, but that didn't prevent Enron, WorldCom, Tyco and Arthur Andersen, did it? It may have even made them more likely as no one was sure who or what should be regulating the situation. Government regulation is just that, the *regulation* of a problem not its *elimination*, and because regulation is not elimination such regulation requires constant expensive and difficult maintenance where things can go wrong. Hence, we pay more taxes for less efficient protection from all kinds of problems. Where we can we need to eliminate problems not regulate them, and in the case of dangerous concentrations of power such as those found in many corporations, we can eliminate this problem. And if we fail to eliminate it, if we leave the fundamental structure of our economic institutions untouched, no amount of regulation is really going to help.[18]

Another way many, again mostly liberals, have offered for gaining control of economic institutions when they are not talking growth or government regulation is to rely upon unions and grass roots protest groups. Through most of the past 100 years it is unions that have typically been the voice of employees, standing as the bulwark against concentrated economic power, and it is protest groups that many believe have impacted, and still impact, political, economic and educational policy of all sorts. As such, promoting union and protest organization membership seems to many the way to increase employee and other power and hence control over economic and other institutions.

Though heroes to many, these organizations cannot do the job that needs to be done. Joining a union or becoming a protestor is doing nothing more than placing yourself in a semi-permanent state of rebellion against the powers that be, it is not getting *control* over those powers. Why has taking to the streets had so little impact on politics and government policy—didn't do much after the 2000 election, did it? Why have unions failed so miserably to better the lot of employees over the past few decades, or even maintain gains gotten in the past— union membership is at 50 year low as unions have been largely impotent in the face of NAFTA, the WTO and the entire process of globalization? Why have student protestors done no better with issues such as class size, tuition increases, faculty hiring and the like? Unions and protest organizations do not get people control; they are not a means for permanently reigning in concentrated corporate and other power. Believing they are is like believing the Founders of this country did not need to write the Declaration of Independence but merely agree anytime the King did something they disliked they would band together and hold another Boston Tea Party. Had the Founders done that, they would have left the King in control, and thus left themselves at his mercy until such time as he made them so unhappy that they had to take action. And risky action at that! But why leave the King in control? Why make risky protest necessary at all? Why base the community around such nasty, rebellious conflict? They did not, and we should not. They took power from the King in one big rebellion, thereby ending the need for any further rebellion, and gave it to those chosen by the citizens—unfortunately not entirely as we are now painfully aware after 2000. We should do the same with our "kings," i.e. those who run big business—as well as big government and "big" education. The point is not to give us a means of rebellion, as unions and protest organizations do, but to make rebellion unnecessary in the first place. The point is not to be organized and ready to strike and protest against those in control, but *to be in control*. [19]

One last suggestion offered for aiding in the control of corporations and encouraging a broader based economic power structure in general, this time one popular with conservatives at the rare moments where conservatives care about such issues—they almost never speak of anything but growth—has been to increase the number of people investing in the stock market; even though corporate scandals have tarnished this suggestion there are still many making it. Particularly for employees in publicly held corporations, it might seem that if they want more control over their economic lives, they could buy stock and thus control who runs their company through stockholder voting. This could also help those who do not work in publicly held corporations. The more people buy stock, the more people control the economy in general. The more people buy stock, the more broad based economic decision making becomes. Students could benefit as well, because many schools depend heavily upon corporate endowments and contributions hence by purchasing stock in the corporations that donate to schools the schools themselves could be changed. This could even help with the problem of corporate influence over politics—a problem we will get to more directly in a few pages. If economic power becomes more diffuse, then it is less of a threat to the political process.

Bandied about in our still Wall-Street-happy society where the stock market continues to be seen by many, unbelievable as it may seem, as the panacea for all ills and the true sign of our "economic health," the suggestion that we gain control through stock purchase is particularly attractive to middle-level management in big businesses and small to middle-range investors. You could almost say that what unions and protest organizations are to workers and other members of the non-elite, equity in terms of stock is to these groups. But this suggestion doesn't work either. Most of us, even those towards the upper end of management or who can have a substantial stock portfolio, do not have enough money alone or in conjunction to buy the substantial blocks of stock necessary to impact corporate decision making in one corporation, let alone in various parts of the economy. The recent experience with Enron, WorldCom, Tyco, Arthur Andersen and the like shows this clearly. Many owned stock in these corporations yet it gave them *absolutely no control* over their corporate leadership because they simply didn't own enough stock. And even if employees and small investors could band together to buy that much stock in one corporation, this still leaves open the possibility that someone with enough money could buy up another large chunk of stock thereby wresting control back from all other stockholders. If someone buys just 5% of a company's stock, they can ruin the company's value by threatening to dump that 5% and hence the employees and small investors who may own a greater percentage of a company's stock are still not really in control of the company. Stock ownership does not diffuse economic power, no matter how widespread it becomes, because the stock market is an inherently unequal environment where the richer you are the more votes and leverage you have—this is what I meant earlier when I mentioned economic Jim Crow.[20] But this discussion is pie-in-the-sky fantasy anyway, because the money involved is beyond the reach of most of us. Major stock ownership, the kind necessary to control a section of the economy or even a corporation, is still the bastion of the extremely rich.

   Our economy has a very serious structural defect that common sense, history and recent corporate scandals show cannot be fixed by fine-tuning adjustments like extended government regulation, unionization, stock ownership or accelerated growth. We have little to no say *by law* in who leads the businesses where most of us work as either mid-level management or labor, and where many of us invest for retirement, and upon which all of us depend in one way or another. Only when we get this say *by law* will our democracy be genuine, and for the first time, near completion. Only when we get this say *by law*, only when we eliminate the structural problem, will we have the control we need in our economic lives.

   To return to the level of international relations for a moment, what I am saying about large business organizations is really no different than what has been an agreed upon attitude regarding nations for almost a century. The fundamental principles guiding international relations are those of National Sovereignty and Self-Determination, namely, all the people of any nation should be able to determine their own course of action without intrusion. On the international stage we accept the Consent Principle for people in a nation; these principles are so fundamental to international relations that one of the few remaining accepted justifications for war is their violation. National Sovereignty and Self-Determination are our explicit, fundamental, guiding principles in international relations, so why not extend this idea to members within other, non-national institutions? Why isn't this principle operative for all groups of people, like those in a large business, not just for establishing and maintaining governments inside national borders? There is no principled reason why this is so. To consider self-determination essential for nations but no other grouping of peoples is absurd and contradictory. We should therefore extend self-determination to the realm of business.

Recent corporate scandals show us that we are beyond the realm of economic fine-tuning, that we need to change corporate structures and hence alter the mechanism of corporate governance, if we are to gain true economic security and opportunity. We must change corporate structure and governance, and we must do so in a way that gives each and every member of the corporate body, from the highest to the lowest, a say in how the body functions. What better way is there to do this than through democracy? We thus have our second reason for completing the American Revolution.

Reason 3: No more 2000's

The American people are a mature people with well over 200 years of experience managing a basically democratic political system. Unfortunately, at many points in our democratic system we are still treated as if we are children. The expression of the popular will is limited by institutions that ensure we as individuals have almost no direct control over anything that happens in our government. We still have the Electoral College. We still have a representative democracy that allows no direct participation of the citizenry. We still have an antiquated primary system, an exclusionary two-party system, a closed debate system, etc., all of which gives us even less impact and treats us more as child-like, amateur spectators instead of essential participants. We do not deserve this. We have risen above it. It is time we establish a system that respects our maturity, one that allows as much participation as is practically possible. Our system does not do that now and as such should change. How should it change, that is taken up in Chapter 2, but that it should change is obvious. We must shake up our democratic system. We must extend the democratic gains gotten in the American Revolution. It is the only way to prevent another 2000 debacle.

Structural change in our politics is absolutely necessary, but we all know the *real message* of the 2000 election; a message made even more real by corporate scandals: money has become so influential in our politics that if we do not seek to further the Revolution, to extend the democratic experiment beyond its current limits, we run the risk of losing our democracy entirely. In fact, what the 2000 election shows is that we have already started losing that control. The recent past in American politics is littered with stories showing that our limited-democratic political system has come increasingly under the control of money. Influence peddling either direct in the forms of bribes—remember Abscam[21]—or indirect and hence more subtle and pernicious in the form of lobbying and campaign contributions, have radically altered the state of democracy in America.[22] There is a real belief among Americans that all politicians are for sale, and whether exaggerated or not, this attitude shows we Americans understand large sums of money and democracy do not mix. We know that if democracy is to work, money must be removed as an issue. The way to do this is by extending democracy in politics and ultimately throughout our society.[23] We must make our politics more democratic, but we must also make the institutions in our economy, the Enron's, WorldCom's, Tyco's and Arthur Andersen's of the world, more democratic as well. No other solution, at least not one that leaves our politics open to manipulation by vast sums of money held permanently in the unchallenged control of any person's or group's hands—a solution like campaign finance reform—will work. It will not work, because wealth will always find a way of creeping back into the system—why else do we have to keep passing new varieties of campaign finance reform?

The idea that concentrated power corrupts democracy, particularly concentrated power in the form of wealth, is not new. It was a commonplace to the Founders of American democracy, and we might call the point a passion with Jefferson. They learned it not simply from personal experience, but from a group of writers who made the point their focus. This was the group of writers who commented on, and critiqued, English politics around the time of the Glorious Revolution of 1688—the revolution that established England's constitutional monarchy. Men such as Harrington, Sidney, Neville, Trenchard, and Gordon—the most famous political writers of late 17th and early 18th Century England—were endlessly pointing out that the attempt to balance democracy and aristocracy fails. It fails because the aristocrats, chief among them in their own day the Hanoverian monarchs, corrupt the democratic system through money. The political question of the day after the Glorious Revolution was not whether the seats of parliament were for sale, but how much. Even the subjection of the King to parliamentary power had not been enough to prevent the abuse of power, according to these men:

> Few of them accepted the Glorious Revolution and the lax political pragmatism that had followed as the final solution to the political problems of the time. They refused to believe that the transfer of sovereignty from the crown to parliament provided a perfect guarantee that the individual would be protected from the power of the state.[24]

The subjection of the King to a constitution and parliament had not been enough to prevent abuse because the existence of the monarch left in place someone with the desire for, and money to buy, influence. These writers drove this point home, and the American Revolutionary leaders listened. They eliminated the traditional landed aristocracy, including the monarchy, and thereby hoped they had greatly lessened the ability of a democratic system to be corrupted by wealth. What they could not have foreseen, as we discussed earlier, is that the coming industrial revolution would produce a new type of aristocrat: the ultra-wealthy. It is these new aristocrats that now threaten our democratic political system—this aristocracy is not exactly a traditional hereditary aristocracy of course, but it is close. If we do not act, as the American Revolutionaries acted, to democratically control this concentration of permanently-held power and hence make it non-permanent, then we will experience, as we have already partly experienced, the increasing erosion of our current, partially democratic system. To put it plainly, if we do not make the Enron's, WorldCom's, Tyco's and Arthur Andersen's of the world more democratic, then they will eventually drag down what's left of our democracy. Democracy does not mix well with extreme concentrations of permanently-held power, no matter what sort of power. We must extend democracy therefore, or run the risk of losing it altogether.

We must extend democracy throughout politics and into the corporate world, into all realms where power is concentrated in the unchecked hands of a few, but we must not seek to eliminate such power. Many on the radical left, in particular anarchists and communists, have seen the same problem with balancing democracy and concentrated economic power, but their response has been to seek the elimination of all such power. *That is not in any way what I am suggesting*. What I am suggesting is that we respond to the current concentration of economic power—and other power for that matter as we will see—in the same way 18th Century Americans, and many 18th and 19th Century Europeans, responded to the then growing concentration of political power.

During the late 17th, 18th and 19th Centuries, in many parts of Europe and its colonies, the era of religious and feudal wars ended and the modern nation-state was born. These new nation-states allowed for a concentration of political power unlike any seen in Europe since Ancient Rome, and unlike almost any that had ever existed before. This concentration of power lead to many abuses, blame for which was often placed on the fact that power was held in the hands of a small aristocracy topped by a single monarch—something with which most of us would agree. To end the abuses, revolutions were undertaken to wrest power from the hands of aristocrats and monarchs and place it on a consent basis, or at least a partial consent basis.

However, in the face of a similar concentration of economic power during the 19th and 20th Centuries, many leftists sought a different solution. Rather than extend consent-based power, they sought to eliminate power relations altogether. They sought a society of complete "freedom" where no person was ever subject to any other. This was their big mistake, as history has born out. All their "utopianism"—I put scare quotes here because I believe there is nothing really utopian about their vision at all—produced was totalitarianism. Why these later revolutionaries sought a different solution to a similar problem is a complex question, one we need not address here. All that needs to be said is that in the face of the failure of the solution offered by radical leftists, we should return to the earlier solution. We should not seek to eliminate concentrations of power, just put such power on a consent basis.

Figure 2 makes this point more clear. We in "Contemporary America" are trying a precarious balancing act between "America 1750," where every institution is paternalistic and modeled on the relation between parents and children in the family, and a "Future America" where only the family is run like a family.

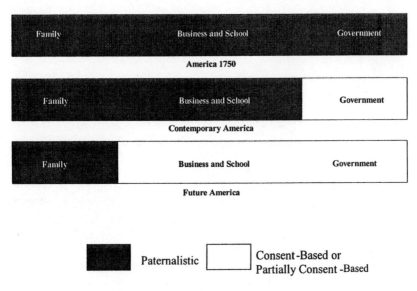

Figure 2

What I am claiming is that we cannot maintain the balancing act of "Contemporary America." That is the lesson of 2000. Either we push forward to a "Future America" or we will slide backward to "America 1750." We cannot stay in the middle because of the corrupting influence of permanently-held power, particularly in the form of wealth. American history shows we Americans feel a need to regulate permanently-held economic power because without such regulation that power becomes too strong and threatens our limited experiment with democracy in politics. Much of the most important legislation of the late 19th and 20th Centuries has had this purpose—anti-trust regulation, campaign finance reform and securities and banking regulation are prime examples. In other words, America has slowly been moving towards "Future America" for quite some time, for the reasons just discussed, and I am simply saying we should complete the move entirely by completing the Revolution. We should complete the move, or if we don't, we move in the direction of 1750. We cannot maintain a middle ground.

Another facet of the 2000 Presidential Election, and almost every election in the U.S. for that matter—one that is largely ignored but shows equally well the growing crisis in our democratic system—is lack of voter turn out. The reason this facet of the 2000 election is ignored is because we take for granted at this point that a huge percentage of eligible voters will not vote. There is nothing new about 50% or less of eligible voters turning out for an election, so this got no airplay during the 2000 election and rarely does in any election. Though it got no airplay, we must wonder at the reason for this astonishing figure. Ask an American why we fought WWI, WWII or a host of other wars, or why we are fighting the current "War on Terrorism," and they will respond by and large that it was, and is, to "preserve our way of life". And what way of life is that? Why our freedom-loving, democratic way of life of course. So why is it that we are so gung-ho for democracy in our rhetoric, and in other people's countries, but so few of us use the very democratic rights we seem to support so strongly?

The answer to this can be found, I think, in the malaise that has settled over America. What malaise you ask? The malaise that has most of us resigned to membership in the first generation of Americans living less spiritually well than our parents—a flat-screen TV and imported SUV don't make up for the unhappiness caused by working a 60-75 hour week, at an unsteady job we dislike, in order to pay for them. The malaise that has us laughing at our own convictions, or worse yet, having no convictions at all—"Generation X" grows larger all the time. The malaise that has us so jaded that we are ready to put down a book like this because it seems "naive" and "preachy". The malaise that has adults, and sometimes children, shooting one another in acts of uncontrolled rage. The malaise that has sales of legal drugs like Prozac, Valium, Paxil, St. John's Wort and alcohol in the 10's of billions of dollars, and when combined with sales of illegal drugs like marijuana and cocaine, soars to the 100's of billions. The malaise that has self-help/spirituality books the fastest growing part of the book market. This is the malaise I am talking about. There is a general sense of unease pervading our community, one difficult to measure yet palpable.[25] How many of us feel our voice, let alone our vote, can make a difference? How many of us are optimistic that our dreams will come true, or that we will even get a chance to pursue them? How many of us feel we are really in control of what happens to us? How many of us feel we are reaching our potential? How many of us like our jobs? How many of us feel secure in our jobs whether we like them or not? How many of us believe our lives will get better into the future? Pressing further than our own futures, how many of us believe that the lives of our children will be better than our lives or our parent's lives?

There is a malaise in this country that is evident everywhere. Beyond the thin veil of patriotism that many of us wear with pride, there is nervousness. This nervousness stems from the lack of control we possess over our lives, and it finds no higher expression than in our politics. We can vote, but so many do not, and they do not because they believe it just doesn't matter. What we must do then is make it matter, make it matter in a way it never has before, and that requires structural change in our politics. It requires structural change elsewhere, as we have seen and will continue to see. But if we are to avoid another 2000 Presidential Election, and I am not just talking about Electoral College issues but the more frightening abandonment of democracy by almost 50% of the population, then we need to change our politics fundamentally. We need to put authority throughout politics—and throughout our economy and educational systems as well—on a more democratic base. By altering certain basic institutions, we must ensure that our political order is as without cronyism, and is as *non-paternalist, non-aristocratic, non-inherited and merit based* as we possibly can. We must make power, in all its varieties, more accessible to everyone based on their talents. This task requires deep change.

The 2000 election makes clear that on a number of fronts our democratic political order is in crisis. It makes clear that a structural defect in the actual institutions of our democratic order as well as the institutions that surround that order have gone a long way toward undermining the limited democracy won for us in the American Revolution. It makes clear that these defects have even undermined the confidence of the American people in the democratic process we now have and possibly in democracy itself. So what then must we do? To my mind the answer is simple: complete the American Revolution by extending the democratic experiment.

This is reason number three to complete the American Revolution.

Reason 4: Help Ease Ethnic, Racial, and Gender Conflict

One of the great problems we confront around the world is an increase in factionalism, or as I have heard it termed: balkanization. Religious, ethnic, cultural and other groups more and more find themselves seeking to break away from any institutional attachment to other groups. Separatism is on the rise worldwide. Just how this should be dealt with is implicit in my earlier discussion of 9-11: international empowerment through economic democracy. An internationally established democratic order—the creation of which multinational corporations must spearhead—not only would allow the diverse peoples of the world to increase their ability to contribute to and control what happens to them, but it would also allow them to have access to democratic forums in which they could better work out their differences. Internationally this is the solution, but what about inside America? Though downplayed after 9-11, the Untied States is still experiencing the erosion of common assumed codes of conduct between groups in the public realm with a corresponding rise in "identity politics". America, as with many nations around the globe, becomes less and less one nation and more a gathering of diverse groups who do not seem to share anything at all, and who press their interests with little regard for, or connection with, other groups—witness the constantly increasing hyphenization of Americans into Italian-Americans, Irish-Americans, African-Americans, etc. This rise in balkanization has lead to increased tension and strife among various groups, and a lack of support among groups that at base should share a common cause—their disempowerment. Look at most large political protests today. They are often little more than a gathering of interest groups, each with their own banner stating their own agenda. Be they ethnic, religious, racial, gender, economic, political or ideological, many groups in America seem either indifferent towards, or at odds with, one another to such a great extent that they lack any common ground upon which to meet and resolve their issues. They lack some common, assumed codes of conduct and any programmatic unity, things necessary for groups to interact in a mutually supportive, non-violent fashion, things necessary in order for that most cherished of American activities to takes place: peaceful, public debate. No cooperation or no agreement on basic rules of conduct, then no peaceful competition, no respectful disagreement. For this reason there has been an increase in the fragmented politics of special interests as well as in violence between groups, and a heightened tension that more fragmentation is on the way. We live in an America that in the past 30 years has seen virulent bipartisanism in politics, race riots, terrorists bombs from the right and left and rates of violent crime unlike anything anyone could have ever imagined possible. So what is the solution in America? Is it the same as on the international stage?

The answer is, quite simply, yes. Completing the American Revolution through the extension of democracy can help reduce America's balkanization by providing an assumed area of agreement among groups. However they may differ on other issues, universal democratic control of our institutions can provide the programmatic unity and underlying moral commitment that can serve as a common ground on which diverse groups can stand, interact positively and solve their problems in a peaceful manner. The reason our current democracy does not serve as this social glue in America is that our own partial commitment to democracy makes questionable just how much America is committed to the ideals of democracy. Many institutions in this nation use other means besides the democratic to resolve their conflicts and distribute power. This provides a negative lesson, saying democracy is just one mechanism among many that may be used to settle disputes and exercise power, and it is not the fundamental moral ideal of America. If different areas of society can rightfully employ different methods of conflict resolution and power distribution, why should two groups in confrontation adhere to democratic process? Why should two factions both see themselves as "American" when it is unclear what America stands for? There seems no reason, and hence conflicts arise and come to be settled by any means necessary, including violence. To overcome this factionalism and the violence it engenders, we must make clear just what America stands for, and what else is that besides democracy? We must make democracy the moral touchstone of this nation, the uniform process for all conflict resolution and power distribution. In so doing we will establish democratic procedure as the genuine moral ground for all people, one that can serve as our assumed common ground and the mechanism to adjudicate disputes. We must make clear what the part after the hyphen in Italian-, Irish-, African-, etc., really means.

This is not to say that all violent interchange would be eliminated; some groups both in and outside America are deeply hostile to one another and to democracy itself. But it does mean that "America" will come to be clearly defined, and what is demanded of you as an American will not be in doubt. Those who choose not to play by our rules can thus rightfully be rooted out and dealt with. Those who choose to play by these rules will have an increased sense of community, or at least a sense that being American stands for something, something giving them commonality with every other person in this nation. And the result of this can only be a reduction in the view of ourselves as a loose association of diverse groups with little in common; a reduction which in turn will yield a rejuvenated public sphere and a decrease in the fear of violence as well as in actual violence itself. However, this can only be accomplished if our commitment to the values of democracy is clear, a commitment that is not clear in our present system.

Too much has been made recently about "diversity" in America, and not enough about unity—other than the somewhat empty, fear-based unity following 9-11. If our current emphasis on diversity is to bear any positive fruit, if people are to learn from one another's differences, then these different perspectives need to have something in common. It is time we start to emphasize some commonality. It is time we look to a single idea that holds together the diverse elements that make up America. Democracy is that idea. It is that social glue. But it needs to hold us together in all walks of life, in all parts of society otherwise it will fail to play the role we need it to.

Extending democracy will also give many an increased opportunity to partake of the material and spiritual wealth of this nation. Many individuals, as well as groups, feel very little commitment to America because they do not see themselves as having an equal opportunity to take advantage of what America can offer. Permanently held power in the hands of a few keeps them all but excluded from the lifestyles they want to lead. If the system becomes more open and merit based, if opportunity increases, if we can help overcome the malaise of which I spoke in the last section, then this will serve to bind us to one another and to the American system. The benefit of full democratization will be not simply a clarification of America's "moral commitment" and increased peace among groups therefore, but a real improvement in people's sense of hope and social standing. And this, in turn, will benefit not only individuals but the overall peace and security of the many groups that make up this nation.

Real inclusion in a clearly defined America forms our fourth reason for completing the American Revolution.

Reason 5: Increasing the Efficiency of Organizations

Democracy can also help with another variety of balkanization that we are currently experiencing as we have never experienced it before. We live in an age where the hyper-specialization of tasks coupled with the explosion of information makes it impossible for one person, or even a few people, to "know it all" or "do it all" in any institution. This means that somehow a vast number of perspectives—each task and different piece of information represents a perspective—must be brought together in order for most organizations to function well. Efficiency demands that people are informed about what others in their institutions are thinking and doing, and there is no better way to ensure that everyone is informed than democratic decision making. Democracy is what can allow information to flow because it requires joint deliberation and decision making, during which time individuals can inform one another of their views on things. Democracy simply makes sense when we need to get individuals in touch, and we have never needed to get people in touch more than we do today.

To look at this point historically, democracy made sense in 18th Century American politics because the community had started to become so specialized, complex, large and spread out that no one person could monitor and run it all. The Founders had to bring together the diverse actors in our community, from the far reaches of huge territories, in order to make sensible decisions. If they did not, decisions would be too parochial, narrow in focus and myopic—as they have almost always been in empires where decisions were made for vast territories by only a very few. The same situation now exists in many parts of the government, as well as throughout our businesses and schools. They have become so large, involving so many actors, in such diverse fields over far flung reaches of the world, that the only way they can be run efficiently is by allowing individuals from various parts of these institutions to deliberate and make policy. No one person, or even one person and their staff, can do this effectively. *Increased specialization and information require democracy in order to maximize efficiency!* Maximizing organizational efficiency provides our fifth reason for completing the American Revolution.

Reason 6: Limited Democracy has Performed So Well, More Would Undoubtedly Perform Better

The last, and in a sense best, reason to extend democracy is that the limited democratization of power in government has been such a rousing success we might expect similar success if we extend it throughout politics, the economy and education. In the span of a mere 200 years—a short span when you compare it to the thousands of years of recorded history—limited democratic political systems have swept the globe. Even systems that are not at all democratic often feel forced to call themselves such because of the assumed unassailable rightness of democracy. This is an amazing feat, given that prior to the American Revolution experiments in democracy had been few, brief and isolated. The Consent Principle and its underlying optimism about humanity are ideas that have gone from questionable to unquestioned. Few coups in the history of ideas, particularly ideas regarding the social world, have been so swift and complete— look at how long it took Christianity, with its ideas about the moral equality of man, to take hold in the West for instance. And the reason that democracy as an idea, and as a system, has come to be so widely accepted is because of the results produced by democracy. The limited democratization of political power has been a major boon to the development of dynamic individuals and their dynamic ideas, individuals and ideas that in their time have revolutionized the world. It is no coincidence, I believe, that the first modern Western country really to experiment with democracy, and where democracy has been unchallenged for over two hundred years, has become the most powerful nation on the planet, possibly the most powerful nation of all time.

Given the success of limited democracy in the political arena, it seems sensible to extend it in politics and try it in other arenas as well. Who knows what types of developments might result from such an extension? If we open up our political, economic and intellectual life to *complete*, *genuine* free interchange for the first time, if we make our system truly competitive and merit based as any truly democratic system is, we may see the biggest expansion ever in the history of ideas and the activity that results from them. The Consent Principle is a simple, rational, guiding principle for the distribution of power, one that can help make other parts of our culture, ones guided by less rational principles, work better. The advent of limited democratic institutions in the political arena minimized the uncertainties involved in determining who should hold power and how that power should be used —we need not just hope our leaders are good ones who do good things—thereby ushering in a period of security, justice and opportunity in which individuals could flourish. I believe that the thorough democratization of our political, economic and educational institutions would have similar effect. When questions are settled by appeal to open, law-governed practices, practices which minimize unfairness and help guarantee, as much as it can ever be guaranteed, that the majority of people will be satisfied by the decisions of those in charge, this promotes the development of the individual. When power is no longer distributed based on the principle that might makes right, this has the effect of allowing things of a more delicate nature to grow, and it is this growth that allows us to progress. When individuals are in power because they have demonstrated merit in a competitive forum and not because of whom they know or how much money they have, their rule is better.

In politics we have abandoned the era of wars of dynastic succession, rule by birthright, internecine intrigue committed behind closed doors or on battlefields, etc. We have abandoned these in politics and have gained security, consistency and fairness in the process. We should now abandon similar activities in other arenas of power.

Unfortunately, however, part of our political institutions, and almost all of our economic and educational institutions, still function much the way political institutions functioned throughout the world hundreds of years ago, and this holds back the potential of many individuals. Ultimately, who holds power in most of these institutions is decided behind closed doors, and these decisions are subject to forces which may be both immoral and irrational. Leaders in businesses, schools and even in parts of the government, are appointed through processes we would consider anathema when choosing a President, Senator or Representative. Why allow this to go on? The American Revolutionary leaders of the 18th Century saw the virtue of placing political power struggles under law governed processes subject to public inspection. They saw the virtue of giving out political power to those who could prove to constituents subject to such power that they deserve to hold it. Why not make all our power struggles, all distributions of power, have the same virtue? What we stand to gain is that those in power will actually be better suited to run our institutions, as they will be chosen based on their publicly demonstrated abilities, not on how they can serve some limited group of people in power. And this in turn will give individuals the impetus and space to develop, much the way the limited democratization of our political institutions created such impetus and space.

All this may seem naïve. It makes it sound as if every bit of progress in the past few hundred years has been the result of democracy. This is certainly untrue. What is true, I believe, is that the more power is distributed based on merit as merit is decided *by us not for us*—the more free, fair and secure the social environment—the more individuals thrive. This thriving in turn translates into progress on all fronts, spiritual as well as material. To return to an earlier analogy, the more we are treated like adults the more we act like adults: taking responsibility for ourselves and developing our capacities as we see fit and to their fullest potential. This is what we have experienced in America already, and we have no reason to think this wouldn't accelerate in a thorough-going democracy.

My naiveté may seem worse however in that I make it sound as if our limited-democratic politics is perfectly clean while business, the academy, etc., are perfectly dirty. I have no such illusion. Certainly democratic politics can be manipulated while the decisions made in private by businesses, universities, etc., can be quite fair and sensible. My point is, however, that in politics it is illegal to manipulate—though not entirely—and this works to minimize such manipulation, thereby resulting in fairer, more sensible decisions about who should hold power. In business and elsewhere this lack of legal restraint makes manipulation the norm, almost a given of these decisions, and as such those decisions tend to be less fair and sensible.

We must also recognize, as I was at pains to point out before, that the corruption of our political system, when it does occur, seems rarely to be a result of the system itself. Rather, it stems more from the fact that most democratic political institutions are surrounded by institutions that are not democratic. These surrounding institutions, particularly those with large amounts of money, serve to corrupt the democratic process. The failure is not with democracy, but with the lack of complete democracy. Institutions where power is permanently held and controlled will always serve to corrupt those in which power is non-permanently held and controlled—again as we have already discussed. I do not see an unproblematic way to balance institutions where power is permanently held and those where it is not. Either all power is ultimately permanent, as it was hundreds of years ago in the West and as the influence of money increasingly makes it today, or it is all non-permanent as I hope happens in the future—again, just exactly what I mean by non-permanent and how we can achieve this will become clear in Chapters 2-4.

The underlying reason democracy is so successful in promoting individual and hence social development is that, more than any other system, it allows a thorough-going dialogue between the private individual and the public, social realm of government, businesses and schools. Our ability to serve our own private, individual interests is dependent upon whether our private, individual interests can be shown to serve the interests of others. This is the only way in which we will be given the resources in terms of time, money, information, education, legal rights, etc., that are always necessary in order to accomplish any of our projects. If we want to build a building, paint a painting, make a movie, write a novel, open a business, develop a product, or any endeavor save for the most limited and personal, we must get the materials, free time, education, legal rights etc., in order to do this.

In a non-democratic system, one like certain parts of our current political system, and our entire economic and educational system, we, childlike, must show that our private projects serve the interests of some small number of people who permanently control those resources in their private hands. And this small number is effectively reduced to one given that they tend to function according to the same principle: judge a project in terms of how much money, honor, fame, etc., it will make for me, the "investor." What this means is that the vast majority of our projects are approved or disapproved, given the resources necessary for their development or not, simply in terms of whether they will provide some private person or group of people money, fame, honor, etc. The most personal aspects of our lives, the dreams, the hopes, and the projects to which they give rise, are thus judged in terms of how much they will aggrandize the power of the already powerful. As such, the private projects that tend to be approved are the ones that will maintain the status quo, regardless of their worth as assessed by other measures. They tend to be the ones that those in power can understand and like. The best idea might be let to wither and die from lack of support, simply because it was not obviously to the advantage of some powerful person or group of people, or simply because they did not understand it. Non-democratic systems promote rigidity in a society and hence hinder the development of the new, and it is this development of the new which is the essence of happiness and progress, both material and spiritual, both individual and social.

In a democratic system, the need to obtain resources by convincing others of the importance of your private, individual project still exists. This is simply a function of living in a society. What changes is that the audience is no longer someone whom you do not control in any way, one who can ignore your input or who is driven by purely narrow self-interest. Given that they are some individual or group who you ultimately control—in a representative democracy at least—who is forced to listen to your ideas and who is acting in the name of their constituencies as well as themselves, the criterion they would apply in judging your private project is much different. They would have to judge your project first and foremost in terms of the interests of the majority. "Will it promote a better society?"—better being determined through democratic process—not simply "will it promote themselves?" And you will have direct input into the decision. Compare this with our current system, where your input is recognized only if those making the decision *allow* you to give it, and even still, they make their decisions based on how your idea, project, etc. will serve *them*.

This is not to say that in our present system those who control resources might not listen to you and have on their minds the betterment of us all. True, but why leave this up to chance? Why hope that we have a loving, caring patron (read parent)? Why allow ourselves to be treated as children are treated? Why not guarantee that we are listened to, that our voices have impact and the interests of the majority are respected—as much as any of this can be guaranteed—by designing the system so that this result is mandated? Why leave open the possibility, in the very structure of the decision making process, that would allow your private dreams to be judged behind closed doors and in terms of how much money, fame, honor, etc., they will create for some powerful individual or group? In a democratic system the structure of the decision making process would be open, and your input would be heard, thereby lessening the chance that the decision would be made in an unfair, arbitrary or irrational way. Democratic judgments are not based on whether they serve some individual's or small group's private interests, rather, they are based on how they promote the interests of the majority of people in a given area, or maybe across the board.

To some of you, this democratic judgment is going to seem too constraining. Judging our private projects in terms of how they promote the majority's interests might not seem much better than judging them in terms of how much they might promote some powerful individual's interests. It might seem we have just traded in the self-serving interests of the one or few for the mundane, low-brow, conservative interests of the many. The "masses," uneducated and unsophisticated, might enforce a mediocre standard to match their mediocre interests, a situation worse in some sense than a standard enforced by the powerful for the powerful. The powerful tend to be more able to appreciate "finer" things and different ideas because they have normally been given the training to do so. Ultimately, the rich may be more progressive and less conservative than the poor. They may be in a better position to judge the merit of an idea or individual.

What we need to recognize is that the modicum of truth contained in this characterization is outweighed by several points.

One is that the potentially oppressive nature of the democratic process is counter-balanced by the openness of the democratic process. Surely the democratic process may result in decisions that pander to the "masses", but at least that pandering must take place in an open, public forum. Contrast this with decisions which may pander to some powerful group, decisions as they are now made in many cases. Here the pandering is done behind closed doors, and is not subject to anyone's inspection, particularly those who are decided against. In both cases there could be pandering, but in the one case it would be done in the open and the other it would not. *This difference is crucial.* It is crucial because the public nature of the one decision would allow the decision to be challenged throughout the entire decision making process by those who oppose it. The private nature of the other decision would not allow this challenge, and would even accentuate the quantity of pandering that might take place.

I can drive this point home by asking you a question: Would you rather that your fate be decided in front of you, in a forum where you have input, or would you prefer that it be decided hidden from your view and without your input? I think we all know which we would prefer, and that is because we believe the open decision, even if it goes against us, is more fair due to its openness and our input. This is why we have a court system and trial by jury, right? Democratic process does not eliminate that the interests of some people will have to be heeded, that is the very logic of decision making—for more on this see Chapter 5. What it does eliminate is a level of unfairness by eliminating the closed decision making process.

A second point concerning fear of the "masses" is that people are much better educated and informed today than they ever were before. Thanks first and foremost to public education, the vast majority of people are literate, have some knowledge of history as well as of other areas of the country and the world. The explosion of media has also contributed greatly to this process. We are said to live in the "information age", a time where the fear is not of too little information but of too much. The world of entertainment, particularly that of movies and television, has contributed to the profound expansion of the "American mind" as well. Even the advances in travel have served the purpose of widening the horizons of the "average" person. One hundred years ago, few people knew much, at least in any direct fashion, about what happened beyond the limited confines of some small geographic area. Now, most people have gone, either physically or at least via movies and television, beyond the horizon. We are aquatinted with more people and places, in both a direct and indirect manner, than any other people in history.

What I am suggesting is that the image of the "masses" as some group of undereducated and undernourished rabble is a myth that we should abandon. Nonetheless, for those of you who fear that people are incapable, in general, of sound judgments on the merit of the private projects of many individuals, I can only say that this same argument was offered against the popular control of government itself. Many in the 18th Century, as we saw above, feared that "the people" would lack sufficient education and reasoning ability to control the destiny of a nation. They believed that democracy would degenerate into rank factionalism and mob rule thus undermining not only freedom but public security. Well, this did not come to pass, and we have no reason to believe that "the people" would not be equally capable of controlling a number of other institutions in this nation.

For my part, I have never met a member of this feared group "the people." All I have ever met are individuals, not one of whom I could have comfortably judged too ignorant or stupid to be able to express their opinions, no matter how different than mine, in a rational manner. By and large, the fear of "the people" is nothing more than a fear of someone with different views than our own, a fear that those who consider themselves "enlightened" should be above, right? Nonetheless, for those of you who persist in your fear of "the people," you who obviously know better than we crass members of the masses, I can only say that democracy will give you the chance to educate us. If you are *so* right about things, then your rightness will shine through in a public, democratic forum. And if it doesn't, whose fault is that? Maybe you do not know as much as you think?[26]

No matter what can be said against democracy, I think we would all agree that it is a better system than any other yet conceived. It is this reason that it has spread all over the face of the globe. All I am suggesting is that given this success, shouldn't we assume more success from a spread of this system? I think so, and hence we have yet one more reason for completing the American Revolution.

Thanks But No Thanks, You're Not Interested

Having read all of this I'm sure some of you are saying in disgust: "Whatever!" You believe we will never get control over our government, and certainly not big business. You believe we'll never reign-in the powerful. You believe we'll never make our society more secure, equal opportunity and merit-based. As far as you are concerned there's no real, ultimate solution to this problem. There is no way that everyone can be given a fair and equal opportunity to gain security and fulfill their dreams. There is no way that the standards used for judging individuals can be decided *by us* not *for us* because those in power will always promote whom, and what, they want to promote. There will always be someone in power over us, someone we must satisfy in order to get ahead and over whom we have no control. Sure, people feel insecure and powerless in the face of those outside their control *by law*. Yes, plenty of people are angry and frustrated that they may not have been given a genuine and fair chance to show their worth. But there is no point in talking about these feelings. There is no point, because there is nothing to be done about it. There is no point to complaining about something that cannot be changed. We might as well learn to adapt to the system we have.

If you find yourself thinking like this, stop. Lose this resignation. Americans did before—that is the real spirit of 76—and we can do so again. Accept what Jefferson is counseling us to do in the passage opening this book. We should not frivolously change our institutions according to him, but when the situation demands change, then change they must. And our situation demands change. ***Do we need any more evidence of this than 9-11, huge corporate scandal and the 2000 Presidential Election?!!*** We *can* express our frustration with our system and we *must* express it, by *really* altering our institutions.

Others of you are not just resigned. To you my views are more than frivolous and foolish, they are a provocation. You think I am a hold over from a bygone era; some sort of radical who never grew up. You don't care about politics. You feel no connection with the American Revolution. You feel no connection with America for that matter. You don't even know what it means to be an American. You say that security, opportunity and happiness do not depend upon completing the American Revolution. What they depend upon is money. You believe that's what life is about in contemporary America. Screw that, that's what life is about everywhere. Nothing more, nothing less. According to you, every person's happiness is their own business, and happiness has little to do with any political/social experiment. "I'm perfectly capable of making myself happy" you think to yourself, regardless of the institutions in which I am governed, work and learn. As long as I am lucky and struggle long and hard enough, I can become a success. Complete the American Revolution?! The hell with that. "Make yourself rich!" you say.

This is certainly the conventional wisdom of many, but like most conventional wisdom it is anything but wise. We all have fears, very real fears. Fears that our security will be ripped away, that our dreams will fade, that our talents will go to waste without our having had a fair and equal opportunity to discover, develop and show what we are worth. We have these fears, but we must stop believing we can overcome them on our own regardless of how the world's institutions are structured. We must stop believing we are going to win the lottery, either literally or metaphorically. We must stop believing an escape into our private worlds can gain us security and happiness; *there is no place to hide. Again, do we need any more evidence of this than 9-11, corporate scandals and the 2000 Presidential Election?!!* Don't you think every investor in Enron thought their nest-egg was secure? Don't you think every millionaire stock broker in the World Trade Center thought they were in control of their destiny? Of course they did, and they were wrong. We must admit that our lives are not in our control much of the time and it makes us sick both spiritually and physically—anyone out there have anxiety, high blood pressure or ulcers? We must admit that self-centered cynicism doesn't help—if it did, everyone would be happy.

Too many Americans have forgotten the ideals of the Revolution and replaced them with the *Myth of the Castle*. The Myth of the Castle is my term for the belief, held by so many, that the way to obtain security and happiness is by hiding inside our own private worlds; worlds made private by walls of money and secured by the laws of the government—the chief law being, of course, that nobody touches your money. And part of this Myth of the Castle, my reason for calling it this should be obvious, is that the more money we make, the bigger and stronger our castle grows increasing both our security and happiness.

It is time we abandon this Myth and return to the ideals of the Revolution. *People, wake up, there is no private place left to run*! Even if you or I make a great deal of money, we are still part of political, economic and educational systems that directly impact our destiny and the destiny of our family. Plenty of those in the World Trade Center were rich, but it didn't help them. Plenty of Enron employees had high-paying jobs, but it didn't help them. Plenty of Wall Street investors had portfolios valued in the millions, but it didn't help them. And most of us will never, no *NEVER*, make that kind of money anyway. Most of us will never even make enough money to gain even basic protection for ourselves or our families. To continue to pin our hopes for security and happiness on the chance that we will makes as much sense as the inner-city kid who ignores school because he believes he will be the next Michael Jordan. *It is time we admit this! We will have to work with and depend on others our entire lives.* We cannot achieve the isolation that the Myth of the Castle suggests we can, even if we make a lot of money, and most of us will not make that much money anyway. Therefore, we must stop clinging to the Myth. We must see that the better way to gain security and happiness is to gain a say for everyone *by law* in how the institutions that we all depend on function. Our security and happiness require a re-structuring of the public realm, not a retreat into the private realm. We are in the same situation now that Americans were in prior to the Revolution and we must handle it the same way.

They could not run away from an unfair system and we cannot run away from ours.

You and I need to restructure the institutions under which we live. We need to make them democratic. This is the only real hope we have that we can gain control over our destinies. Of course we will never gain total control of our destinies. We will never achieve a complete guarantee that our dreams will be fulfilled. But there are degrees of control, degrees of opportunity, and that is how our lives, and our happiness, connect with the American Revolution. Completing the Revolution will give us greater control of our lives, a greater opportunity to achieve our goals, and hence a greater chance at happiness. It will give us greater control and opportunity by opening new lines of communication between the private, individual world of our hopes, desires and dreams and the public, social realm in which they can be fulfilled; communication that will give them the best chance of mutually supporting, not conflicting with and destroying, one another. This is the social system we need, and if we pay close attention, one the American Revolution has shown us how to design.

By merely attempting to complete the Revolution we will at least overcome our present state of social stagnation. Stagnation we have been consigned to by the worn-out theories of conservatives and liberals alike. Stagnation that prevents us from developing, or even believing we can develop, institutions better designed to allow people in our society the fair, equal and real opportunity to fulfill their dreams and gain security. Conservatives and liberals both believe they have the proper vision of society and it is simply the moral failing of their countrymen which prevents its implementation. They are wrong. Our current failing, as much as it is a failing, is a failing of intellect, not will. We simply have not yet designed the right system for relating individuals to the community, the private to the public. We have not yet developed the proper system whereby everyone has a fair, real and equal chance to rise to their fullest potential and realize their dreams. We have a hint at what it might be, from people like Jefferson, but we have not yet fully taken the hint.

Beyond the cynical and skeptical among you, there are a few remaining groups who will dislike my suggestion that we complete democracy in the political sphere and extend it to the economic and educational sphere. One of these is the group that benefits from the current system. This is the group equivalent to King George III and the English aristocracy in the 18th Century. To you I say that increased democratization does not mean a necessary loss of control. *What it means is only a loss of guaranteed control.* To those who are currently in power in politics, the economy and the academy, if you can continue to demonstrate that you should be in power, then you will remain in power. The only change in your status is the requirement that you demonstrate your merit for your position, and you demonstrate it at regular intervals in a public forum. More on this in coming chapters.

Another group that will dislike extending democracy is comprised of those who believe that a completed democracy would require a complete equality of status: no rich, no poor, no better, no worse; a permanent pass to the school cafeteria as I once heard socialism (*which I do not advocate* as I have already said) described. But this is just a fundamental misunderstanding of democracy. Democracy does not demand complete equality of result, only equality of opportunity. Everyone must have the same chance to rule, everyone must have the same chance to excel—in whatever institution you find yourself—but what you do with that chance is up to you and to the extent of your talent. Democracy will not force everyone into the cafeteria, it will only demand that those who are at the four star restaurant did something to deserve their meal, something recognized in an open forum. Again, more on this in coming Chapters.

One last group that will dislike what I have argued is those who believe a completed democracy will be mob rule. The mob is too ignorant to run things according to many—a view shared by some of the Founders of this country as we have seen—and worse yet, the mob may take the law into their own hands and trample the individual—as James Madison feared it might. Both concerns are legitimate. I have already said something about the first concern in the above discussion of the impact of education and new technology on our society, as well as with my claims about how democracy is actually more efficient and sensible in our age of increasing specialization and information. Nonetheless, I return to this objection in both Chapters 2 and 3, in particular in Chapter 2 where I discuss "natural" and "historical" elites. As for the second concern, I take this up in Chapter 5 when I address several "theoretical" problems facing democracy. Though I call this problem a "theoretical" one, I do not mean to suggest it isn't important; just how important I take it will be obvious to you after you have read Chapter 5.

Conclusion

If our concern is with our security, with the control of our destinies and the freedom of opportunity to develop our talents, as so many of us claim now and as was claimed in the 18th Century, then that demands an absolute acceptance of the Consent Principle. The Consent Principle is the only fair way of balancing individual projects with membership in particular institutions and society in general. It balances these by making institutions and ultimately society something resulting from our wills and not something alien imposed upon us against our will by some surrogate parents. Without the Consent Principle, institutions and society are going to be externally imposed limitations on the individual. The only way an institution or society can allow the individual to thrive, the only way we as individuals can be ruled, and still be free, is if the rulers are chosen by those who comprise the institution. The only way we can be ruled and still be free, in other words, is if we rule ourselves. Rulers chosen by those over whom they will rule, the very point of the Consent Principle, is the key to balancing the individual with institutions and society in general.[27]

To balance the individual and society we must universally accept the Consent Principle. What I believe this means, when the rubber hits the road, will become clear in the coming Chapters. Also, for those who want more by way of a justification for the Consent Principle, I direct you to the last Chapter of this book. There you will find a "philosophical" argument for the Consent Principle, and for extending it into other realms, as opposed to the largely historical and practical argument you have just read. By "philosophical" I mean only it is an argument that stems from issues regarding the justification of the judgements regarding quality or merit.

I can end simply by restating that it is in a universal democracy that I believe our future resides. It is in institutions founded on the Consent Principle that we will finally successfully balance the private interests of the individual with the public interests of the community. Balance in such a fashion that, though not utopian, allows for our private projects to be judged based on merit. When our society completes the trajectory upon which it started over two hundred years ago, the anger and malaise that has descended upon it will be overcome. A more universal democracy can give you and me the best possible chance of accomplishing our dreams in a free and fair manner. It is what will give us the control that we desire and that will further invigorate our society. It is what will end our frequent feelings of powerlessness and cynicism and allow us to begin helping ourselves in large numbers. It is what will finally allow us to achieve the status of adulthood in all walks of life. Let's undertake the most fundamental change in the institutions that comprise our society in over two hundred years, a change Jefferson himself seems to suggest is inevitable and good in the passage opening this book.

Notes

[1]The argument that the electoral college is not anti-democratic but a leveler between populous and non-populous states is totally uncompelling. Numbers of electors are determined *by* population, therefore they cannot be a way of negating inequities *in* population. The electoral college exists for one reason and one reason alone: to *check* the will of the people.

[2] As was already hinted, the loading dock, shipping department and in fact the entire company was downsized shortly after this incident due to a move overseas, and the entire factory where I worked no longer exists.

[3] Samuel Eliot Morison, *Sources and Documents Illustrating The American Revolution, 1764-1788, and the Formation of the Federal Constitution,* (New York: Oxford University Press), pg. 133.

[4] See Bernard Bailyn, *The Ideological Origins of the American Revolution* (Cambridge, Mass,: Harvard University Press, 1967), chps 1 and 2.

[5] Bailyn pp. 278 My addition in brackets.

[6] The quote is from Murray Bookchin, *The Third Revolution,* (New York: Cassell), pp. 242-243. For Madison's notes, as well as various private correspondences and debates regarding Constitutional ratification, see Morison, pp. 233-362.

[7] Bailyn, pp. 283-284

[8] First pasage from *The People the Best Governers: Or, a Plan of Government Founded on the Just Principles of Natural Freedom* (Hartford, 1776: JHL Pamphlet 68), pg. 3. Second passage from Bailyn pp. 288-289.

[9] For the story about Washington's toasting habits, see Bookchin, pg. 184. The quote is from a letter to Washington from Gouverneur Morris. Morison, pg. 306.

[10]My inversion of the typical meanings of left and right is intentional. I hope it will help minimize the lazy thinking that results from the overuse of terms.

[11] The central focus of Paine's *Common Sense* is an attack on the notion of inherited power—his attack consumes the second, and I believe central, chapter of his pamphlet.

[12] This is not to suggest that the only reason for the adoption of these structures was to limit and check democracy. There was also the need to check the abuse of power by the representatives of the people themselves. This second task only becomes necessary however, if a representative form of democracy such as the one adopted is chosen. A representative system like the one outlined in Paine's *Common Sense,* one where representatives could not vote in any other way than the one dictated by the constituents they represented, would not face the same problems. It might face different problems though, but more on that in latter chapters.

[13] For specifics on what democratic governance of corporations means, see the Appendix and more so Chapter Three. But please notice, I said democratic governance *not* state control or the elimination of the free market. In fact, what I am supporting is an increase in free markets—genuine free markets not the markets we have now which are neither

free nor markets. Democracy is really just free market thinking and thus when I advocate democracy I am absolutely *not* advocating government control or worse yet, socialism.

[14] Again, for complete details see Chapter 3

[15] For a similar view on this point, see Robert Dahl's piece in *Democracy*, Philip Green ed., (New Jersey:Humanities Press, 1994) and C.B. MacPherson's in *Democracy: Theory and Practice*, ed., (Belmont California: Wadsworth Publishing Company, 1992).

[16] Even if you open your own business you have to get financial backing. This means you still have someone judging and controlling you, someone over whom you have no control because all banks work basically the same and thus you can't threaten them with moving to another bank. Not to mention, the dream of owning your own business, though nice, is not a real option for most because they have neither the collateral nor the experience. And for those few for whom it is an option, they face a bankruptcy rate that is well over 50% for new small businesses, meaning most of them will end up back in big business.

[17] For a similar analogy with a similar message, see Michael Walzer's, "The Case of Pullman, Illinois," in his *Spheres of Justice*, (New York: Basic Books, Inc., 1983) pp. 295-302.

[18] This is not to say that government regulation should go away. Government regulation is essential to a fair and safe society—see "Specific Suggestions for Restructuring the Economy" in Chapter 3. But, government regulation can only be successful *if* fundamental change takes place that will allow it to be successful. When it comes to the power of corporations and the like, fundamental change, not some government regulatory Band-Aid, is crucial.

[19] By leveling this criticism of unions and protestors I do not intend to demean the valiant efforts, and limited successes, of the many who have sought, and still seek, to make more fair our economy, schools and society in general. I intend only to point out that at this juncture in history a new solution to this problem of control is not only possible but necessary; a solution suggested by the American Revolution itself. The day of the labor union and protestor has passed, as evidenced by the declining membership and increasing weakness of these organizations, though I do believe that labor unions could maintain a limited role in certain business organizations. For a more complete treatment of this, see Chapter Three.

[20] For more on this, see Chapter Three.

[21] For those who do not remember, it was a Justice Department sting operation in the 1970's that caught several congressman accepting bribes.

[22] You might want to check out some statistics, particularly concerning the dominance of big business in our society in general and specifically over the government. See Charles Derber's *Corporation Nation* (New York: St. Martin's Griffin, 1998), David C. Korten's *When Corporations Rule the World* (West Hartford, CT: Kunarian Press, Inc., 1999) and Jeff Gates', *Democracy at Risk: Rescuing Main Street from Wall Street* (New York: Perseus, 2000).

[23] What this means exactly I attempt to make perfectly clear in coming chapters. However, for a quick summation, see the Appendix.

[24] Bailyn, pp.46-47.

[25] For some statistical evidence of this malaise, see Juliet B. Schor, et al. *Do Americans Shop too Much?* (New York: Beacon Press, 2000), and Juliet B. Schor and Douglas B. Holt *The Consumer Society Reader* (New York: New Press, 2000).

[26] For more on this, see my discussion of "natural" and "historical" elites in Chapter 2.

[27] I believe the American Revolutionaries were implicitly using reasoning to found a government that a later Enlightenment hero, Immanuel Kant, would explicitly use to attempt to found morality.

Chapter 2
How to Complete the American Revolution:
Democracy and Politics

Like blueprints, the following three chapters will sketch how to build something. My intent is to show what various institutions should come to look like given a commitment to moving the American Revolution further along, move it further along by basing less of our institutions on a paternalistic model and more on the Consent Principle. However, these sketches need the expertise of certain skilled professionals—political scientists, lawyers, economists and educators—to make them actual. They do not give a complete vision of society but they are the necessary first step towards providing such a complete vision. The situation with these blueprints is no different than with actual blueprints. Read them with this in mind.

My analogy with blueprints does break down in a substantial way however. Unlike blueprints, these sketches contain justifications for each part of the sketch. I do this to make clear why I suggest certain specific structural and other changes in politics, the economy and education. Without these justifications it would be unclear why I believed certain changes are necessary. I also give these justifications so those who disagree with my vision can see my reasoning and be convinced, or show how to do things better. Much of what is said here is very open ended. These are educated suggestions but there may be other and more sensible ways for our institutions to embody the Consent Principle, and I welcome the input of others. In the very democratic spirit I champion so much, I see what follows as an invitation to debate so that all of us may decide how things can be done better.

Isn't our politics democratic already?

On to the specific subject of this chapter. Here we will concern ourselves with two questions. First, what would a political system that fully embodies the Consent Principle look like? Second, how can such a political system be brought about? Before we answer either of these questions however, I want to address the apparent strangeness of the first.

Doesn't the American political system, at all levels, already embody the Consent Principle? O.K., maybe there are a few glitches like the Electoral College, but in general doesn't our system require open, competitive elections in which citizens vote for the candidate they believe is best qualified? Haven't the vast majority of limits to the democratic process been removed in the past several hundred years of American history by amending the Constitution and passing other pieces of legislation, as I myself pointed out in the last chapter? If any part of our society seems to treat us like adults, allowing us to decide for ourselves who is best qualified to run things rather than having that decided for us, it would seem to be the political system. So what else needs to be done?

To see what needs to be done let's start by reminding ourselves of something from our elementary school civics classes. The original models of democracy, upon which we were weaned as children, were those of Ancient Athens and Puritan New England. These two models of democracy shared a single idea: democracy meant the direct participation of all citizens in the governmental process. Democracy, to be more specific, provided each citizen with a forum in which it was not only "one man one vote", but "one man one voice". Each citizen had the right to express their views on any issue facing the government, and it was that debate which resulted in a vote thereby establishing the policy of the government. There was no buffer between the people and the government. What the people decided after open debate, the government did. Classic Consent Principle.

These two models acquainted us with democracy in its ideal form, and it was through them that we came to understand our American system. In particular we came to understand that our system differs from these more ideal systems in an important way. Our democratic system is representative and not participatory. We live by the principle of "one man one vote" not "one man one voice." But why does our system differ in this way? Why do we have a representative rather than participatory democratic structure? Why do we have some compromise system and not the ideal system?

One reason was made obvious to us in school. Participatory democracy, though a lovely ideal, was not workable in the later American Colonies and is certainly not workable in the large and vastly complex modern world. There were then, and are now, simply too many people, spread over too vast a territory, in order to make this work. How can we hear what 1 million people, or worse yet 250 million people who are spread out over hundreds if not thousands of miles, have to say on an issue? It was feasible for the Ancient Athenians or early, European settlers of the United States to have participatory democracies because they lived in small communities. In the later colonies and in the contemporary world, the community has grown in size. Participatory democracy is a nice ideal but impossible in practice.

Another reason was not pointed out in school but might be obvious to many of us now that we are adults, particularly those of us who spend a great deal of time in meetings. Participatory democracy would be nice in that it would allow everyone to speak their piece, but it would result in an endless array of meetings where debate never ceased and thus nothing would get accomplished. Any system where power is to be exercised must, if it is to work, eventually allow power to be exercised. This is just what a participatory democracy would not do. So much time would be spent ensuring that the group decides on what constitutes the best course of action that little or no time would be left to actually take action. It would be nice to hear what everybody has to say on issues that effect them—this would be the "feel good" system of the year—but this is not possible without creating a system that moves at a snail's pace. And the first problem exacerbates this problem. As numbers and distances increase, inefficiency increases. With more people, spread over more area, we would need more meetings, involving more participants, arguing more positions. It is bad enough to debate every decision to be made, it would be worse yet when the number of times this must occur, and the number of people involved, becomes enormous.

A third reason is one that we would have never heard in school, not simply because we would have had difficulty understanding it in our younger years, but because it questions the virtue of participatory democracy itself—something a bit subversive for civics class. To some, participatory democracy is not only practically difficult it is far from the democratic ideal that most people assume it to be. In other words, this reason in favor of representative democracy does not stem from a concern about implementing participatory democracy, but the wisdom of a participatory system itself. Many have argued, as we saw in the last chapter, that opening decision-making power to everyone might invite disaster. It might, because many of "the people" seem incapable of making sensible decisions. People with no qualifications are easily swayed by flashy arguments or worse yet, short sighted appeals to self-interest. Some people are simply more intelligent and naturally qualified to lead then others. Even if they are not "naturally" more qualified, they have obtained better training and as a result are in a better position than others to govern. Not to recognize the superiority and expertise of certain people is to allow society to be run in large measure by the less talented and qualified. Rather then participatory democracy leading to a community's taking a profitable course of action, in most cases it will do just the opposite. Bad policies would be the result of a thorough-going participatory structure. Therefore, if we are to have democracy at all, we must have a representative system in order to check the impact of "the people".

These are the reasons we have our current system and not a participatory system. These are the reasons offered for differing from the democratic ideal—for those who believe it is ideal at all. These are the reasons that many believe our system to be the best *possible* system available to us. But are these good reasons? Having made plain the basic difference between our system and the systems of the past, and the reasons for these differences, what we need to do next is analyze these reasons. We must see if the participatory model is ideal, and if it is, can we design a workable system which more closely approximates that ideal. With that done, we can then address the second overall question of this chapter concerning the means of bringing about a more democratic political system—of going from our present to our future in other words.

Closer to the Participatory Ideal

Let's take on the practical reasons offered against participatory democracy first. Let's assume what many would assume, that a participatory system is the best democratic system, and see how we might confront the two practical problems we face in having a participatory system.

We should start addressing these practical problems by recognizing their seriousness. Often times, practical difficulties are seen as something easy to handle. The idea is that once we get clear on theory practical issues fall into place, they take care of themselves. They are not seen as important obstacles. I want to fight this idea. These problems are hard ones, and if not dealt with well they will form a serious impediment to the enactment of any of the ideas discussed in this book. Another point to keep in mind regarding practical problems of the sort under consideration is one made by the famed Ancient Greek philosopher Aristotle. Aristotle suggests that we should not look for greater precision in a subject matter than the subject matter will allow. We should not look for answers to problems in politics that work like answers to problems in mathematics. Problems are very different, and what is going to be acceptable as a solution in one case may be very different than what is acceptable in another. Our problems at this point are practical in nature, and are not going to be solved in ways that are absolutely clean and clear. They will involve compromise. They will involve risk of failure. They will involve uncertainties. We are not going simply to "solve" every problem once and for all. Our subject matter is vastly complex and extremely subtle, and we should recognize the limitations this imposes on our ability to solve certain problems.

With these points made, let's confront the two practical problems that face participatory democracy.

We are told in the study of American government, and democracy in general, though participatory democracy in most cases is the best, fairest system, it is really not a viable form of government. At a certain point a threshold is reached where there are simply too many people to allow participatory democracy to function. This belief is accepted, almost without question, and as a result we are told that if we are going to have a democracy, we must accept the next best thing to participatory democracy, i.e. representational democracy. This is taken to be common sense, but is it?

I do not doubt that at a certain point the number of people in a community prohibits the effective working of a participatory democracy in that community. I also think that no matter how technologically advanced we might become, there would be no way to overcome this. When the number of people becomes too great, we cannot involve every member of a community in every decision that their community faces for several reasons.

First, due to time constraints, it would be difficult for everyone to vote on issues, let alone allow them a voice in the issues that were raised and the solutions proposed—as real participatory democracy would require. Even if we could work out some technological means of bringing vast numbers of people together, potentially from great distances, there would not be enough time to allow the open interaction necessary in a participatory democracy. On any given issue, if 10,000 people wanted to speak for an average of 5 minutes per person, that amounts to 833 hours of discussion. Assuming an 8 hour work day, that discussion would take over 100 days. And these are low estimates. If the number of people involved in a decision was in the 10's or 100's of millions, then many more than 10,000 people could want to speak, and they would in all likelihood take a lot longer than 5 minutes per person. And these numbers do not include time for debate. What this means is that for any given issue it will take on average, and this is a generous estimation, 1/4 to 3/4 of a year or more for a decision to be made. This is certainly not a viable option. Nothing would get done.

A second problem is that to turn the responsibility of governing large institutions, of whatever variety, over to everyone, would be to overburden individuals. Governing a complex institution is a tremendously difficult task, one that requires full-time devotion to the understanding of the institutions involved and the issues that confront those institutions. To make everyone responsible for such a complex task would be horribly inefficient. It would take people away, in many cases, from what they want to do, and it would result in much redundant effort. How many people should we require to exert this extreme effort? If everyone, won't this take them away from other individually and socially important tasks?

Given these two reasons, it would seem that that the first practical objection to participatory democracy is correct. There are too many people to make a universal participatory democracy work, and this cannot be helped even by technology. How about the second objection?

Here the situation is more complex. The mere fact that decisions must be made collectively does not mean that such a system will be inefficient or slow—that we will spend all our time meeting and debating not acting. When groups are small enough, a participatory democratic process can be the most efficient. It helps us bring to bear many perspectives on a given problem, and it encourages open analysis of those perspectives by the most minds. It also makes people feel as if they are a part of whatever decision is eventually made, thus making it more likely that they will enthusiastically support the decision and energetically take action based on that decision. It is for these reasons that when people attempt a project where no existing social hierarchy is in place and only a few people are involved—the few people involved are taken to be equal in status regarding this project—democratic decision making is the norm. If you get two non-experts building a bicycle for instance, they will work as a team, which entails making decisions together.

The second objection gains much more credence as the numbers of people involved increases however. The more individuals involved, the less time will be spent listening to each individual and the more time will be spent allowing every individual to be heard. This will lessen the quantity, and ultimately the quality, of each individual's input, and increase the time in which debate will take place. When two people build a bicycle their input can be lengthy and have great effect. If 100 people build a bicycle, the input of each individual will be reduced in quantity and hence effect, while the total time listening to people will increase. Thus, more time will be spent on lesser quality input. On top of this, a certain amount of alienation will set in among the individuals involved. Each individual will have less say in any decision, and will thereby feel less a part of that decision.

Our discussion of these two problems demonstrates there is actually one main practical problem with participatory democracy: size. Therefore, if we are to have any participatory democracy—as our democratic ideal would seem to demand—this problem must be dealt with. The best way to deal with it, I believe, is to establish an ideal size—both in numbers of people and geographic area—that will allow participatory democracy to work efficiently. Participatory democracy could then be achieved simply by keeping the numbers of people and distances involved in most government institutions below the proper ideal, or threshold, size. This threshold number should guide the design of political institutions so that as much participatory democracy could take place as possible. As long as we keep our political institutions below the threshold size, then participatory democracy could work often and well.

Though something to shoot for in designing our political institutions, this answer does present us with two problems: One, how can we identify this threshold, if we can do so at all? Two, what do we do in the case of institutions that are simply too big to keep under the threshold?

Establishing this threshold would be a fairly simple, though a tedious and laborious affair.[1] For each type of governmental institution involved (executive, legislative, judicial), and for each level of each type of institution (local, state, national,), a trial and error method should be employed until the threshold is established. The basis of this method would be to run trials with actual groups of people making decisions, and then see how they felt about the process afterwards, and whether the process was efficient. If they felt comfortable and the process was efficient, in other words they felt their input was meaningful, they were satisfied with the decision, and they reached the decision in a reasonable amount of time, then we are below the threshold. As soon as the majority of people show signs of dissatisfaction, then the threshold has been reached. You then run several more experiments to confirm your results, and that becomes the size which should be used to guide the structuring of each type of political institution. As often as possible, we should structure our political institutions so as to keep them smaller than the threshold size for their proper functioning as participatory democracies. This would be far from a fool-proof process, but over time it would allow the proper "settling out" that would make our governmental institutions increasingly better as participatory democracies. It has the added advantage of being a democratic way of establishing the proper democratic political organization. The people actually involved in the democratic process will be the ones making the decision about what numbers work the best.

The response to the second question is a great deal more complex. When political institutions are too big to structure according to some threshold number, then a variety of representational democracy *must* be employed. We have no choice on this matter. Given this, we confront the question: what kind of representational democracy? This might seem a strange question to ask. It is often assumed that there is only one basic variety of representational democracy. If true, this would solve our problem, but there is a second variety of representational democracy that is not often recognized as representational, one that is presently at work in the Untied States as a matter of fact. Not only is there a second variety, I believe this second variety should be expanded into that most central branch of government, the legislature, in order to make that system more participatory in nature—this is not the only change I will recommend but it is the central change as I make evident in the next section. In order to argue these points I will identify the different means of representation, weigh their advantages and disadvantages in light of our commitment to making our system more participatory, and then show how they can be combined to make a better, more participatory, system.

"Improved Representation"

When we talk about "representational democracy," the type of system that springs to most people's minds is what can be termed a "parliamentary" system.[2] It involves the election of representatives, by the citizens of a certain geographic area, who govern in the name of the citizens. The second type of representative system, the one not often thought of as a representational system, is the current jury system of the United States. This jury system is based on the idea that citizens of a community should not be represented by some group who it elected and who speaks in its name, but by a random selection of the citizens themselves. Rather than assuring that the citizens are heard by making certain people beholden to the citizens through election, the jury system allows some randomly chosen sub-set of the citizens to speak for themselves. In no sense are the jurors actually expected to speak in the name of the entire citizenry. They are expected to speak for themselves. But juries work to represent the citizenry in that over time enough of the citizens participate in the juries so that these become an expression of the "community's voice".

The advantages of the jury form of representation are obvious for those who hold out the participatory ideal of "one person one voice". The jury system allows ordinary citizens to speak on and decide issues based on their own debate. The jury system maintains the important participatory democratic ideal that each citizen has not only one vote but one voice, and it is your own voice, in conjunction with the voices of your fellow jury members, that guide debate and make decisions. The system not only allows but makes necessary the actual input of every member of the jury, an input that far surpasses anything allowed by a parliamentary form of representative democracy.

The obvious disadvantage of juries for supporters of participatory democracy is that they would not allow every citizen in the community to speak on a given issue. Currently, various juries, at various levels of the judiciary, make decisions that are not open to debate by every citizen. If we were to expand the jury system outside the judiciary, the same limitation would arise. Though true, there are several things that might mitigate this disadvantage. One is that over time, almost every citizen is now, or would be in an expanded system, called to serve on these juries, thus ensuring that every citizen has input at some time on some level. Even though your input may not be constant in any one forum, there is now, and would be, an opportunity for your voice to be heard on the various juries in which you participate throughout your life. So many of these juries are, and would be, necessary, that any citizen could expect to serve a number of times in their active political life. A second mitigating factor is that the system could be designed to allow the input of non-jury members, particularly in very important decisions, through a mechanism such as a public hearing or a plebiscite. Also, current juries call witnesses, hear evidence, etc. all ways in which non-jury members might have a say in the decisions being made. In an expanded system the input of non-jury members could be made in the same way, or even broadened. A third mitigating factor is that the randomness of the selection lessens the chance of some people coming to dominate because they serve again and again on juries—we must worry about corruption and abuse of power if everyone cannot speak and vote on issues. In a random selection, various people are called to serve and in an expanded system it could even by mandated by law that once you served on a certain type of jury you could never again serve on that type. This random selection also helps avoid juries with a slanted perspective—always a fear in any jury based system. Random selection almost guarantees that multiple perspectives get represented, avoiding a jury heavily weighted towards one side on an issue.

Though far from ideal—we already know what our ideal is and why it is impossible in all cases—juries have many advantages over the parliamentary type of representative democracy. The problem with the parliamentary system is that it puts certain citizens in the position of speaking for others, rather than speaking for themselves. The consequences of this are many and almost all bad. First, it is unclear who is responsible for the decisions that are made. If this system is to be at all democratic, the representative must determine what the citizenry "wants" and then attempt to speak in its name. The representative is to function merely as a spokesperson. But this removes responsibility for all decisions from the representative, and puts in on the citizens. But how can vast numbers of citizens ever be held responsible for anything? They cannot—if they could, then we should hold every German citizen who voted for Hitler in 1933 responsible for the Holocaust—which leaves the question of just who is responsible for the actions of the government unanswered. A second problem concerns determining the will of the citizenry. Often times, this will is only vaguely expressed, and this only every few years. What this means is that just what the citizens want is going to be left open to vast interpretation by the representative. The representative thus can either misjudge or actually distort what he or she believes the citizens want, leading to a situation in which the representative can make decisions that are their own, not the will of the majority. And they can do this while acting as if they are not responsible because they are merely "following orders". A third problem is that the voice of the citizenry can be distorted through various means such as media, special interest groups, political party machinery, etc. In this situation, even if the representative is trying their best to act on the will of the membership, they may not be doing so because this will has been distorted. And finally, some or all representatives might see their role not as expressing the will *of* the citizenry but thinking *for* the citizenry. Their role being, in their minds, to vote based on how they see things irrespective of what the citizens want. In such a case, the amount of democracy in the system is reduced to nil, drawing closer to the aristocratic systems the American Revolution was fought to overcome.

All these problems have the same common cause. There is some attempt being made to allow the citizenry to express their will on the issues that affect them. This cannot be done directly, for the reason of size outlined in our discussion of participatory democracy, so this is done indirectly through the election of "mouthpieces." The installation of these intermediaries introduces to the system the problems of speaking in another's name. It raises questions of responsibility, possible miscommunication, abuse of power and the resurrection of aristocracy, questions which do not arise when someone is taken to be speaking for him or herself.

There are only two real advantages to the parliamentary system. The first is that it allows professionalism and hence promotes efficiency. When an institution is large enough to merit a representative system of control, that institution also becomes very complex. A parliamentary system allows certain people to become professionals at the running of such large institutions. They can study the institution they control and become experts at handling its problems. This expertise then increases their efficiency and effectiveness. The second advantage is that it allows everyone who is not a representative the time to concentrate on other activities. When a citizen's responsibility is only to participate in the election of a representative once every couple of years, they need not dedicate much effort towards understanding the issues. This allows them to concentrate on other issues that may be of great importance to themselves, the community, or both.

However, these advantages are disadvantages as well. The first advantage, professionalism in the leadership, can lead to rigidity in the leadership that then makes the government unable to respond to changing voices and circumstances. It can also lead to a professional class of leaders who become increasingly removed from the membership they are intended to serve— witness the "millionarization" of the American Senate and Presidency over the past 50 years. The second advantage turns into a disadvantage in that the citizenry, those who are being represented, become increasingly ignorant about the issues. This ignorance can then lead to bad policy because when the representative acts on the will of the citizenry, they are acting on a will that is often poorly informed.

Both the jury and parliamentary systems of representation have advantages and disadvantages. Can we combine these two systems in order to make our current system of representation have most of the advantages and few of the disadvantages? If so, how exactly would this combined system function? What would be the place of elections? How large would the juries be? How often would they meet? How would they be chosen? What would be the role of political parties? It is to these and similar question that I now turn.

Restructuring the Government According to Improved Representation

To start our discussion of the actual structure of representation, let's see how we can incorporate the advantages of a jury system into our current system of representation; incorporate them so that we obtain the best of both systems while avoiding the worst.

First, we should retain our current model of representation for the executive branch of government.[3] The President and all executive officers at all levels of government should be, as they are now in most cases, directly elected by the citizens of their districts for terms ranging from two to four years—any impediments to direct election such as the Electoral College should be eliminated. This helps ensure that experts at enforcing the law are in control yet are at the same time under the control of those they govern. This also allows the consistency of policy that we need from the executive branch without allowing undue entrenchment—individuals never leaving positions. To further avoid entrenchment, we should place term limits on the executive such that no one is allowed more than two consecutive terms of office—regardless of length of term.

Second, we should retain the current model of representation for all upper houses in our legislative bodies. Institutions like the U. S. Senate should retain their status as directly elected bodies, ones where members serve for longer terms such as the six year term of a U.S. Senator. This, as in the case with the executive, serves to maintain the professionalism and policy consistency that helps make government effective and efficient. Also, as in the case of the executive, term limits should be placed on the upper houses to avoid entrenchment. A two term limit would seem adequate.

Third, we should maintain our current jury system in the judiciary and expand the current practice of electing judges to the bench. In some districts judges are directly elected by the citizenry, but in other districts, and particularly the highest court in the land the U.S. Supreme Court, citizens are allowed no direct voice in appointments. When citizens are not allowed a say in appointments this makes appointments little more than patronage in many cases, and often ensures that judges are out of sync with the communities they serve. In order to avoid these problems, while still maintaining the high professionalism and as much political neutrality as possible in our judges—also the central reasons to maintain tenure (job for life) for judges—I suggest we expand the current direct election of judges, but also require that those judges obtain the approval of the executive officer and upper house in charge of the district they will serve. For instance, there should be a general election held to fill spots on the U. S. Supreme Court, but the results of those elections must be approved by the President and the Senate.

Fourth, political parties should be allowed to function much as they do now—though hopefully more than two— in order to help streamline the election process. Candidates for various offices must be narrowed and some consensus on the key issues in an election must be reached, or elections will be a messy and indecisive affair. Political parties can help with both these tasks. Precise qualifications for a political party to take part in the elections process—appear on ballots, gain access to debates, etc.—will have to be set by individual districts based on measures like quantity of signatures on petitions and professional polling numbers. More importantly, these parties will have to be publicly financed, through tax dollars, as all parts of elections will have to be publicly financed, to ensure no undue influence from money. In particular, access to television and radio airtime will have to be strictly regulated and equally distributed—this being a function of both what is necessary for more fair elections but also the fact that the airwaves are publicly owned in the first place and thus should serve the public interest.[4] Such changes in financing and campaigning will not only help avoid corruption, it will also foster the development of more parties as the existence and plausibility of a party will be based on their platform not the money they raise. For those worried about free speech issues—that money equals speech as a number of courts have argued— private financing could be permitted, but public funds then used to match the money given by private citizens. Hence, if one candidate on the ballot raises 10 million dollars in private money, and their opponent only 6 million, the public financing system would then make up the remaining 4 million. This would apply to any candidate on the ballot—for criteria establishing ballot access see above.

Beyond these basic structural similarities, and for the reasons we have outlined, I believe the following substantial changes should be made. The lower houses of all legislative bodies should be converted into juries. The U.S. House of Representatives and other comparable bodies should no longer be elected by the citizens but should *be* the citizens. Citizens chosen by lot should serve for designated lengths—different lengths for different levels of government— debating and voting on legislation proposed by the upper house and by jury members themselves. The lower houses should be chosen by lot, but they should continue to play the same role in governing that they currently play. They should be part of the legislative process, and part of the overall system of checks and balances that keeps any branch from gaining too much control. Importantly, they should maintain the "power of the purse," that is, they should control the government's money. This ensures they are the most powerful part of the government and it only seems fair given the money being spent is *their* money— *our* money.

In order to ensure that jury members have the knowledge necessary for effective and efficient management of government, we should make the term of jury service long enough for each jury member to become acquainted with the complex issues they must discuss—removal of a jury member should be allowed only after a court hearing if there is plausible evidence of their having violated jury ethics or are, or have become, incapacitated. This term must be made long enough to ensure the proper education, but not so long so that jury members themselves become entrenched in their positions or are kept away from their careers and lives for two long. Part of this term should be spent in formal study, and in consultation with the outgoing jury in the institution in question. Depending upon the institution in question, the term of a jury service should run anywhere from several months in smaller institutions, to several years at the level of the Federal Government. The upper house, as a more professional, constant body, should also be used to help educate members of incoming juries. They should play the role that judges play in courtrooms today, informing the juries about the intricacies of procedure, and helping to maintain an orderly environment for debate.

By converting the lower houses of our legislatures into juries, we would eliminate the "one man one vote" mentality of our present system—we would obtain a more participatory structure—and we would avoid the entrenchment that our current system engenders. We would do this while still maintaining a high level of professionalism in the government. In order to further maintain this balance, we must ensure political parties, political action committees and lobbies of any sort should be made illegal among jury members and have no contact with members. It is also important that no one speak on another's behalf. The point of a jury system is make each citizen speak for themselves, not to have them represented by one another, or to have them spouting a party line. Legislative juries would be no different than judicial juries are right now in these regards. This is not to say that a jury member could not be a member of a political party or other group. It is only to say that political parties, political action committees, lobbies, etc., should not be allowed to organize, recruit, spend money on, etc., any member of a jury. In fact, to further avoid outside control, for the period of jury service, no jury member should be allowed to receive any "gifts" from any individual or group associated with issues being voted upon. Again, this is no different than the way juries function in their current form in the judicial branch of government.

We can ensure a more participatory structure while maintaining professionalism through the use of juries, but can we make the service in these "legislative juries" something that is not odious to the average citizen? Can we ensure greater participation without asking ordinary citizens to abandon projects in which they have personal interest? Most people hate jury duty right now, can we avoid this in the future considering the vast expansion of jury service I am proposing? I think this can be done if we structure jury service much like an amended variety of other public service programs as they are now conceived. Two obvious examples are the current jury system in the United States, and the military draft that we have used and continues to be used in various nations. Individuals should be called to service for an appointed time, but now they should receive some significant reimbursement for their lost time, and with a guarantee that their lives can be picked up where they left off at the beginning of jury service—a law would have to be passed to ensure both of these. With these provisions for compensation and the return to one's normal life, jury service would not be too overbearing to the average citizen. In fact, many would like it, I believe, as it would give them a chance to have real impact on the government. Regardless of how much individuals like jury service however, it should remain as it now is, mandatory, though the normal exceptions will be allowed—for illness, etc. Jury members should also be chosen at random, based on any number of systems that have been employed with great success—and for the reasons we have outlined.

With these methods we can incorporate the advantages of a parliamentary system, and we can also avoid the disadvantages. Individuals would not become entrenched in their positions because they would be in power for an appointed period of time. Once their time is up they can return to their normal activities. Because they would be given a guarantee that they could return to their work after jury service, the inevitable interruption would be lessened, and hopefully the lost time would benefit their development.

One last concern is the issue of jury size. The proper size of a jury, once it is established that a system of representation is necessary—that the district in question is too large to be run as a participatory system—will vary from institution to institution. Nonetheless, the number for any given governing institution can be obtained quite easily. A jury should never exceed in size the threshold number established for a participatory democracy in that type of institution. Each jury is to work exactly like a participatory democracy in that every jury member is to be able to raise issues, speak on issues, and vote on issues. Due to this, we can designate jury size as the size most likely to allow participatory democracy to function well. Every jury should be as large as possible to ensure that we get as many perspectives as possible, but the jury should never exceed the threshold number for a participatory democracy. My guess would be that, at its present population, the U.S. House "jury" would have approximately 1000 members.

Combining Participation and Improved Representation in Our Government

With these basic guidelines for representation set out, we can now provide an actual blueprint for how our government should work at all levels:

On the local level—the level of counties, wards, parishes, etc.— government should be participatory in nature. Local communities should be run by the people who live in them, and each citizen should be allowed to raise issues for discussion, engage in discussion, and vote on solutions. All the duties of government that cannot be handled by direct participation, such as the policing, regulating and judicial functions of government, should be carried out by those voted to do so by the participatory body.

Out of these local units should be constituted larger governmental units. These larger governmental unites could be regional in very populous States such as New York, California, New Jersey, etc. Or, they could be entire States, if the States are not too populous, as in the case of North Dakota, Nebraska, Alaska, etc. These larger units could by participatory in structure, if they do not exceed the threshold size for participation. If they do exceed that size, then they should be run by the system of Improved Representation just outlined. The function of States or other regional units should be to decide on issues throughout their wider geographic area, including the settling of disputes between the various local, participatory-democratic organizations.

The States or larger regional units should in turn be subject to the Federal government. The Federal government, which would undoubtedly be structured according to Improved Representation—we all know 250 million people or more is too large a number for direct participatory democracy—should then be the final authority over all the smaller units. It should have all the responsibilities that are possessed by the current Federal Government.

The basic relationship between the smaller units and the larger units should be one of "suzerainty". Suzerainty amounts to a hands off attitude by the larger units towards the internal affairs of the smaller units, while allowing control by the larger units of the relations between the smaller units. Given this, the only time a larger unit should involve itself in the internal affairs of a smaller unit is when some citizen of a smaller unit believes they are being treated unfairly by that unit, when two units need to work together to solve an issue, or when there is some larger policy issue that effects an area greater than that controlled by a single smaller unit. Given this is basically the system we now have, no change need really take place in the relationship between smaller and larger government levels. Worked out over the 200 plus year history of the U.S. system, the relationship between levels of government, while hardly perfect, offers much. As long as the other changes suggested above are enacted, nothing here need get altered greatly.

Through this system I believe it is possible to achieve the democratic goal of allowing the maximum amount of open interaction between individuals in the determination of all judgments—the ultimate goal of participatory democracy. This system will unquestionably have flaws. But it may also be the most vibrant system in the contemporary world, one that allows people to determine their own lives to the greatest extent yet known.

The Elitist Objection to Participatory Democracy

Having shown how we might make our government much more participatory without decreasing efficiency, even when representational in nature, we must now turn to the "theoretical objection" against participatory democracy itself. We must question what we assumed while addressing the practical problems facing participatory democracy, namely, that the more participatory a system the better it is. The desire to question this assumption, the real issue in this "theoretical objection" concerning the wisdom of the people, will become pronounced in some after reading what I have just written. "My god," they will proclaim, "you want the average American to have *more* say in what goes on in this country! Surely this will lead us to ruin. Most Americans don't vote now because they aren't "interested," (read able to think at a level that makes politics interesting to them) so now we are going to drag them kicking and screaming further into governing this country?! Surely this will mean our demise! Every X (fill in the blank with the type of American you dislike the most) will surly elect Y (fill in the blank with the worst possible individual you could imagine as President) or pass law Z (fill in the blank with the worst possible law you can think of)!" This worry, which many of you are experiencing right now even though you might feel ashamed to say so, the very same worry we touched on in Chapter 1, is ultimately based on a belief in the existence of an elite that is more able to govern than the rest of the citizenry— some group of people who are more intelligent and talented than most of us. In order to respond to this objection—which we can now refer to as the "elitist objection"—we need to discuss whether such an elite exists. And if it does, whether the democratic system we have just outlined would be the wrong form of organization.

To open this discussion, we should notice that two different types of elite could exist. One we can term a "natural" elite. A natural elite is one that exists independent of whatever humans might have done or will do— membership in such an elite being determined by forces beyond human control, i.e. genetic makeup. Examples of naturally elite individuals in music, science and athletics would be Mozart, Einstein or Michael Jordan, and in the case of governing we might point to Abraham Lincoln or George Washington. The second type we can term an "historical" elite. An historical elite is one that exists mostly as a result of something humans have chosen to do. In this case, whether you are in the elite or not is the result of forces that humans can and do control, i.e. distribution of wealth, educational opportunity, etc. An example here might be Bill Gates, Donald Trump or Henry Ford II, and in the case of governing take many American Presidents since World War II. We must keep our discussion of these two types of elite separate. We must, because the claims about the existence of each type of elite, and the effects of each type on participatory democracy, might be different due to their supposedly different origins.

A "Natural" Elite and Participatory Democracy

The claim that there is a natural governing elite—mostly those people more intelligent than the rest of us—and that as a result we should not support participatory democracy but rather a representative or even aristocratic system, can be argued against in several ways. First, we could respond by denying the existence of such a natural elite. Denying the existence of a natural elite is to assert the basic equality of persons. Such a radically egalitarian idea would transcend any assertion about the equality of persons under the law. Rather it would emphasize that *no one* is really more intelligent or talented than anyone else in a substantive way—at least not when it comes to what it takes to govern. This is a position that was popular with the political philosopher Thomas Hobbes, and has increased in popularity recently with the rise of "political correctness"—it is very politically incorrect to suggest in any way that some people are better than others when it comes to governing or anything else for that matter. It has been quite common throughout history to see all differences between people as the result of upbringing and historical circumstance—it is all nurture not nature in other words.

Asserting such radical egalitarianism would be a bad response to the elitist objection. What is the proof that people are equal? It would seem that evidence actually weights heavier on the side of the existence of a natural elite rather than against it. In many walks of life some people do just seem naturally better than others, and often are, and should be, put in charge of those who are less good. We can see this again and again in music and athletics, mathematics and literature, public speaking and political leadership. Some people are just better at things than other people.

This could be challenged from the radical egalitarian perspective of course. The radical egalitarian could claim that a natural elite is being confused with an historical one. What looks like natural difference is really just a difference in socio-cultural background. Mozart, Einstein, Winston Churchill and George Washington just had a certain upbringing and the time was ripe for the type of genius they exhibited.

If the radical egalitarian takes this road, then they are doing two things. First, they are admitting that there is a difference in people's qualities, and thus opening up the chance that this historical elite should be put, or left, governing. They are admitting that some people are better and that maybe we should not support participatory democracy as a result—something the radical egalitarian would most likely not want to do. Second, and more important, they are merely trading in the discussion of a natural elite for an historical one. Though a legitimate step to take, they have really not advanced their cause but simply shifted the focus of discussion—a discussion of historical elites that is off the point here and that we will undertake later in the chapter.

A second challenge that the radical egalitarian could level against this criticism is that the evidence for the existence of a natural elite is actually no good. The evidence for a natural elite is of two sorts. One is social scientific evidence based on claims about genetic make up. Blacks are pitted against whites or Asians against Westerners in tests of various human qualities, tests that supposedly demonstrate that these qualities are genetically based—not just intelligence but everything from homosexuality to obesity has been claimed to be based ultimately on genetics. The second type of evidence is that which we appealed to above: anecdotal. It just *seems* that some people are more naturally talented at things than others. Ask anyone and they will be able to tell you stories about people who are better at certain things, or more self-confident, or more self-disciplined, or any of the other qualities that make someone more effective at leading people.

The radical egalitarian could attack these two types of evidence in the following ways. Social scientific research on the quality of persons has all the inherent weaknesses of any social scientific research: difficulties in sampling, prejudicial interpretations of data, unclear causal relationships between social phenomenon and underlying physical factors, etc. Such difficulties always face social science, and they are particularly poignant in this instance. When anything as controversial as human quality difference is being argued for based on social scientific research, these weaknesses are going to become glaring. It is for this reason that all previous social science research on human quality difference has failed ever to convince even a majority of experts or people in general for that matter. We have heard many times about the "discovery" of the intelligence gene, or the fat gene, gay gene, alcoholism gene, etc., but these discoveries are quickly and quietly forgotten as they are subjected to rigorous testing. It is very difficult to prove that something as complex as behavior has such a simple, single cause. Thus, if social scientific evidence forms the basis of claims regarding the superiority of certain people, then the case for the existence of a natural elite is going to be very unconvincing.

As regards anecdotal evidence, the radical egalitarian could respond prospects are little better. It may just *seem* that certain people are better, but this does not mean that they *are* better. Many cultural prejudices could be at work in the interpretation of stories about quality difference. For instance, the superiority of boys over girls in mathematics, which many claim is a natural superiority, could just as well be explained as a result of upbringing. Boys are taught from a young age that mathematics is "manly," whereas girls are taught mathematics is a "boys" subject. What may seem the obvious conclusion to draw from a certain story might be obvious only to people of a certain background. Anecdotal evidence is always the most unreliable evidence. It is certainly not something upon which we could establish as controversial a claim as that some people are naturally better than others.

Even if correct, this radical egalitarian critique of the evidence for the existence of a natural elite does nothing but return us to my initial criticism of radical egalitarianism. It returns us to this criticism because a critique of evidence of the sort just outlined would cut both ways. If this challenge undermines the evidence for a natural elite, then it undermines the evidence for equality, because what little evidence there is to support fundamental human equality would seem to be the same as that offered in support of a natural elite. Making the appeal to social scientific research and anecdotes no good in one case makes them no good in the other. By taking this avenue of approach the radical egalitarian would thus throw out the baby with the bath water. The result is that we are returned to where we started: looking for evidence that people are basically equal.

The case against radical egalitarianism is far from conclusive, but it need not be made conclusive. There is another, better response to the "elitist objection" against participatory democracy based on the existence of a natural, governing elite. This response does not involve a discussion of the complex question of the existence of a natural elite. It is more practical in nature. It is an attack upon the worry that motivates the "elitist objection" to participatory democracy.

What the "elitist" really worries about is that if we adopt a participatory democratic structure, we will repress the more intelligent and talented among us, thereby inviting disaster because the less intelligent and talented will govern. We will repress the intelligent and talented because they will be forced to conform to the will of the majority, who are less intelligent and talented. But this worry is unfounded for the following reason. If there is a natural governing elite, some natural intelligentsia who "knows" better, then participatory democracy can let them shine. It can let them shine because those who constitute this elite will be given the opportunity to convince people of their superior quality. If they truly *are* superior, then they should be able to demonstrate this is some way that is convincing—particularly given their audience is supposed to be less intelligent and talented than they are. And if they cannot give such a demonstration, upon what basis are they claiming to be of superior quality? That individual who claims to be an artistic, scientific or political genius, yet has never painted a decent painting, established a revolutionary theory or lead a nation, lacks grounds for their claims to membership in an elite.

An example from the world of sports is helpful—a world that will provide us even more insights when we appeal to it in the chapter on the economy. If Michael Jordan is really better at basketball than I am, if he is really a member of a natural basketball elite and I a mere basketball peasant, than he should have no problem showing this in open competition on the basketball court. Give him and I a free and fair competitive environment, one where we received similar training and time to develop our skills, and his natural talent at basketball is going to shine through if it exists. Change the case. If I am a better natural public speaker than Michael, this too should be evident when we both speak to almost any, but the most slanted, of audiences. In other words, if someone has a talent, and they are made to compete fairly against those who are less talented, there will be little question about their superiority. Open competition allows those who are the best to show this. That is all participatory democracy provides, a free, fair and open competitive environment. As such, any "elitist" should have little fear of such a participatory democratic structure.

Ultimately, a democratic system need make no assumptions regarding the fundamental, natural equality of persons. The only thing democracy requires, in terms of equality, is that everyone is given an equal *opportunity* to direct the decisions that affect themselves and those around them. It makes no assumption about who will be able to take advantage of that opportunity, and it will allow a natural elite, if it exists, to assert itself. It will also allow human equality to shine through, if it is the case that people are equal. Whether people are of the same quality or some are superior, a democratic system can work just the same. A democratic system can work in either case because it is ultimately merit based, merit as determined by the community in an open forum. This means whoever has merit will be able to show this, regardless of whether it is a few individuals or almost everyone at one time or another.

A fully democratic society could let a natural elite assert itself, if it is designed properly, thus the worry about repressing the more intelligent and talented is unfounded. And because the worry that motivates the "elitist objection" to participatory democracy is unfounded, this undermines the objection itself. This worry is, in fact, doubly unfounded. It is doubly unfounded because, I believe, participatory democracy could allow a natural elite to assert itself better than in any other system. Those naturally better qualified could, due to their superior ability, convince those of inferior ability that they should give them substantial control. The amount of control that is possible to accrue would be limited only by the ability of a natural elite to convince people that they should be given control—within the restraints discussed in the system of Improved Representation. This system leaves open the possibility that the truly superior individual can have control far greater than any normal, hierarchical, bureaucratic system, or a system where some historical elite dominates. Thus, the worry that a participatory democracy would repress those of natural ability, and hence lead to mediocrity or even disaster in government, is further undermined.[5]

On the relationship between institutions of governmental power and a claimed natural elite, we as supporters of participatory democracy share much with, of all people, Plato. In his *Republic*, Plato bases the ideal state upon an educational system intended to identify a natural elite. Plato is an avowed elitist.

But what he also believes is that a system must be designed that does not presume the superiority of any particular individuals—he does not believe that an actually ruling elite and the natural elite are at all the same. His entire state is a means of allowing people, from whatever background, to demonstrate their "natural" merit.

Our democracy can be based on the same notion that an individual's possession, and quantity, of talent must be demonstrated not assumed. No person need be assumed to have more talent than another, but if they do, then they will, or should, be allowed to go as far as that talent will take them. This was Plato's idea, and it is a fundamental idea behind democracy as we are construing democracy.[6]

Though what I have said might have force, some are still going to balk at this idea that a properly designed democracy will allow a natural elite, if it exists, to assert itself. The reason they will give is that a member of the natural elite may not be able to convince the common person of their superior quality. They may be too advanced for the common person, and the only way they could make the common person understand their ideas would be to water them down. It is almost a cultural cliché to speak of "geniuses," or even the very intelligent or talented—those people we would want most to govern—as misunderstood in their own time, only being recognized for their talent late in life or after they are dead. They simply cannot be understood by common people exactly for the reason that they are uncommon. The genius may just be incapable of communicating with the mediocre, or they will be forced to change their ideas in order to be understood and thus become mediocre. Either way, the result will be entirely negative on the person of extraordinary talent. Thus, a natural elite will not shine through in a participatory democracy, and may even be hurt be such a system.

This concern is a general one, applying to the world of governance and many others, but is probably brought into focus best by using an example from the world of fine art. I know we are concerned with a natural governing elite but with the world of art this concern can be made the most clear and then easily applied to the political case. If this causes you concern as you think these worlds are different in some sense, simply replace the artistic genius in the following scenario with someone who has a revolutionary new idea about how to organize ourselves politically or economically.

Imagine an artist who feels compelled to paint in an entirely new style and seeks funding and support from their community—they apply for an NEH grant let's say. This style is different than anything seen before, and therefore is something to which people are unaccustomed. This fact, the style's difference, makes it almost certain that most "common" people would be unable either to understand it or appreciate it. This difficulty in understanding and appreciation could actually be a part of the point of the style. It is considered a rarefied aesthetic, one not meant for everyone. In a participatory democracy, or our system of improved representation, one where "the people" control the NEH, what will happen to this artist?

The answer would appear to be that this artist will not thrive. Their attempts to convince others of the value of their work—their task as the member of some system allowing participation—will be fruitless because almost everyone will fail to possess the vision that is necessary in order to see its value. And they do not want to spend their time trying to convince people of their talent anyway. The result will be that this artist will not receive the material support necessary in order to be able to produce his or her art. Hence the art will not be produced. The member of the natural elite, as exemplified here by the artist, rather than shining through will actually be thwarted in a participatory structure. The only way they will thrive will be to conform to the requirements of the majority, a requirement that will repress their natural superiority.

I have three responses to this.

First, the need to conform is already required of the "genius", or anyone with different ideas for that matter. No one who attempts to communicate their beliefs, feelings, etc., is immune from the need to heed the call of their community. They are not, because it is only through relation to the community that they are granted the time, the materials, and often the motivation, to work. Given this, we must ask what is the best response to the requirement of conformity: One, to attempt to eliminate the need to conform while allowing the "genius", i.e. the member of the natural elite, to excel?; Two, to make the "genius" conform to social pressures in the present implicit, clandestine way?; Three, to make the "genius" conform to social pressures in an open forum?

One is inadequate because it is unclear how the genius is to be given the means to produce their work by society, without having to conform to social pressures, i.e., the market. If people are to pay for creative production, be it a movie, painting poem or piece of public policy, they are going to need a reason to do so. This reason will often, if not always, be that such production plays a "positive" role, of some sort, in their lives. What this means is that creative production will have to conform to what people can understand to some extent. They will have to be affected by something like a piece of art of a theory, which means that in order for the artist or intellectual to work, that artist or intellectual will have to be sensitive to social need. Some level of conformity will be required if creative production is to be possible.

Two, to continue along the way we are going, is to deny the problem. At present we do make the genius conform to the requirements of social "taste," as that taste is expressed through the market. We do this, but we do not explicitly recognize that what we are doing is making the "genius" conform. Because we are normally not opening up their creative production to some form of community judgment, i.e. a vote, competition, etc., we believe that somehow they are not really being required to conform. But they are. And in hiding this, we leave open the chance that the mechanisms of conformity, such as the market, are guided by forces other than a concern for the quality of the creative production.

We are left with number three, admit that social conformity is something that does take place and therefore it should take place in a free and fair way. Denying this situation will not make it go away, and in fact, to get it out in the open may help the "genius." It may give them a means of having their work judged in a way where the main concern is the work itself. Where the critical judgment is out in the open and based exclusively on the work, not simply on whether it is marketable, or some critic likes it, etc.

My second response concerning the relationship between the "genius" and the community is that our image of this relationship has become consumed by a certain "ideology of genius." This ideology is based on the belief that the "genius" and the "common person" are at odds and ultimately in conflict. Or, if they are not in conflict, they are at least not capable of any meaningful communication. It is for this reason that the "true genius" must starve in his or her lifetime, and that the scientist must be "mad." These people are simply beyond the understanding of most of us. This assumption forms the basis of our current view of genius, but how much does this it make sense? Is the "genius" so different from everyone else that they cannot be understood by most of us? Or, is this ideology just a reaction on the part of the public and others that stand to profit from this view of genius, a reaction had to make "geniuses" and their production seem more important and special?

I believe that we should abandon this view of genius. Genius has not always worked as this ideology would lead us to believe. At many points in history geniuses from various fields have been recognized as geniuses in their lifetime. Not only were they recognized as geniuses, but their actual creative production was amply understood and appreciated by large segments of the population. Examples abound. Various "natural" political geniuses were recognized in their own time by "the people". Pericles of Athens and Cicero of Rome, two examples from the Ancient world have already been mentioned, and when we move to more modern times Franklin, Jefferson, Madison or Adams are examples as well.

Move to other spheres of genius and examples become more numerous. Many fine artists, particularly artists from the Italian Renaissance, were recognized as great in their own day. Their production was sought after not only by the elite, but by the community—Michelangelo's "David" was originally commissioned by the city of Florence for example. The same goes for the literary and artistic production of Ancient Greece. Be it sculpture, architecture, plays, etc., the great artists of the day were recognized and sought after by the public. Still another example is Shakespeare. He was admired by people from various walks of life when he was alive, and is still considered by most one of the greatest literary figures of all time. And still another might be the music of such Jazz greats as Louis Armstrong or Charlie Parker, appreciated by many people when they were alive, and still recognized as true innovators in their musical genre.

My third, and most important, response to the claim that participatory democracy will stifle the natural elite is to grant the point and ask: Now what? If this is the case, if there is a natural governing elite, one that neither can nor should explain itself to the democratic mass, then why do we not accept fascism? If talent and democracy conflict on some fundamental level, then there is no reason I can think of to have any democracy at all. Not only does this require the rejection of any of the reforms I have suggested, but it also demands that we rid ourselves of the democracy entirely. In fact, it demands the resurrection of a system like the one the American Revolution replaced. If the elitist is correct, and democracy necessarily suppresses talent, then we must return to the paternalist model and not seek to combine democracy with any other system but end democracy here and now.

To conclude, for those who worry about the effect of increasing our democracy due to the natural endowments of the citizenry, this is a very dangerous game to play. To play it is, I believe, to get caught on a slippery slope at the bottom of which is exactly what we in the United States and many across the world have fought against on many fronts over many generations: paternalist, authoritarian dictatorship.

An "Historical" Elite and Democracy

We have seen arguments as to why, even if a natural elite exists, this has no negative effect on our call for more participatory democracy. But what about the effect of an historical elite on a more participatory system? If there is such an elite might democracy result in its losing its privilege to people who are less qualified? Might democracy drag down those who have been better trained, resulting in a rising tide of mediocrity? Given the existing intellectual stratification of the U.S.—which is undeniable—might not opening up every decision to majority rule result in decisions being made by people who are less qualified? It might not be that the citizens lack natural talent, but they may lack education and training, so won't more democracy lead to rule by those without the skills to govern?

As we did in the previous case, we could respond to this objection simply by saying that this historical elite, if it is truly elite, should be able to make its presence felt in any democratic system. Rather than this elite suffering in a democratic system, it should be able to thrive as our democratic system is out to identify quality ideas and people. Thus, if someone is better trained than someone else, they should have no problem showing this in some open forum. When the well-educated, person of "substance," confronts someone less educated then they should have no problem beating them in debate. Right?

Democracy need make no assumptions about who has quality, what quality is, or how it is distributed. That is the point of a democratic system, and thus an historical elite could exist, and excel, in a more participatory democratic system. Its superior talent should be recognized, unless the point here just the one we spent many pages covering, namely that talent and democracy cannot co-exist, in which case this ground has been covered.

However, we can not end here. We are faced with a question in the case of an historical elite that we were not faced with in the case of a natural elite. A natural elite by definition, whether it exists at all, is not the result of human choices; an historical elite, which definitely exists, is the result of human choices. This means an historical elite is possible to eliminate from American society and human society in general. We could choose not to continue to have such an elite. This raises the question: should we choose to continue this elite or choose to eliminate it?

The reason for continuing it would be that more qualified people could run our institutions at the present time. In the short term we would have the advantage of being lead by those trained to do so. The reason against continuing it would be that such an elite might prevent us from promoting the equal opportunity for everyone, and hence meritocracy, that we, as democrats, are out to provide. We would not have equal opportunity because the current elite would continually end up in control of those things that are necessary for the development of talent, i.e., responsible positions, material resources, education etc. They would thereby tend to monopolize, and cause a concentration of, talent. They would tend to overwhelm those who might have talent but lack training. An historical elite would get in the way of natural talent. These are the reasons for maintaining an elite and the reasons against it, so which alternative is best?

I believe we should act to eliminate the current historical elite over time. One reason for my belief is our consideration for promoting equal opportunity, a key point in favor of participatory democracy. Simply put, we need to create a system where, as much as possible, blood-based relations do not dictate position. This is the main thrust of our discussion in Chapter 1, and it remains so now. Another reason, and the more important one here, is that the only reason not to eliminate the elite is a concern that such a removal will result in power being held by less qualified people. This is a genuine worry, but it is a worry that can be overcome when we realize that the increasing leveling of talent in a society need not mean the creation of mediocrity. Bringing down a stratified elite could mean instead the creation of an overall raising of talent to a level unlike anything that has been achieved before. *Leveling need not require settling*. The elimination of the elite would be accomplished not by bringing them down, but by bringing everyone else up. We would thus end up with more talent not less. As long as there is no attempt to eliminate the privilege of certain groups all at once, we could through a stretch of time enact reforms that would allow everyone a chance to excel. As well, eliminating this elite holds out the possibility that more talented people will come to the fore as they will no longer be held back by an historical elite—the main point in favor of eliminating an elite as was just pointed out. The elimination of an historical elite may cause some mediocrity in the short term—over one generation perhaps—but in the long term in may promote the greatest boon of talent yet seen.

, This presents us with the question of the nature of these reforms. If we do seek to eliminate our historical elite, how can this get accomplished? This is a complex question, but we can at least suggest some answers here. Eliminating the present elite can be accomplished partially through a comprehensive system of education (more on this in the Chapter 4). Elimination of intellectual class lines can also be helped by overturning our intellectually stratified social system, particularly in the work place. It is taken for granted that a person does predominantly brain work or brawn work. Due to this assumption, we accept as natural a hierarchical work structure where some people who do no manual labor control others who do. By eliminating the assumption that you do primarily brain or brawn work, we can create a work environment that is more intellectually mixed, and the more intellectually mixed our work, the more capable everyone will be of making decisions. Exactly how this mixing might occur would depend upon many factors of course—most importantly the nature of the tasks—and thus we cannot be too specific here, though Chapter 3 does address this point in discussing the democratization of the workplace. Suffice it to say it is important we see that any democracy is going to have to remove some intellectual stratification.

What falls to us now is the attempt to enact the system outlined. Or, to repeat the second question with which we started this chapter: How could such a government be brought about?

Going from Here to There

What we face is no longer a question of how things *should* be, rather it is a question of how we go from how things *are* to how they *should* be. On this question, the question of how a group of people can self-consciously alter the institutions which comprise their society, there has been a commonly given answer: Step outside the existing system. This "stepping outside" can occur, and has occurred, in two different ways. On the one hand we have the model of Tolstoy, Gandhi and Martin Luther King, Jr. This is the model of peaceful, conscientious objection. The point here is that laws are to be broken, but they are to be broken in a non-violent way and only to demonstrate the ultimate immorality of certain laws. These laws are then to be changed by the existing system, or some close relation, in most cases. On the other hand we have the model of Adams, Jefferson, Washington, Murat, Danton, Robspierre, Marx,

Lenin, Mao, Ho Chi Minh and Malcolm X. This is the model of violent revolution; the "by any means necessary" and "ends justify the means" lot. The point here is to break the law in as violent a means as possible in order to change not just the law but the very system itself.

Am I advocating either of these? No. My reason for this is that both actions are too extreme. The change I am advocating in the structure of the government can be brought about through legal means. There is no need to break the law, we can effect the outlined changes through the current political process. To put it in a slightly different manner, the law-breaking stage of the American Revolution has already occurred. This law-breaking stage was wholly necessary, I believe, for without it power would never have started to be based on the Consent Principle. But this has occurred and it has made all other law-breaking unnecessary. All furtherance of the Revolution can now build on what the earlier stage of the Revolution has gotten for us, and this means no need for law breaking. *What we need now is not law breaking but law making. What we need now is evolution not revolution.* The leaders of the earlier stage of the American Revolution have provided us not only with *reasons* to change our existing system and a *model* for how to change our system—as we have already seen—but with the institutional *means* through which we can change our system.

This is not to suggest that acting on some or all of the ideas outlined so far would be easy. It is only to suggest that our efforts should be concentrated in certain areas as opposed to others. Here is how we should start:

1.   Re-form or form a political party according to a program that includes, but is not limited to, a-d listed below:[7]

   a) The United States Constitution and all State and Local Constitutions and Charters should be amended to effect the creation of participatory or Improved Representative systems that include the abandonment of the Electoral College, creation of legislative juries and the direct election of judges.

   b) Laws should be enacted regulating political groups (parties, action committees, lobbies, etc.). This should include their formation, funding and their relations between elected and jury representatives.

   c) All elections should be publicly funded—for the source of this revenue see the end of the next chapter. This should include a basic level of funding for all candidates qualified to be on a given ballot, with matching funds given to all candidates equal to the highest level of private contributions in order to avoid violating 1st Amendment rights.

   d) All internet, television and radio airtime should be distributed equally among candidates.

2.   All political action of the party should be guided by the ideas set out in the program in order to provide a unified program to the potentially different constituencies that might exist inside the party.

3.   An extensive power base that will ultimately constitute the basic party membership should be sought through the dissemination of the party program in any medium available. Such media should include the world of journalism, entertainment, academia, and especially the internet, etc.

4.   Monies to further the ends of the party should be sought from any and all sources, both large and small, that will contribute.

5.   The party should run in a democratic fashion with an Improved Representative structure.

Notes

[1] To see an attempt at this read Robert Dahl, "The City in Future Democracies," *American Political Science Review*, 61 (December 1967), pp. 953-970. Though his method differs some from what I suggest, they could complement one another.

[2] For our purposes right now, the difference between the "European-type" of parliamentary system and the American congressional model is unimportant.

[3] We might want to include some form of jury representation in the process of nominating Presidents, as per the suggestion of James S. Fishkin in his *Democracy and Deliberation* (New Haven: Yale University Press, 1991). I think this unnecessary however, because it seems more important to me to use the jury model in other spheres of the government, as I will make clear shortly.

[4] Regardless of the public regulation and financing of elections, this system will not be fair, that is open and not controlled by money, unless the economy is democratically reformed. For suggestions on the nature and extent of hat reform, see Chapter Three.

[5] Also, a truly democratic system is going to be one where competition is fair. Each citizen will be given similar access to the resources necessary in order to compete. What this will ensure is that if there is a natural elite, more of its members will be identified, as they will not be held back by a failure to obtain resources. How many Mozarts or Michael Jordans has the world failed to enjoy simply because the situation of their birth never allowed these individuals to develop their talents—simply because they were held down by an historcial elite. For more on just how this equal opportunity might be achieved, see Chapters 3 and 4 in this book.

[6] The essential difference between Plato and the supporter of democracy is two-fold. One, Plato believed that once you have demonstrated your merit that shows you are an aristocrat, and hence you are assumed to have that merit forever. The democrat believes that the demonstration of merit is on going, not a once-and-for-all decision. Two, Plato believes that the judgement about who has merit should be limited to fellow members of the elite only. The democrat believes that everyone should be a part of the decision.

[7] For other planks, please see the end of Chapters 3 and 4. For a complete version of the program, see the Appendix.

Chapter 3
How to Complete the American Revolution:
Democracy and the Economy

On to our next blueprint chapter. In this chapter we will answer the following sorts of questions: How should we ensure individuals have their economic power and position based on judgments of merit made *by us*—those over whom they will have that power—not *for us* by some surrogate parent(s)? How should our answer to this question result in businesses being organized and run differently, if at all? What impact should this have on relations between business and government or labor, if any? Should the world of finance work the same or differently in a democratic economy than it does now? Should IBM, Kmart and Merrill Lynch run the same as the local factory, the Mom and Pop store and the small savings and loan?

Before we proceed, we should notice that as in the previous chapter you may be a bit puzzled initially. Our politics may have looked as democratic as it could possibly be and our economy may look the same—my arguments to the contrary in Chapter 1 not withstanding. Don't we already consent to our economic institutions either by accepting or denying work from them or by buying or not buying their products? Aren't we always free to leave a job, start our own company or take other steps in the face of an economic situation we do not like and to which we do not consent? Doesn't our money act like votes in that a purchase is like a vote? When I buy a Whopper and not a Big Mac haven't I voted for the Whopper in essence? And if I don't like either, am I not free to withhold my consent for these products by withholding my money?

Unlike the previous chapter, you may be more than puzzled. You may be suspicious or even frightened. Any time someone discusses altering the economy Americans get very nervous—we cling very tightly to the Myth of the Castle. What has been said so far might lead you to believe I am out to touch that most cherished of our rights: the right to own property. Maybe you even remember that "economic democracy" was a euphemism for socialism/communism in the past. A thought may have crept into your mind in fact: "Is this guy some sort of commie?! Is he out to resurrect the godless system we spent countless dollars, years and lives defeating?!"

Well, come to this chapter with all the puzzlement, fear and suspicion you like. We are going to address these issues head on. We are going to address them as well as the practical issue of bringing about the changes suggested. Without addressing the practical issue, our speculations would remain speculations in the worst sense: idle.

The "Ideal" Democratic Economy

To start, we must notice that we do not have something we had in the previous chapter. In the economy we do not have a single democratic ideal about which most people agree—one that faces primarily practical problems of implementation. Rather, we have three very different ideals: capitalism, socialism/communism—hereafter referred to simply as socialism—and the welfare state. Supporters of each have claimed theirs is the perfect economic compliment to democratic politics. Is one of them right?

To answer this question we need to determine what an "ideal" democratic economy would be like—ideal not utopian hence the scare quotes—and then see how this relates to these other ideals. Unlike Chapter 2 in other words, we cannot simply state an ideal with which everyone is familiar, justify that ideal to those who doubt it is ideal, and then show how to make it, or some close approximation, actual. Instead we have to outline an ideal first, see how closely it resembles what others have considered ideal, and then show how we might bring about this ideal, or some close approximation.

First, then, an "outline" of an ideal democratic economic system. If our economic system is to be truly democratic—based on the Consent Principle and not paternalism—it must share the values of the political system set out in the previous chapter. The economic system, like the political system, must be dedicated to allowing an equal opportunity for individuals to compete and show their merit—no one can be assumed to have greater merit based on their birth or other criterion. Yet, when some individual has demonstrated merit in an open, competitive forum, our system must allow them to win economic power—for at least a certain period of time. The truly democratic economy, like the truly democratic political system, is one that is merit based with merit being decided *by us* not *for us* in open competition. But once merit is decided that must result in control for some period of time. This is an economic system, like the political system in the last chapter, not about the elimination of power but about putting power on a democratic, that is consent, basis.[1]

The economic system embodying these values will be the one that allows individuals equal access to those goods which promote the development of their talents and ideas, i.e. education, housing, health care, natural or social resources, capital, etc. It will also be that system where those individuals whose ideas win support from others in open competition will be given the resources necessary to develop those ideas. It is that economic system which will allow, to put it simply, both equality and inequality. The equality is an equality of opportunity in competition; the inequality is an inequality of success after competition. The economic system must block as little as possible the development of individuals either prior to competition or afterwards. There must be a balance between promoting the competitive advantage of all individuals while allowing those individuals whom can succeed to do so.

This is an outline, in faint form, of an ideal democratic economic system. A point causing sadness in some and joy in others. Sadness in some because they see this balance as impossible. Any economic system allowing inequality of success will eventually eclipse equality of opportunity—someone's getting richer means someone else gets poorer—while any system demanding equality of opportunity will ultimately eliminate inequality of success—equality means no one gets richer. We must have inequality or complete equality, but not both. Joy in others because they believe we have already achieved this balance in our current American system. Our combination of free-market capitalism, limited from excesses through anti-trust legislation, unions and a welfare safety net—what we are calling the welfare state—is just such a system. Our system may need a little refinement here and there, but we have managed to strike the essential balance.

It is time for neither sadness nor joy. This balance is possible but not yet actual. In order to see why, we need to analyze the ideals of capitalism, socialism and the welfare state. In doing so, we will see how each misses the democratic mark and in turn learn how to hit that mark by overcoming their weaknesses.

Capitalism over Socialism, but Neither is Democratic

Neither socialism nor capitalism allow, even theoretically, the equality of opportunity and inequality of success demanded by a truly democratic economy. Capitalism is closer, but neither is ideal. Here's why.

Socialism has two major problems. The socialist economy presumes the "merit" of certain individuals prior to any activity, economic or otherwise.

Simply the fact that an individual is born human and sentient, hence has needs, means they deserve to have their needs satisfied—"to each according to their need" is the principle they advocate. The standard of "merit" for a socialist is the mere possession of humanity. To put the point bluntly, any human, merely because they are human, has an equal right to produce and consume. This is not a system based on open competition intended to show merit. This is not a system based on competition at all. Socialism thus violates the democratic principle of determining merit because it presumes merit prior to, and with no, competition. Status and power is granted by virtue of birth.

The second problem with socialism is that it does not allow inequality of control in the economy. Everyone is presumed to have merit, equal merit, regarding control over what is produced and how it is distributed. As socialism violated the democratic requirement that merit be demonstrated in open competition, now it violates the democratic requirement that once merit has been shown it should allow inequality in economic power. The socialist presumption of equality is not only a problem because it is a presumption—equality is not something that comes about after competition—but it goes against the notion that when merit is demonstrated it should be rewarded with a greater amount of control.

On to capitalism. Given the requirements of a democratic economy, it would seem that capitalism fulfills them better than socialism. This is true. However, capitalism still does not fulfill all the requirements and thus must be modified, if our economy is to be made genuinely democratic.

A capitalist economy does allow that merit in having economic power is something that must be shown. Its use of a market as the place where merit is demonstrated is even more democratic. The players in any system are allowed to compete with one another *en route* to the demonstration of merit, and the winner is "chosen" by the actors in the market; a competition that does not *initially* presume a winner prior to the actual competition. I say *initially* because as a capitalist system runs, things become quite different.

In an ideal capitalist economy, the best possible according to someone like Adam Smith, every player in competition would start from a position of rough equality.[2] They would then bring to an open market the goods or services they would like to sell, and by free competition the victor(s) would be decided by the actors in the market. The problem is that a capitalist system, even of the ideal type, eventually undermines free competition. The capitalist understanding of the free market undermines the very premise of open competition on which an ideal capitalism is based. Capitalism is, in other words, self-defeating. Here's why.

What the victor wins in the capitalist free market is wealth, capital, private property, call it what you will. The winning of wealth, the accumulation of capital, amounts to an accumulation of power. This accumulation of power results in an ability to then control the market, particularly if there is an even tacit agreement with other actors in the market who have accumulated wealth about how they will act. And this accumulation of wealth only spirals upward. As more wealth is obtained, the potential to accumulate wealth increases, in turn leading to the accumulation of even more wealth. What happens is that after time some actors in the market are able to have an undo amount of influence over the market, thereby making the market unfree. Capitalism results in a violation of the democratic requirement that competition must be free and open. As capitalism progresses, some actors are taken out of the market and are actually able to control that market. They no longer have to demonstrate their merit against all comers in open competition.

To make this point more clear, let's look at an example.[3] Suppose there is a market that involves two competitors. They are in competition over the selling of fresh-brewed coffee. One competitor has an almost unlimited amount of capital, the other has only enough to open a shop or two and begin to sell their product. Who will win this "competition?" The competitor with the capital will win. They will be able to dominate this competition because they will be able to out "market" the other coffee shop. They will be able to sell their product closer to cost or even below cost in order to get a bigger "market share." They will be able to advertise their coffee and thus develop a greater demand. They will be able to build more coffee shops, hence sell in a wider market, gaining even greater name recognition and profits. In all areas of the market they will have a leg up, and though not 100% guaranteed of success, they will dominate the vast majority of the time.

By extrapolating from this scenario—a scenario intimately familiar to most Americans—we can see that the accumulation of capital is going to allow a situation like this to develop in every market.[4] Eventually, in almost all markets the winner will be decided prior to any competition because certain actors control the market. Capitalism is only merit based if the market is free, but capitalism as a system ensures that all markets eventually become unfree. Unfree not because of the great bogeyman of all capitalists, government intervention from outside the market, but because of actual actors in the market itself. It is one of the great ironies of capitalism that those who claim to love free markets actually ensure their destruction. Capitalism makes for unfree markets, hence unopen competition that skews the determination of merit.[5] Capitalism amounts to a system where eventually some individuals or companies are granted, to borrow a notion from academia, economic "tenure." Unless they do something incredibly stupid, they will have their position of power in the market for life.

To this you might respond: "But haven't those with capital demonstrated their merit, as evidenced by their accumulation of capital, and isn't this enough?"

No, this is not enough. First, it assumes that the possession of capital at present is always the result of having demonstrated some merit in the past. We will see reasons to doubt this shortly, but for now just think of inheritance. Second, even if merit has been demonstrated in the past, this fact does not show that the merit demonstrated in the past could still be demonstrated in open, free-market competition now and in the future. It is commonplace to see academic tenure as a recipe for laziness, disinterest and inadequacy in Professors, and "economic tenure" has the same result in the economy. Merit is something that should be demonstrated each time a decision regarding economic power is to be made, if a system is to be truly merit, that is free-market, based. A system that is truly merit—free-market—based will be one that focuses on the present not the past. The problem with capitalism is that as it develops it comes increasingly to focus on the past. The capitalist allows past economic activity to be a determining factor in present economic status.[6] The capitalist allows past economic activity to have an effect, in fact a crucial effect, on present economic activity.

The difference between a competitive system that focuses on the present versus one that focuses on the past, as well as the superiority of the former, can be brought out by appeal to an analogy with athletics; typically classic present looking systems. That individual or team which won the championship last year is not presumed to be the champion for all times, nor are they given undue advantage in determining the winner of present or future competition. What an individual or team has done in the past is not considered at all when it comes to the determination of merit in present athletic competition.[7] This is not allowed in athletics, and even the suggestion sounds ridiculous. It is not allowed in athletics because too many factors contribute to performance to assume that these can be maintained from past to present. In athletics this is not allowed but in capitalism it is allowed, and takes place all the time.

The capitalist system also allows that when merit has been demonstrated in one area of economic activity, this means that whoever demonstrated that merit is allowed to have a say in all other areas of activity as well. Capital, once made liquid, is neutral regarding its uses. Your having accumulated wealth by making cars, computers or coffee does not mean you can only spend that wealth in the car, computer or coffee industry. Rather, it means that you can spend your wealth in any other area you choose, and thus potentially control the market in other areas that have nothing to do with the area in which you originally demonstrated merit. This seems very misguided. Again the analogy with sports is appropriate. As we do not allow winners to have a greater say in the outcome of next years competition in their own sport, we would consider in ludicrous for them to have a say in the outcome of other sports. But this is exactly what capitalism allows by the accumulation of neutral wealth, of power, in the form of capital. That person who has one good idea about cars, computers or coffee is left with enough wealth to control other areas of competition. Thus automobile and computer manufacturers, or a coffee retailer, can increasingly come to dictate what happens in the world of art for example.[8]

The accumulation and stratification of permanently-held power allowed by capitalism not only has an effect on competition at a time but across time. To put it simply, in a capitalist system the past not only dramatically effects the outcome of present competition it does the same with future competition as well. It has an effect on the future in that the person who accumulates wealth not only does so for him or herself, but does so for those whose "victory" they would like to ensure in the future—most often their children. This "victory" is ensured through things such as the establishment of a large estate that can be inherited and the endowment of certain institutions that will help "groom" those people they want to advantage in competition—often exclusive schools and clubs. In this way, the inequality that begins with one person or group demonstrating merit can be transferred not only in one market at a time, and across several markets at a time, but across time in many markets. The accumulation and stratification of power, and hence the elimination of open competition, thus takes on an ever more permanent status. It is for this reason that I said above that the mere possession of capital is no necessary indication that merit has been demonstrated by its possessor. Maybe the person who has capital is an ignoramus who got lucky enough to inherit money and position, or simply met "the right" people because they were members by birth of "the right" club. Capitalism allows in economics what we Americans would never allow in politics, that someone has power simply because they were born into it.

This is not to say that in a capitalist system wealthy individuals are immune from losing their wealth and power. There can be a fall from grace,[9] though most often this is to those who have greater economic power hence supporting the point I made above that those with superior economic power dictate success in the market. Nonetheless, irrespective of the loss of wealth, the simple fact is unaffected that at any given time in any capitalist system that is at all developed there is a certain economic strata of the population who are in the position to control the markets in which they want to participate. This control can take many forms: manipulating the market through the use of capital; having the ability to try risky yet rewarding ventures that others with lesser wealth could not undertake; having been prepared better than your "competitors" for the competition that is to take place; etc. Capitalism allows such control without the demonstration of merit, and actually fosters it by allowing the accumulation of permanently-held economic power through the accumulation of capital.

The basic point is that an ideal or pure capitalism shuts down what it claims to promote: free markets. Capitalism leads to a situation in which competition is no longer open. One of the requirements of a democratic system is that competition between players is open, that no one gets an undue advantage from the system itself. Capitalism violates this principle. The capitalist system, as it progresses, comes systematically to advantage certain players and thus renders the system unopen. As I said before, capitalism undermines itself. Capitalism runs headlong into the requirement that everyone must get an equal opportunity both at success and failure. When you can control the livelihood, the educational opportunities, the access to resources, the access to capital, etc. of those against whom you are competing, there is no longer equal opportunity. Strangely enough in fact, it seems capitalism and socialism share the same basic flaw: one's birth determines one's economic status. Socialism starts with this point assumed whereas it is a by-product of capitalism, but in either case the problem is ultimately the same. This is the essence of what makes them both undemocratic systems.

What is needed then is a system that does not allow birth to determine our economic position, a system that ensures the economic heights to which you rise or fall are of your own making. To which you might respond: "But don't we already have such a system in America? Isn't this the point of the welfare state? Doesn't the welfare state maintain the balance between equal opportunity and unequal success that a democratic system demands? " It is to this I turn now.

So What's Wrong with the Current American System?

Why might someone see our current American economic system as the democratic ideal? What about this system would lead them to believe it balances equal competitive opportunity with inequality of success? The answers to these questions follow fairly easily from an examination of the past one hundred or so years of American history.

The problems with a pure capitalism, problems like those discussed above, were quite evident to Americans by the early part of the 20th Century. The combination of corporations into trusts that dominate markets had begun to cause extreme concentrations of power in the hands of a few, threatening competition in the economy and even democracy itself. In order to re-invigorate the economy and protect democracy, anti-trust regulation was imposed under the "guidance" of Theodore Roosevelt, legislation that broke apart trusts and eliminated monopoly control of the marketplace. This might be the first sign to someone that our current system, with such anti-trust regulation still fully in place, approaches the democratic ideal of open competition.   Anti-trust legislation seems to prohibit the dominance of any markets and thus ensures vibrancy, yet, it also allows that an individual or company can gain a great deal of economic power in a given market. This legislation seems to ensure just what we were claiming had to be ensured, open competition without the eclipse of success.

When this legislation is combined with legislation created to help the poor, legislation such as that enacted during the period stretching roughly from

1930 to 1965, the resulting economic system might come to look even more democratic. The most important pieces of this legislation were those making it legal for workers to unionize. By allowing members of the working class to bargain collectively for a better deal at work, and thus improve conditions for themselves and their families, this allowed a redistribution of wealth that helped the working class become and stay more competitive in the overall economy; an improvement that seems to be just the sort of improvement demanded by our democratic ideal. It is what can make possible the merit-based social mobility that is at the heart of a democratic economy. The "blue" collar worker now sends his or her child to college, and hence the "blue" collar of the parent is replaced by the "white" collar of their child. And when such legislation gets bolstered by social legislation covering many who are either unemployed or not represented by a union—Franklin Roosevelt's New Deal culminating in Lyndon Johnson's Great Society—the democratization might seem to be complete. Even if you are out of work, or can not work because you have to take care of your family at home, you are given the support you need to help get back on your feet and help your children get ahead. This safety net ensures that you can pull yourself up by your own bootstraps, meaning only that with effort each American becomes able to compete on a roughly equal footing in a given marketplace.

As the 20th Century progressed, the anti-competitive aspects of "pure" capitalism were apparently addressed one by one. This is why many believe that our current welfare-state system is the perfect compliment to democracy. A belief that is as understandable as it is wrong. To see why it is wrong, let's go through each of the major types of regulation imposed on "pure" capitalism during the 20th Century. Let's see how they do little in the service of making competition equal and hence ensuring that power is merit based.

Anti-trust regulation does not eliminate the permanent accumulation of economic position and power. In fact, it helps ensure the permanency of such power. It does this by allowing our economy to be filled with sets of mega-corporations dominating markets, thereby making markets appear competitive when they are just as controlled as they were by monopolies. We *feel* as if markets are competitive because there is more than one company, and this eliminates the public outcry against the controlled markets that exist when there are monopolies, but replacing one monopoly by a set of mega-corporations doesn't open up the competitive environment much. Examples abound from Coke and Pepsi to McDonalds and Burger King, but nowhere is this more evident than the automobile market.

Anti-trust law ensures that no one automobile manufacturer can buy out all others. But it also ensures that there will be very little genuine competition and true vibrancy in the automotive industry by making it perfectly legal that only a few extremely powerful companies dominate with a steady, relatively inflexible market share. GM cannot buy Ford or Chrysler, but GM, Ford and

Chrysler are allowed to exist in a state of relative stasis, a stasis that allows no new comers into the market and keeps GM, Ford and Chrysler right where they are. Anti-trust regulation does not ensure competition it ensures laziness, laziness that then breeds mediocrity. This is why the American automobile industry has failed to produce any new alternatives to the traditional internal-combustion engine that gets 20-50 miles per gallon. This is why our transportation system gets progressively worse, clogged by the same basic vehicles that have made very few technical advances of any note in over 50 years. There is very little competition and hence very little innovation. Why should GM, Ford or Chrysler innovate and risk loosing market share when they can comfortably produce the same basic cars year in and year out, never having to worry about new comers because anti-trust regulation ensures the static market? And anti-trust regulation doesn't even touch the issue of businesses coming to be powerful in multiple markets. It only regulates companies in a single market, not across markets. Hence, if GM wants, it can become a major force in the insurance industry, banking, movie making, or anywhere else for that matter. Anti-trust regulation creates a set of dominant companies for which competition is increasingly unknown. Even foreign competition becomes less and less of a factor because there is no international anti-trust regulation. This allows major players in markets in the United States simply to join with competitors around the globe—Daimler-Chrysler for example—creating huge international concerns with the power of nations. Anti-trust regulation is a failure if it is supposed to ensure competition. It is certainly a failure at ensuring what is demanded by a truly democratic economy: equal opportunity in competition. "Little guys" with good ideas do not get, save for only the rarest of circumstances, an equal chance in our economy. If our economy is to be democratic, they must get a chance *all the time*.

As for legislation allowing unions, in Chapter 1 we discussed the ineffectual nature of unions in ensuring a better deal for their members, and hence in making them competitively equal. Unions are not a means of getting power for their members and of ensuring their members are on an equal footing in the economy. They don't even ensure that their workers will be treated fairly, have job security or continue to improve in wages and benefits. Nothing makes the ineffectual nature of unions more evident than the phenomenon of globalization.

In the face of increasing union demands, demands that if met might have made workers and their children more competitive, companies simply relocated. The first relocation was from north to south inside the United States, and then from first to third world. Companies just by-passed unions, and unions were powerless to do anything. The result was of loss of decent jobs for their members and hence an ultimate worsening of material conditions for union members and their children—it is tough to raise a family when you go from working for U.S. Steel to Wal-Mart. Unions have been almost uniformly ineffectual in the face of globalization, and the reason is that they do not really ensure power and hence cannot provide equal competitive advantage to workers. They do not make their members more equal. They certainly do not ensure what a truly democratic system demands: equal competitive opportunity for all.

This leaves the actual welfare system of the welfare state. Of the three parts of the welfare state on which we are focusing, this is the most laughable in terms of helping us approach our democratic ideal. Rather than making economic opportunity equal for all, the welfare system merely ensures that the economically worst off among us do not get any worse—and this is in theory mind you. There is no attempt to make the recipients of the welfare system equally competitive to the rest of society. The welfare system has simply created pockets of poverty where no one, or very few, die from starvation, but where no one, or very few, escape their poverty. It has "ghettoized" whole groups, creating cultures that see the notion of competition as ridiculous because they know the deck is stacked against them in the first place. It has created zones of poverty where from education to job training, from health care to housing, opportunity is substantially less than for those born to privilege. Hence, it fails, and quite miserably, to do what is needed in a genuinely democratic economy: give equal opportunity to all, especially children, regardless of the position they hold at work or of the family into which they are born.

To sum all this up, the welfare state is an attempt to ameliorate the negative effects of capitalism *without* changing their causes. It allows the permanent accumulation of capital to occur, and thus for unfair "competition" to result, only it attempts to make the results of this unfair competition less severe. Our current system allows vast amounts of permanent privilege because it does not open up the competitive environment—it is not really a merit based system—and it keeps those who are semi-permanently ignored by the system content enough so that they do not revolt. It allows the child of the CEO of GM to go to private schools and get every benefit of wealth, while it keeps a child, a child who may have equal or more inborn talent than that of the CEO's child, in substandard housing and substandard schools. Yet, even though they are substandard, at least the housing and education exist so that there is no substantial social unrest from the lowest levels of society. But this is not what our democratic ideal requires. Unlike our democratic ideal, the welfare state is not an attempt to base the economy on the demonstration of merit. It is an attempt to make sure that the distribution of economic power changes little, and that it is increasingly not guided by merit at all. It is a system that keeps certain people advantaged in competition—it is good to be Henry Ford's or Conrad Hilton's great grandson or daughter I bet—and certain people disadvantaged, generation after generation. It does exactly what a truly democratic system should not: it makes birth definitive in the possession of economic power. Our current system is not a cure for the cause of a problem; it is a Band-Aid that helps alleviate some symptoms.

The underlying difference between our ideal democratic system and the welfare state can be brought out by means of a metaphor. The welfare state plays the role of fixing the damaged goods that are produced by a damaged machine. As these damaged products—markets monopolized by corporate giants and a semi-permanent underclass—roll off the machine, our system attempts to fix them one by one with varying degrees of success. What our system never does is fix the damage in the machine that is causing the bad products in the first place. It allows the bad products to continue to be produced day after day, with the ebb and flow of life dictated by the latest popular theory about how best to fix the damaged products. The democratic system, on the other hand, must be an attempt to fix the damaged machine not the products that the machine produces. It must offer an alternate means of economic organization so that the problems with the traditional machine can be eliminated. It must attempt to end the production of bad "products," and to offer a new means of dealing with the inevitable defects that arise.

The Role of Government in the Economy

We have been analyzing the relationships between the ideals of capitalism, socialism and the welfare state in terms of how they do, or more accurately do not, allow a balance between equality of opportunity and inequality of success. We have seen that none of them allows this balance to be struck. To gain more insight into why they go wrong, and to start to see how we might do things better, I want to alter the focus of our discussion a bit. I want to turn to the issue of the relationship between government and the economy. The central issue in American politics over the past one hundred years or more, and one can be seen as at the heart of the difference between capitalism, socialism and the welfare state, it is also one that can launch us into our search for a better system. I therefore turn to it, and I do so by way of another analogy with sports.

To the capitalist, the government should have the same role in relation to the economy that spectators have in relation to a sport. As spectators sit on the sidelines, hoping that the competition between teams is fierce and hence enjoyable, so the capitalist believes the government should merely watch the economy, hoping for the same fierce competition. About the only way the government should get involved in the economy, according to the capitalist, is the way spectators get involved in a sport. Part of the spectator's ticket price goes towards maintenance of the field, security and other essentials that allow competition to take place, and so government should give money to maintain basic infrastructure—roads, ports, etc.—and the institutions necessary for basic business practice—a mint, patent office, police force, etc.

The socialist believes exactly the opposite of the capitalist. As the capitalist believes the government should be a spectator, the socialist believes government should be one of the *teams*, maybe even the only team. The role of the government is not to watch competition take place but to actually control the action by being one of, if not the only, competitor. Unlike the capitalist who believes the government should leave the economy alone, the socialist believes the government should *be* the economy. This is what leads to the government policy most often associated with socialism: nationalization.

The supporter of the welfare state has yet a different view. If the capitalist sees the government as a spectator and the socialist as a team, the supporter of the welfare state sees the government as a referee. The role of the referee is to make sure that the players on the field, regardless of how well matched or hopelessly mismatched they are, adhere to certain rules, and if anyone gets injured, they are taken off the field. To the supporter of the welfare state, the government is not there to make the economy more competitive in any ultimate sense, it is there simply to make each competitor, not matter how good or bad, follow the rules they have agreed to follow and to minimize injury.

The problem with these views on the relationship between the government and the economy is that none has government playing the role a democratic economy needs it to play. What a democratic economy needs of government is for it to ensure the vibrancy of competition. In a truly democratic economy the government must foster as much competition as possible. Rather than standing on the sidelines, actually playing the game or making sure competition is "fair" and helping the occasional injured player off the field, the government should set down rules to ensure that each team, as well as each individual athlete, is maximally competitive. The model here is that of the league. In a truly democratic system, the role of the government in relation to the economy should be like that of the NFL to football, the NBA to basketball, the NHL to hockey or Major League Baseball to baseball, only to a much greater extent. The role of the league is to establish the rules of their respective sports, but it is also to ensure that the sport remains as competitive as possible by establishing salary caps, draft systems, etc. This is exactly what the government in a democratic economy should do, only more so. Government should have the role of enforcing laws guaranteeing fair commerce, product safety, and the like—as every capitalist, socialist and supporter of the welfare state would agree—but it should also make sure the economy is structured so that it furthers the quantity and quality of competition. Government should be that body, like the league in a sport, looking out for the health of competition itself.

By looking at things in this way, we can see exactly where capitalism and the welfare state go wrong in relation to democracy—of course socialism starts out wrong as it doesn't see competition as important at all. The capitalist believes competition is fostered when as many influences as possible from outside the economy, particularly the government, are kept out of the economy; an idea that might seem to make sense at first glance. Leaving people alone might tend to bring them into a greater amount of competition with one another because it would allow certain selfish desires to be unleashed, especially the desire to get rich, thereby establishing the motive to compete like hell. The problem is, genuine competition requires more than just the *desire* to win, it also requires an *ability* to win, and that's what the capitalist fails to see. By keeping outside influences out of the economy, what is produced is an economy where many have the desire to win, but few have the ability. Their ability is undercut, often before it has even been recognized by anyone, because that ability is a threat to others who also have the desire to win and the resources to undermine the ability of their potential competitors. The "winners" in a capitalist economy want other people to have the desire to win—that's what makes them work hard—but they do not want them to have a real chance to win—because that will threaten their superior position of wealth and power. The result is obvious: very little genuine competition and a great deal of frustration.

As for the supporter of the welfare state, they believe competition is fostered by the same basic motivation as the capitalist. They simply add that if those who have very little ability to win are not taken care of to a certain extent, then they will eventually undermine competition through increasingly violent upheaval. In order to keep competition going there needs to be the appearance of fair play, the appearance that everyone has the chance to develop their abilities, even though this may be only an appearance. The problem is that because this is only an appearance, the welfare state has the same basic result as capitalism. Many with the desire to win have little ability to win—even though given half the chance they might be quite competitive—and thus competition fades away.

What we need is an economic system that helps everyone develop their abilities and use them in a fair competitive environment, we need a system that fosters competition yet maintains the opportunity to win. In order to see how it is possible to design such a system, to design a system where the government can play the role of a league in a sport, I want to turn to yet another analogy—one suggested at the beginning of this chapter. It is with this analogy that we will really start to see how we might design an ideal democratic economic system.

The Comparison between Capitalism and Voting

A capitalist economy might seem analogous to democratic politics in the following way. In a democracy each citizen possesses a vote. We decide on the policies of the government, or the people that should hold office, by allowing citizens to cast their votes. Those policies or candidates that receive the most votes win, and are implemented or obtain political office. In capitalism, we can look at the possession of capital—currency being the most obvious example—as we look at the possession of a vote. We decide on what policies or people should hold economic power in the same way we decide on who should hold political power. We cast our currency (vote) for the goods (policies or people) we would most like to have (support). Those goods—meaning the people who created them—that receive the most currency thereby obtain economic power, just as those policies or people who receive the most votes obtain political power. In this way capitalism appears to be as open a system as democracy, in fact, the perfect compliment to democracy. Though they are analogous in this way, there are important disanalogies from which we can learn how capitalism is different, and how it might be modified.

The first disanalogy is that in democratic politics you do not get to keep what you win, whereas in capitalism you do. When you win an election for example, what you are being granted is the use of a certain office, and you must continually undergo reelection in order to prove you continue to deserve that office. With economic power the situation is reversed. What you win in economic competition is considered your property permanently. It is something about which you never again have to demonstrate you merit regarding its ownership. Won once, property is yours for life if you choose to keep it, whereas political power is something for which you must keep demonstrating your merit.

Second, the use of political office in relation to your competitors is very tightly restricted by law, whereas the use of property is not. In the case of political office, what you can do with your power is normally dictated by the rules of a constitution of some sort, and in particular, it is explicitly stated that you cannot use your power to control elections. The situation with property in a capitalist economy is reversed. There are almost no restrictions on what you can do with your property in relation to your competitors, and almost nothing is said about your ability to control the outcome of present and future economic competition in the market. It is perfectly legal to use your property, your wealth, to out-maneuver your competitor and eliminate your competition altogether. There is no sense in capitalist economics that your possession of wealth commits you to the maintenance of an open competitive environment. Just the opposite. The advantage of wealth is assumed to be that it makes life less risky, it moves you above the fray, by allowing you to eliminate your competition.[10]

Last, in democratic politics you cannot accumulate votes. Your victory in an election does not make your vote count for more. It is a basic democratic principle that each person is allowed one, and only one, vote. A present office holder may be able to use that office to sway people to give him or her their votes in the next election—the supposed power of incumbency—but their own actual voting power is never more than just their single vote. In capitalism, this situation is again reversed. Victory in capitalist competition amounts to winning capital. This capital is then accumulated. The victor in capitalist economic competition thus comes actually to possess more "votes" than those who have lost. This is not just a matter of gaining or losing influence. Your position in the economy actually becomes more or less powerful. It is as if by winning an election in politics your vote now, and possibly forever, came to be worth one million votes to everyone else's one vote. A democratic system in which this was allowed would not be democratic at all. But this is exactly what takes place in capitalism all the time. To put it in terms of our analogy: capitalist economic systems make legal the throwing of the economic election.[11]

Given the way in which these two systems are analogous and disanalogous, the way to overcome the problems with capitalism is to make it conform more to the model of democratic politics. We must design an economic system whereby victory in competition does not lead to the eventual eclipse of competition. We must design an economic system that supports those who have demonstrated merit in an open forum, yet does not result in the ultimate elimination of the need to demonstrate merit. This can be accomplished by creating an economy where victory in competition does not result in the permanent accumulation of capital, property, or in a word, power. Victory in competition must yield economic power in some form, but that power must be something that continually has to be earned, not power that can be translated into some neutral medium that can be accumulated and held forever. To put this simply, the possession of permanently-owned capital or property, at least on any large scale, is inimical to capitalism. To be plain, private property as we now understand it is what shuts down the free market. It may sound absolutely crazy to suggest, but that is exactly what I am suggesting. Capitalism and our current understanding of private property can not go together. If we want to have genuine free market competition, if we want who merits economic power to be established by the actors of the market, then we must alter our current conception of private property. We must make property something that is not permanently held. [12]

Making Capitalism Competitive:
Modeling the Economy on Politics, Sports and the
Public Library

We can foster competition and control based on merit without that resulting in the accumulation of permanently-held property or capital by looking at economic "office", economic power, the same way we look at political office or power. As with political power in a democracy, economic power should not result in the permanent ownership of that power—the current President of the United States does not own the office and neither should the President of a company.[13] Economic power should be nothing but the ability to control certain goods, services, etc., for a set period of time. After that period of time is up, if that power is desired by more than one person, there must be a competition to determine who will obtain it. In this competition all the participants count equally, even those who have held that power previously. In such a system, power would be distributed based on the ability to use that power well, an ability that must be determined through some form of open competition in front of those over whom that power will be held.

We have a number of actually functioning models of such an arrangement. One we have been examining: the distribution of political power. In the case of political power, such power is not permanently owned by anyone, it is something that we allow a person to use for an agreed length of time based on our judgments of their merit. When that time period is at an end, those who desire that power must then compete for it, including the person who may have already been allowed to use that power for some time. The person who then wins the ability to use that power is determined based on open competition in a public forum.

A second example of the distribution of power based on open competition is an athletic team. We have used the analogy with athletics before, but in this case I want to concentrate on the competition between players on a team, not teams in a sport. A sports team is made up of various positions, occupation of which is a variety of power. It gives you the power to play. These positions can have different functions—as they do in sports such as football and baseball—or they can each play the exact same role but are ranked according to their ability to play that role—as in the case of tennis or golf. In either case, the position that an athlete occupies is something that they occupy only as a result of permission from the team, or some official in charge of the team. This position is not something they own, and they occupy the position only as long as they can prove that they are the best person available to occupy that position. Once they can no longer prove this, normally by losing in some head to head competition with the others who want that position, they are removed. Their having occupied that position gives them no "rights" in regards to that position, regardless of how long they have occupied it.

A third example of such an arrangement for distributing goods is an institution that has worked quite well in the United States for over one hundred years: the public, lending library. The public lending library allows that a resource is permanently owned by no one, thus making that resource open to everyone's use. Any person is allowed "ownership" of a book for a set period of time, during which they can use the book as they see fit. But that ownership is not permanent, and it is subject to some restrictions about just how the book can be used—you can't throw the book away for instance. Strictly speaking, no one has permanent ownership of the libraries resources at all. The resources are managed by the government, but the only thing the government does is maintain the facilities in which it oversees the use of this resource by individuals. The point is that the government plays the role merely of setting up the situation in which this resource can be used by everyone, but the government does not use the resource itself. Or more to the point, the government has no more access to these resources than does any other individual or group. They are simply one more "competitor" amongst many, and they do not have any privileged position in competition. As such, no one can really be said to "own" the books, by that meaning have permanent and unquestioned control of them.

The use of politics, athletic teams or the public library as examples of how to organize our economy in general might seem very limited. For instance, the public library has a criteria for victory in competition which is not applicable to the entire economy: first come first serve. In any economy, most of the resources are going to be sought by multiple parties at the same time, thus first come first serve will solve nothing. Another reason the public library might seem a bad example is that in an economy most resources are not reusable in the way that books are reusable. Many goods can be used only once and thus to win use of them once is to win them for all time. In the case of sports teams there are problems as well. A sports team is an institution inside the larger institutions that make up the economy. Failure in athletics does not mean that you are removed from the economy at large. But it would mean that if this system were applied to the whole economy.

These, and other, disanalogies exist. But they do not pose substantial problems for the application of the basic principles behind democratic politics, athletics or the public library to the economy in general. For instance, we can establish a dual criterion for the ability to use goods, obtain services or jobs, etc.—hereafter all things that confer economic power like capital, goods, services, jobs and the like, will be referred to simply as "goods". One is first come first serve. If no one else wants a specific good at a particular time, then that person should be given the use of that good. If some good is desired by more than one party at a time, then we can fall back on the criteria used in democratic politics. We should open up the question of who will get the good to those who will be affected by the decision—those who have the good—and allow then to make the decision based on an equal competition held between those who want the good.

The fact that capital, goods, services, jobs, etc. are limited and that some may be unrenewable or even usable only once, does not pose a significant problem either. When some resources are renewable then competition will occur again and again for the use of that good. When the good has only a limited time of use, then that good will get used by those who win the competition for it until the good is used up. Once it is used up, then there will be no more competition over that item.

We can also structure the economy in such a way that failure in competition does mean removal from the economy. This would not only be possible, it would be necessary, because failure could not mean having no economic support. It could not mean this because if it did, failure would completely disadvantage some people in comparison with others, thus making competition unopen. This system must have some safety net built in which keeps people competitively active even after a loss. Just how to accomplish this will be discussed shortly.   The important point here is that this and the other problems that might exist as a result of disanalogies are far from insurmountable. We do have perfectly good working examples of how capital, goods, services, jobs, etc., can be distributed in such a way that this does not result in a permanent accumulation of power, examples that can help us apply this to the case of economics.

Individuals and Competition

So much for our initial discussion of how we might allow competition to result in power or "property" without that leading to unfair competition. Will this alone ensure that competition is equal? We have seen how we might, in theory, be able to maintain economic inequality in the control of resources without allowing their permanent accumulation, but how do we keep opportunity equal?   A second question that we need to address is what would be the motivation for participating in this economy? If wealth and power cannot be permanently accumulated, then why should we bother to become economic actors at all?

The establishment of a basic equality in education and living standards for people can deal with the first problem, particularly children. The model I would use here would be none other than Plato's *Republic*—surprising that Plato keeps surfacing in a book on democracy. In Plato's *Republic*, as we saw in the last chapter, the point of the state is to identify a certain elite who should be given absolute power.   This is accomplished through an educational system where every child starts on an equal footing; they are given no undue advantage over their peers as a result of their economic, social or familial background. They then undergo an education which is intended to let the better students be identified and thus give them the burden and privilege of running society.

What I would keep from this model is the basic educational requirement. The point of education would be entirely different—this system is not about identifying an elite that is given absolute power—but the notion that people are given equal training to play a role in society would remain. This educational structure will be discussed in the next chapter.

Beyond an education that allows the maximum possible development of their abilities, there should also be some safety net for those who lose in competition.   There should be some means by which people could sustain themselves when they are in the process of competing to get into a certain institution and/or earn the use of certain capital, goods, etc. This is necessary for two reasons.   First, without such a net certain people who have lost in competitions would eventually become competitively disadvantaged.   It is difficult to demonstrate your merit when you have nothing to eat. It is the responsibility of this system to ensure that competition is open and this means that some floor must be maintained for every person in order to keep them able to compete. A second reason is that competition is a risky business. If there is no means the allay some of the risk, then this system will ultimately stop fostering the development of new ideas. It will stop fostering creativity and the experimental "spirit." It will stop fostering the development of individuals. It will do so because the most creative, daring ideas are often the ones that stand the greatest chance of failing, either failing to gain support from other people, or failing when there are actually tried. If this failure entails that the person who has failed will be heavily disadvantaged then they will not try again. The basic idea is that if there is no way to limit risk, people will stop taking risk and the system will stop producing new ideas and bold adventure.[14]

This last point raises the question of the motivation for acting in an economic system such as this. Capitalism, the closest system to the one we are designing, functions as a result of both positive and negative motivational forces. Ideally the positive forces are creativity, love of competition and enjoyment of wealth. Capitalism offers a means of developing the self, of coming to try the new and hence of coming to identify with the institutions that one lives in because they result from your creative act. It also offers an environment in which one's merit is tested against others. It gives people the opportunity to see your worth by directly testing it against the worth of others. Beyond this, it produces a great deal of wealth which can be enjoyed in many different ways.

The negative forces are greed, vanity and fear. For those who are not positively motivated by capitalism, this system is little more than a means of taking personal risks. These personal risks are taken, ultimately with one's material livelihood, for the exclusive purpose of eventually not having to take risks anymore. When you need not take risks anymore, "free time" is supposed to result, and some more meaningful life is to be found outside the capitalist system. The individual in capitalism is thus often driven by fear and greed. The fear is always that your basic material well-being will be harmed, and that you will never achieve freedom. As a result, greed sets in. The individual gets an overwhelming urge to accumulate as much as possible in order to ward off this fear, and to guarantee free time. And because the ultimate goal of the system in such a case is the empty goal of not being in fear, of simply removing yourself from the system, of being "free," no sense of what to do with yourself is ever established. This leads to a growth in vanity. Once fear is overcome—though it is never completely overcome—the only motivating force in life is to worship what you have spent your whole life trying to obtain, i.e. wealth. The only thing many people really know how to do is accumulate wealth, they have never really thought much about what to do with freedom.

In the democratic economic system so far outlined here, the attempt would be to overcome the negative motivations and accentuate the positive motivations of capitalism.[15] The positive motivations would still be present; in, fact they would be heightened. This is a system built around the development of the individual. It attempts to give the individual maximum room for growth and control over their own life by putting success firmly in their own hands—and success will still result in wealth, just not permanently-held, exclusively private wealth in most cases. The point of this system is to make people more creative and then let what one has created live or die based on the case you can make for it. It opens up the possibility of allowing your worth to be demonstrated fairly. In capitalist "competition" you may wonder whether you had an advantage, and hence your victory becomes tainted.[16] In this case, competition is made open hence assuring that victory is dependent exclusively on merit. And to boot, when you win you get luxury!

Regarding the negative motivations of capitalism, the fear that sits at the bottom of a capitalist economy would be removed by two things. First, this system would allow a greater amount of control over your own life. Your life would not be subject to control from forces larger than, and with absolute power greater than, that had by yourself. You will be confronted by people who are better than you at things, but at least this will be something that you can see acted out in front of you, not something that will come as surprise. Fear is most often driven by the unknown, something that will be greatly diminished in this system. A second factor that would diminish the fear inherent in capitalism is the establishment of a certain economic floor. Every person, to be kept competitively "healthy", must be given a certain level of basic economic support including food, shelter, education and medical care.[17]

The elimination, or at least limitation, of the fear that acts as a primary motivating factor for many individuals in capitalism will dramatically lessen the other negative motivations behind capitalism. Without the fear, there will be no drive to the extreme accumulation of goods that is seen as necessary, to ward of disaster, in traditional capitalism. Hence greed will be significantly diminished. It will be significantly diminished, but not eliminated. For those who maintain a greater desire to have control of certain things, that desire will be allowed, only it will have to play itself out in open competition. The diminution of fear that works to limit greed will also work to limit vanity. The point of this system is not the empty one of eliminating fear and possessing "free-time", thus we will not be driven quite so fast to the empty worship of "things" that can fill up our free time.

Specific Suggestions for Restructuring the Economy

Now that we have shown the problems with socialism, capitalism and the welfare state, as well as how it is possible to balance equal opportunity with inequality of control—in theory—it is time to get specific. It is time to address directly questions like those we broached in the opening paragraph of this chapter and have been with us since I suggested democratizing the economy in Chapter 1.

We should start by noticing that when structuring economic institutions, as when structuring political institutions, there are two main characteristics on which we must focus. One is the type of economic institution. The second is the size of the economic institution. When structuring our ideal democratic politics we saw that different types of political institutions require different structures, and the same type of institution can require different structures as sizes change. The situation is the same in the economy. Accordingly, let's focus on the simplest economic institutions at various sizes and then proceed to the more complex at various sizes.

The simplest economic institution is the proprietorship or partnership. The proprietorship or partnership is owned by one or a few people, people responsible for all the financial liability of the business. As these people are personally accountable for paying their rent or mortgage, their utilities, car payment, etc., so in their business they are personally accountable for all debts incurred by the business. There is no attempt in these businesses to buffet themselves from such accountability.

When these businesses are small, regardless of their function—manufacturing, service, finance, etc.—they should continue to function very much as they do now. [18] The business should be the permanent property of the proprietor or partners, something that can be inherited, and something where the profits are accumulated by the owners. Though this may sound as if it goes against the basic democratic principles we have outlined so far, it really does not. Businesses such as these are like families. In fact, they are often extensions of families. It is very difficult to tell where the family ends and the business begins. Many or most of the employees are family members, and if not actually members of the family they are treated as such. Given the close relation between these small businesses and the family, demanding democratic reform of these businesses would be like demanding democratic reform of the family. This is not our goal. We are not out to democratize the family. What that would even mean is unclear. As well, it is not small proprietorships and partnerships that cause real, anti-democratic problems in the economy. They do not negatively impact the free market. Their influence in a given market is almost always small, and as we increase the size of the market geographically, it becomes miniscule. Small proprietorships and partnerships are exactly the sorts of businesses Adam Smith and other supporters of capitalism had in mind when they championed capitalism as a free-market system. They saw, as we should see, that these businesses do not shut down free markets; they are the essence of free-markets. Thus, for these reasons they should change very little. [19]

Small proprietorships and partnerships should continue to be subject to the regulation and taxation of the state—typically that would be the participatory democracies we outlined in the previous chapter—as well as to the possibility of unionization. These businesses, though rarely threats to the free market, can nonetheless threaten communities and their employees. If there are no building codes, regulations concerning waste removal, zoning prohibitions, etc., then—even though small—those businesses could become annoying or life threatening to members of the community. Also, due to the demands that any businesses, large or small, place on the services of the community—fire, police, water and sewage just to name a few—they must be taxed. This rate of taxation will be determined by the local government—again most likely a participatory democracy. Small businesses can pose a threat to their employees as well. Just because a business is small doesn't mean it cannot pose a threat to the body or livelihood of its employees. This means that the employees of small proprietorships and partnerships must have the option—though they would most likely use it rarely—to unionize unimpeded. Unions should be modeled on the political institutions set out in the last chapter. Locals should be participatory democracies, while regional and national chapters should be modeled on the improved representation outlined in the last chapter.

Proprietorships and partnerships larger in scale—though very rare nowadays—pose a problem. Such businesses maintain the personal liability of the ownership, yet they are of such size and stability that this liability means little. More importantly, these businesses can pose a great threat both to the freedom of the markets of which they are a part and to their employees, employees who have become increasingly anonymous due to the size of the organization. Our only option is to regulate such businesses in the following ways.

Unionization of their work force should be not only permitted but encouraged—local and Federal Government might help them organize, through grants, for instance. Employees should be helped to unionize, and unionize unimpeded if they choose, but the decision will be theirs. Second, these businesses should not be inheritable. Such businesses should be possible to create and the wealth, position and power they engender enjoyed, but this should not be passed to other people chosen by the ownership.[20] These businesses, when the owner wants to sell, retires or dies, should be sold to the employees of the businesses and converted into corporations—see my discussion of corporations and "economic citizenship" below.[21] Third, these businesses should be forced, through a rigorous program of taxation, to support small business loans to businesses of lesser scope—no matter whether these smaller businesses are proprietorships, partnerships or corporations—in their market; much like successful sports franchises have to support smaller franchises in less lucrative markets. Fourth, these large-scale proprietorships and partnerships should be prevented from engaging in unfair competitive practices intended to create monopolies. Practices presently limited or eliminated by local, state and federal anti-trust legislation should be continued and advanced.

The reasons for these regulations should be obvious. We are permitting a great deal of personal freedom in the creation, running and enjoyment of the profits of these larger proprietorships and partnerships, yet we are minimizing their impact on their employees and their competition.   The allowance and encouragement of unionization helps ensure that employees have some representation to protect them from an unfair, unhealthy or abusive work environment. The prohibition against inheritance minimizes the impact of these owners on future competition.   It ensures that others, particularly family members, will not obtain undue competitive advantage and hence skew the determination of merit.   Everyone knows that the children of the talented are often themselves less talented, and the prohibition on inheritance in this case ensures that anyone, regardless of their relation to someone in a large-scale business, must show their merit in competition with others.   In other words, after the original ownership of the business has sold, retired or died, their children or other close relations and friends can certainly compete for control of the business—again see my discussion of large scale corporations—but they are not guaranteed of control.   As for the other regulations, they minimize the impact of these large scale proprietorships and partnerships in present competition.   By ensuring that they do not unfairly hurt but actually help their competitors, this will help further free-market competition.

This is how both small and large proprietorships and partnerships should be structured, as well as how these businesses should relate to labor, government and other businesses in the market. Though a substantial part of our economy, we are far from done.   What about corporations?   The corporation, unlike the proprietorship and partnership, limits the personal liability of their owners.   The corporation is created as something separate from the owners, not something for which they must be personally accountable.   If a debt cannot be paid by a corporation, the creditor cannot collect from the personal wealth of the owners.   Due to this, the corporation, even when small, is very different from the other businesses we have discussed so far. The owners of corporations, no matter what the size, are asking something of the community, asking them to admit a new type of entity into their midst—they have removed business from any real connection with the family.   Also, corporations are the businesses that most often grow to incredible size and can develop the power of small nations.   They frequently have amazing amounts of influence and control throughout the country, and in many cases, the world.   It is "corporate capitalism" that is the real threat to free-market competition.[22]   It is corporate capitalism that the founders of this nation could not have envisioned and which they would have seen as true threats to freedom.   It is corporate capitalism and the institutions that support it that have been plagued by scandals, the scandals discussed in Chapter 1, scandals truly global in dimension and hence deeply threatening to all of us. Given these features of corporations they should be changed in the following ways.

The price for being allowed to incorporate, regardless of the size or nature of the corporation (manufacturing, service or financial) is that the corporation should be "unowned" and employee managed. To say the corporation should be unowned is to say that any corporation should be like a democratic government. As no one owns all or part of the United States government for instance, even its current citizens, so no one should own all or part of corporations. That means no employee(s) can claim permanent, private possession of the corporation or any part of the corporation. Further, no person who does not work for the corporation can claim such possession either. Rather than being owned by anyone, the corporation, again like the government, should simply be managed. If the corporation goes out of business, then its assets should be liquidated where possible, with all employees paid their wages first, and creditors second—for the nature of credit in this economy, see my discussion of stocks and banking in this Chapter.

The managers should be all the employees. Whether the corporation is composed of a few people or thousands, ultimate power inside the corporation should rest in the hands of all employees, and their fortunes should be hooked directly to the success of the corporation. This means employees should not be divided into worker/laborer and management, those who own and those who are hired by the owners. Their should be no direct control of the corporation from outside, and *all* employees—regardless of rank and position—should be "economic citizens" of the corporation. [23] By an economic citizen I mean that the employee/citizen of the corporation should have the same rights and responsibilities as the citizen of a democratic state. They should possess all the rights that allow them to control either directly or indirectly the policies of the corporation in their immediate section and overall—voting power, freedom of speech, freedom from arbitrary treatment, etc.—and accrue all the responsibilities of an economic citizen in general as well as of the specific position they hold in the corporation—perform their assigned tasks, adhere to regulations, etc. [24]

If the corporation is small enough, it should be run as a participatory democracy. Each person's salary, position, responsibilities, etc., as well as the overall policies of the corporation, should be established after open debate among all employee/citizens. [25] As soon as the corporation, or in many cases even a section of the corporation, becomes too large, then employee/citizens should control them through the system of improved representation outlined for government in the previous chapter. Section heads, up to the chief officers of the corporation, should be directly elected by the employee/citizens, and there should be randomly chosen "corporate legislative juries" that set the policy of the corporation. Everyone, regardless of their job in the corporation, should have the right and responsibility to serve on these juries, and complete equality should exist between jury members. To be clear, all jury members, regardless of their position prior to being chosen to serve on a jury, should have the same time to speak, their vote should count the same, etc.

In order to get hired and become an employee/citizen of a corporation, you should be voted in. If your job is to be in a certain department—and the department is small enough—then that department's members must hold an election to accept or reject you. You will be allowed to speak before the body in question, as will your competitors for a position if there are any, and then a vote will be taken. If you are voted in, you will then be an employee/citizen with the rights and responsibilities of any employee/citizen, as well as with the rights and responsibilities of the position you fill. If you are not voted in, then you can return to your status as unemployed—see below for my discussion of the unemployed. If the department is too large for everyone to vote on your admission, or your job is to range over a section of the corporation or the entire corporation itself, then you must be voted in by the legislative and executive bodies that represent the employees you will control. Again, if you are voted in, you will obtain all the rights and responsibilities of an employee/citizen as well as the rights and responsibilities of your position.

What exactly are the rights and responsibilities of any employee/citizen in general? If the corporation is small enough; employee/citizens should be allowed to participate directly in the running of their section of the corporation as well as the entire corporation. This includes setting departmental and corporate policy, hiring and firing, determining what employee/citizens get what percentage of the profits if there are any, addressing corporate failure or bankruptcy, etc. If the corporation is too large to be entirely participatory, then each employee/citizen should participate directly in running their department, section, etc., and when these become too large, to serve on juries that set policy and elect those who should implement that policy.

As for the rights and responsibilities afforded an employee/citizen based on their particular position in the corporation, these should be set by the employee/citizens of the corporation according to the above mentioned procedure. These rights and responsibilities should include completing the tasks of their job, and obtaining the pay and benefits that go with the job.[26] That is, as I alluded to above, the pay scale and benefits for each member of your department, section or the corporation at large, should be set by the employee/citizens responsible for running these various parts of the corporation. Decisions regarding pay and benefits should be neither bottom up nor top down. Each employee citizen should be allowed input on these decisions regardless of the position they occupy, except in larger corporations where it should be the juries and elected representatives who decide.[27] Though pay and benefits should be worked out by the employee/citizens themselves or their representatives, it should be made mandatory that corporations provide complete health benefits and education for each employee/citizen of the corporation and their children— education through college at least. This can be made mandatory by not granting a corporate charter to any group seeking to incorporate and that will not provide such benefits.

So much for the structure of individual corporations. What should the role of the government be in regards to corporations? Corporations should be regulated by the government in the following ways: One, the government should establish the procedures for the formation of corporations. This should now include the requirement that to be granted the legal status of a corporation a business must be employee-managed. Two, the government should ensure that the rights and responsibilities of each employee/citizen are respected. Each employee/citizen and the corporation should have an explicit contract that states the rights and responsibilities of both parties, and the government should enforce these contracts. Third, the government should regulate corporations to the extent necessary to maintain product, environmental and other safety. Fourth, the government should guarantee that the competition between corporations is free and fair. Fifth, government should tax corporations to the extent that the government deems necessary to pay for their regulation and other essential services.[28]

Other than these regulations, many of which are already in place, the free market should reign. There should be a minimization of anti-trust legislation. This is one of the benefits of founding a corporation as opposed to a proprietorship or partnership. Given the democratic nature of these corporations, the market has less to fear from their dominance of the market than it does from businesses that are permanently owned. It would be much less likely that employee-managed corporations would collude to control the market than ones that have few owners or managers. However, if at some time after free-market competition between democratic corporations a market is dominated by one corporation, then the government may step in. This would be at the discretion of the citizens of the district(s) in which the corporation operates.

How about the relation between corporations and unions? There should be no allowance for unionization by employee/citizens. Unions should be forbidden as no extra-corporate entity should have a say in corporate policy other than the government, and the government only in rare instances. This is another benefit of founding a corporation.

The need for unions in corporations will have disappeared, so this is not as shocking as it might seem. The democratization of corporations ensures the representation of all members of the corporation. Either each employee/citizen will speak for themselves in a participatory body, or they will be represented through the system of improved representation. This guarantees much better conditions for all employee/citizens of the corporation, and it guarantees them much better representation. It is also much more efficient, as it would eliminate strikes and other labor disputes that arise in the current contentious climate of contemporary corporations.

The financing of corporations should continue much as it does now. Corporations should be able both to borrow money from banks—which themselves will be restructured like any other businesses according to the guidelines we are setting out—and issue stock. The only differences between current financing and democratic financing is that stock ownership should no longer confer ownership of the corporation. Rather, stock should be seen as an agreement to pay a certain percentage of the profits of the corporation to someone who has leant the corporation money. Either that, or stocks can work much the same way as municipal and other government bonds.[29] Either way, owning stock should give the stockholder no say in how the corporation is run, or who runs it. That is the role of the employee/citizens. The financing of corporations should be much like the financing of expensive theater productions. As often as possible, employee/citizens should buy stock in the corporation as this would give them added incentive.

Our discussion may have prompted a worry which we should address at this point. Will employee/citizens be intelligent enough to properly manage a corporation? Businesses can be very difficult to run, particularly as they become more technical in nature, and it may seem that the necessary expertise and far-sighted planning might not exist in the employees at large. How can someone who knows little about a business make decisions about that business? Or at least this, shouldn't we allow those who know the most to make the decisions?

My only response is to point back to the discussions of similar worries in the previous two chapters. Many have expressed these worries in regards to allowing the citizens of a government rule that government, as we have seen. The only difference between that and what is being brought up here is in the earlier cases the worry was about politics and now it is about the economy. But what difference does that make? It would be very hard to maintain that businesses are harder to run than governments, so if my earlier arguments were sound then little more need be said now. Beyond this, businesses in our democratic system would be unlike governments in that you would not be an employee/citizen by birth, you would have to be hired by some corporation to be an employee/citizen. The basis of such a hiring decision would be knowledge of the business, or at least some aspect of it, and hence employee/citizens could be counted on to be better informed than your average citizen in government. This worry is simply something we should move beyond at this point.

We have been concerned with structuring manufacturing, service and financial businesses of various types and sizes, but we have ignored a major part of the economy. What are we to do about the economic aspect of the government itself? Many people work for the government. How are the employees of public schools, police and fire departments, government regulatory agencies, the military etc., supposed to function? Should these all work the same way? Should some work like business and others not? The problem here is that the ultimate leadership of these institutions in our system should be democratic organizations, either of a participatory or improved representational variety. Given this, it is unclear that the employees of these institutions could be employee/citizens because these institutions are already run by the citizenry at large. The employees of the government already have a say in who has power over them simply by being citizens. Their say is watered down however, as their say is mixed in with that of every other citizen. Something that seems unfair as they are working day to day in the institutions whereas the average citizen is not. This would be the equivalent of allowing everyone in a corporation have a say over who is the boss in a department of 15 people. It just doesn't seem fair. So what can be done?

Democratic bodies should be the overall managers of the government agencies in their districts, but most of the other managers and employees of these agencies should be employee-elected.   Save for the very top level of management, all government employees should have the same rights and responsibilities in these agencies as employee/citizens have in corporations. For instance, the mayor of a town should be elected by the citizens, and he should manage the Department of Sanitation overall. The actual person who heads the day to day operations of the sanitation department should not be appointed by the mayor however, but should be elected by the employees of the department. These two officials, one who is concerned primarily with the interests of the citizens at large, the other who is concerned with the interests of the employee/citizens of the sanitation department, must work closely together to ensure maximal efficiency and employee happiness. At times this relationship could be contentious, but that is a check and balance system that would simply have to be dealt with.   This is the only way we can ensure democracy in government while allowing the employees of government democracy in their workplace. The only government agencies that should not be run in this fashion are the military, emergency services—police, fire, rescue squads, etc.—and schools. For the structure of schools, see the next chapter. The structure of the military and emergency services should remain as they are now to ensure efficiency.

We have talked about rights and responsibilities of those employed by governments and corporations as well as proprietorships and partnerships. What about those who are unemployed? In any free market economy, at any given time, there will be a percentage of the population out of work. Even when democratically run, businesses will fail or shrink in size, people will be fired for performing badly, people will quit because they dislike their job, and all of these will cause unemployment. Should the unemployed have any rights or responsibilities? In our system, should a citizen who is not an employee/citizen have any economic rights and responsibilities? We have already suggested that they should, but we must be more specific now.

The responsibilities of the unemployed should be to continue to compete for work or accept retraining. If it is shown that at any time they have shirked this responsibility, then their economic rights could, upon review, be taken away. These rights should be as follows. The unemployed should be granted a government stipend that allows them enough money to either compete for a new job, or get retrained for competition in a new field. This training should be corporate—or government—sponsored if necessary, and it should ensure that at its completion, the newly trained candidate is on an equal footing in competition with those seeking the same type of jobs. Such support should last until a time when the candidate finds employment, or proves to be "unemployable".[30]

The "unemployable", should be broken into two categories. Those who are unemployable due to physical or mental disability—this includes the elderly who have no retirement package granted them as former employee/citizens—or those who are unemployable due to social circumstance. The first group should be guaranteed acceptable, state-sponsored care in order to see if they can be made employable again. This should include hospitalization, rehabilitation, and other like programs that may make them able to compete for employment in the market place again. This state-sponsored care should be of indefinite length—particularly for the elderly. As for our second category, those unemployable due to social circumstance—single parents would be example—these should be given the services necessary to remove the social impediment. For instance, there should be state-sponsored universal day care. This should be continued until employment is found, or until an individual shows that they are not unemployable due to social circumstance but due to physical or mental disability.

Going from Here to There

We are left with an important question: how do we go from our present system to the democratic system outlined above?

One thing that needs to be repeated from the last chapter is that law breaking need not be a part of this process. Certainly the transfer from our current system to a democratic system will cause some fear and hostility. But the law breaking that might seem necessary to effect such a change of power has already taken place. This was the opening phase of the American Revolution, the one that occurred in the 18th Century. It was this violence that allowed the beginnings of power based on consent. Due to this however, we can now extend consent-based power by peaceful means. What we need to do is use the power that is already based on consent to establish new spheres of consent-based power. The process here would be similar to the process suggested at the end of the last chapter. All change should be sought through the democratic channels of the government. *Changes in the economy should be enacted by the evolutionary process of democratic politics not the revolutionary process of violent overthrow.* Making the economy more democratic, like making the government more democratic, is part of the evolutionary, law making phase of the American Revolution, not part of its revolutionary, law breaking phase.

The steps that could be taken in order to accomplish this transfer of economic power are the following:

1) The following suggestions should be part of the political program started at the end of Chapter 2.

2) Laws governing corporations should be passed mandating that they be unowned and employee managed—all employees at all levels should be made into "employee-citizens." This law should include the conversion of current stock and other corporate ownership into lending agreements that allow for a certain percentage of profits to be taken, and certain provisions for disbanding unions in corporations and eliminating certain government regulation of the market. It should also mandate that any entity granted the status of a corporation should provide its employee-citizens with healthcare, daycare and education/retraining for themselves and their families, and where possible housing.

3) A law should be passed eliminating the right to all "luxury" inheritance—luxury being defined as any possession beyond the national average for a possession of that sort. This law should have a grandfather clause built in such that all those currently in the process of inheriting, those who have actually been named in a will, trust, etc., that is now being executed, should be allowed to inherit.

4) A "Citizen's Economic Rights Amendment" should be passed. This should include a guarantee of unemployment insurance, health care, housing and retraining to all those who are not covered by other arrangements—as employees of proprietorships or partnerships where these are guaranteed, or as employee/citizens of corporations where they are mandatory. These should be paid for by passing the following laws:

   a. Legalization of all recreational drugs. A state monopoly should be created responsible for the manufacture, distribution and sale of these drugs. Once established, this monopoly should be dissolved and turned over to private corporations.

   b. Legalization of prostitution that is managed in the same fashion as legalized drugs.

   c. The military should be restructured from its current four-service model to a unified command. All redundant command and procurement should be eliminated.

   d. The U.S. should create treaty organizations across the globe on the model of NATO that minimize the demand on the U.S. to finance a great deal of the world's security obligations.

e. The current Federal Income Tax should be replaced by a Federal Sales tax of 10% or more to ensure that anyone spending money was taxed and to give money to spend as they see fit.

5) Incentives in the form of reduced corporate taxes and the like should be granted democratic corporations that vote in the following "humanitarian" policies as well as policies that help encourage competition:

a. Term limits for high level corporate leadership.
b. Maximize the number of employees receiving "luxury" corporate housing, cars, etc.
c. Establishment of minimum and maximum corporate wages.
d. All employees should be made hourly.
e. Double-time for all work over 40 hours,
f. Minimize the intellectual stratification of work into brain and brawn work. Where possible, those doing "brain" work should also be required to do brawn work. And no one in any corporation should be trained to do exclusively brawn work.

Notes

[1] Notice already this difference from socialism. Socialism is about the ultimate elimination of economic power, in fact, the elimination of all relations of authority and dominance in the economy and otherwise. Economic democracy is about putting economic power on a consent basis, not seeking its elimination.

[2] This presumption of rough equality in an ideal economy was also active among American Revolutionaries, for example Thomas Jefferson. It is for this reason they saw capitalism, in the form of a market-based economy and private ownership property, as important for the maintenance of democracy in government. Democracy in government along with capitalism, a capitalism based on rough equality, seemed complementary.

[3] Our example will be fictitious to keep things simple. For a good real-life example, though one more complex, see David C. Korten's description of how Walmart functions in many communities in his *The Post-Capitalist World*, (West Hartford, CT: Kumaritan Press, 1999), pp. 164-167.

[4] Keep in mind, competition in a "market" can be between businesses or potential businesses, or between individuals in a business. Two people vying to get the same job or promotion in a company could be seen as a market for instance. How the accumulation of wealth would effect the competition between two people for a job is easy to see when we consider the different education that wealth allows. More on this shortly.

[5] Not only does the eclipse of free markets in a capitalist economy follow as a result of theoretical reasoning such as we have just done, but it happened historically. Anyone familiar with the "Gilded Age" in the United States, the period around the turn of the 20th Century when robber barons controlling trusts all but owned the economy, will know of what I speak.

[6] This is made plain throughout one of the most famous recent defenses of capitalism, Robert Nozick's *Anarchy, State and Utopia* (New York: Basic Books, 1974).

[7] This is not always the case. In some sports past performance is considered in the present, but is considered in order to *disadvantage* those who have performed well in the past. For instance, last year's Superbowl winner is given the last draft pick. This is to ensure that competition between teams remains vibrant. Capitalism does just the opposite however. It favors past winners. Hence it losses vibrancy.

[8] Have you paid close attention to who has sponsored most art exhibitions in recent years? And certainly this has a great impact on the art "market": what art gets produced is determined by what art gets bought.

[9] As there can be for a King or Queen, but that doesn't make monarchy any more palatable to us, does it?

[10] In an ideal capitalist economy, there are no anti-trust regulations. Markets are supposed to be "self-regulating."

[11] This undermines the claim that capitalism is democratic in many instances because it allows stock ownership permitting the election of management.   Stocks can be accumulated, votes cannot

[12] Something to notice: socialists have concentrated on private property as the great "wrong" of capitalism. They are mistaken. Privacy is not so much the problem as whether property is permanently held. We must focus of permanency, not privacy, as the central issue.

[13] For specifics on this, see "Specific Suggestions for Restructuring the Economy" in this Chapter.

[14] Notice how this justification for social support systems differs from those in socialism or the welfare state. We are not supporting people here because it is the nice thing to do, or because if we don't we will have to fear them. We are supporting them in order to keep the economy competitive and hence healthy. Rather than social support being a drag on the economy, it should be seen as an essential part of its efficiency.

[15] For an interesting discussion of the impact of democracy, particularly in the economy, on the characters of individuals, see Carole Pateman, *Participation and Democratic Theory* (Cambridge: Cambridge University Press, 1970) pp. 22-44.

[16] The same question that is supposed to plague those who benefit from affirmative action programs. If it plagues them, then it should plague the children of the wealthy—as it so often does—because wealth is just a variety of affirmative action.

[17] Our method of paying for all this will be made clear at the end of the chapter.

[18] Larger and smaller can be defined by certain economic measures with little difficulty. For instance, number of employees, size of geographic market, average size of a business of that type in the United States, etc.

[19] Similarly, there should be little change in the small-scale, permanently held, private property that goes along with small businesses and personal/family life. Objects, such as the individual or family car, the single family or individual home or condo, etc., should be the exclusive property of the owner and inheritable—up to a certain limit. For the nature of this limit, see the next footnote.

[20] The same goes for the personal "luxuries" of such proprietors and partners. Property, such as vast estates, vacation homes, large-scale investments, etc., should not be inheritable. The reasoning here is obvious. Such wealth would give undue advantage to those who inherited it. Determination of just what constitutes "luxury" could be made in the courts by comparing "average holdings" across the country with the items being judged for luxury status. If the average home in the United States were worth $100,000, and the one given in inheritance is worth $1,000,000, it is a luxury. All items where luxury value and average value cannot be separated—a single large "luxury" home that served as a sole residence for instance and which cannot be divided in any way—should have the amount that is luxury taxed by 100% before the property can be inherited. If this tax cannot be paid, then the entire item should be taken by the business or government to be used as it sees fit. Of course, it should go without saying that no sizable "gifts" would be allowed in the system as a way of circumventing the inheritance laws.

[21] Profits from the sale would either go to the ownership if they retired—there personal fortune at their death would be taken by he state—or if they are dead, would be put back into the business.

[22] My thanks to Robert Dahl for the term "corporate capitalism".

[23] Again, my thanks to Robert Dahl for the term "economic citizen".

[24] A more lengthy discussion of these rights and responsibilities follows shortly.

[25] I would suggest that all votes after debate on these issues be confidential to ensure no one feels intimidated.

[26] As in the case of proprietors or partners in large businesses, the "luxury" wealth accumulated by an employee citizen should not be inheritable. At the death of an employee/citizen, their luxury wealth should be returned to the corporation or the government. The reason in this case is the same as in the previous case.

[27] Decisions regarding employee salaries and other benefits in corporations should be made as they are now currently made in government. As often as possible, benefits should include the use of a house, car, etc. In other words, as you rise in the corporation, you should be granted "company" luxury homes, cars and the like; homes, cars, etc., which are your property for a set period of time and which you can use and alter as you see fit—short of selling or destroying them. The reasoning for this is two-fold. First, this creates added incentive to advance. Second, this will lesson the need to take back "luxury" property in order to prevent inheritance. To put this all in the simplest terms, many employees of corporations should have the same relationship to their house and car that the President of the United States has to the White House, Camp David and Air Force One. As long as you have your position, then you can use these. When you move on, you will obtain the benefits of a new position, return to the non-luxury property you own or obtain government housing.

[28] You might think it strange for me to suggest a role for government regulation of corporations given I sounded hostile to such regulation in Chapter 1. Actually, it is not strange at all. I was only hostile to government regulation as a solution to the problem of powerlessness in the economy in general. Government regulation that does not alter the basic structure of businesses would be ineffective, and I am against it. Once the basic structures of business--and government for that matter--has been altered, then I fully support government regulation of many types. In particular, I think it essential regarding the environment.

[29] Modeling stocks on municipal bonds is an idea I got from Michael Walzer in his "The Case of Pullman, Illinois" from *Spheres of Justice* (New York: Basic Books, Inc., 1983) pp. 295-302. For those who do not know, municipal and other government bonds are ways in which private individuals can loan money to a government with a certain guaranteed return, but *without any* say in who runs the government or how the money is used. The only difference between such bonds and stocks as I outlined them above, is that stocks would carry no guaranteed return. You would get a return only when a profit was made.

[30] This will help ensure the fundamental democratic requirement of equal opportunity in competition. It will *help* ensure it. The most important guarantee of such equal opportunity is equal education. For more on this, see the next chapter.

Chapter 4
How to Complete the American Revolution:
Democracy and Formal Education[1]

Though the last blueprint chapter, and the second to last chapter overall, this is the most important chapter in some sense. I put it towards the end not because it is less important, but because without the previous chapters it would be difficult to see just how important it is. Three reasons make this chapter, with its focus on formal education, so important.

First, during the process of formal education more individuals are judged, and in more important ways, than at any other time in our society. Almost every individual in this country receives some formal education, at which time they are judged advanced, normal or remedial, promising or underachievers, ready for the "fast track" or "dirt track"; judgments that in many cases set them on a path determining the direction of their lives and the role they will play in society. Given this, if we are to ensure—as we have been out to ensure since Chapter 1—that the judgments of individuals and their ideas is as fair and open as possible by making them democratic, we must democratize the formal educational process. We must democratize schools. We must make sure that those who make judgments in schools have their authority to do so based on the consent of those over whom they have that authority, not as surrogate parents.

Second, we are concerned with allowing citizens an equal opportunity to show their merit in political and economic competition. For this equal opportunity to be genuine, each citizen must have an equal opportunity to receive a formal education. Only such equal educational opportunity can guarantee citizens the chance to develop the skills, both in communication in general as well as in more technical areas of expertise, which can allow them to compete on an equal footing in politics and the economy. Without such opportunity, competition would simply be unequal. This is not to downgrade the importance of the "economic rights" I previously argued should be allotted every citizen. These can help keep equally competitive, in the economic realm at least, those who have lost in prior competitions. However, in order to make citizens equally competitive in the first place, or in order to successfully re-train them for new competition if that becomes necessary, they must have the equal chance to receive formal education. They must not only have an equal opportunity for an/ education, but that education must be equal in quality. Teachers, resources, classroom size, student to teacher ratios, etc., particularly at the primary level, must be roughly equal.[2] Equality of quality, not just of opportunity, is important in formal education because without it students will not have an equal chance to show and develop their talents. Students must have an *equal* opportunity to have an *equal* education, or our system will prejudice the demonstration of merit; something we cannot allow if our system is to be truly merit-based and competitive.

Third, without this equal opportunity in schools we will not only create inequality of opportunity in politics and the economy, but many citizens will be unable to make sound, sensible decisions in the various democratic institutions my reforms would have them inhabit. The success of any democracy, and particularly the systems outlined here, depends upon the existence of a literate, inventive citizenry that can communicate their ideas and debate them in public. This is a very high demand to make on a citizenry; a demand that can only be met by providing a uniformly sound, formal education. If we do not provide such sound formal education, formal education that prepares people to succeed in a democratic environment, then our democratic systems will deteriorate into tyrannies. The tyrannies will be those of ignorant mobs, most likely under the sway of unscrupulous and self-serving demagogues. It is the worry about this sort of tyranny that motivates the concern I addressed when defending the "average American" in Chapter 1 and in my discussion of elites at the end of Chapter 2. Some would seem ready to go so far as err on the side of a "tyranny of the elite" if the alternative is a "tyranny of the mob," and this concern about the ability of citizens to handle the responsibility my reforms would place upon them needs to be addressed in some ultimate form beyond what has already been said. That can only be done through a discussion of formal education.

For these reasons, formal education is a central element in our democracy, and hence this is a crucial chapter in this book. But, how can we get our formal educational system to play this crucial role successfully? How can we structure our schools so that authority is consent based? How can we ensure that our schools give all citizens equal opportunity to succeed? How can we ensure that our schools produce literate, inventive, "good" citizens? It is to these questions we must turn in this chapter.

Before we address these questions we should acknowledge, as in previous blueprint chapters, that the questions to be addressed here may trouble some of you initially. To speak of producing "good citizens" has an extremely judgmental air about it, one that even smacks of the totalitarian. Who are *we* to say what sort of person is a *good* or *bad* citizen and then act to *produce* the good and not the bad? Isn't education about freedom, and shouldn't we get out of the way of students to allow them to develop as they want, particularly given we are good democrats? Isn't democracy about freedom, and thus judging students, or anyone else for that matter, is contrary to the very spirit of democracy?

In response I can only remind you that the very premise of this book is judgments of individuals and their ideas are, and ultimately must, be made. Democracy is not about eliminating judgments; it is about making judgments in a particular way. Democracy is about ensuring judgments are made in a fair and open manner, one where the merit of individuals and their ideas is judged *by us* not *for us*. We are not, nor could we be, out to end the making of judgments altogether. To believe that somehow we can get by without making judgments of one another is a myth, a myth that is not only intellectually unsound but practically dangerous.[3] We must admit that we make judgments, and that we make them all the time in schools in particular, thus leaving us with the question: what types of judgments are we going to make in schools, and how can we ensure they are made democratically?

One other point we should notice before we start is again, as in the previous two chapters, we cannot simply design one uniform democratic structure that will work in all cases. One thing that prevents this is schools come in different sizes. As we have seen, different-sized institutions often require very different structures, and the situation is no different here. Another thing preventing this is schools are populated by crucially different age groups. To put this simply, in schools we are not always dealing with adults—unlike governments and businesses. In fact, normally we are not dealing with adults at all. Formal education is, except for post-secondary education, education of the young. Thus, in formal education we are dealing mostly with a group who has yet to develop a definitive set of interests or the maturity that allows them to promote, defend and take responsibility for, themselves. For these reasons one structure is not going to work for all schools. We have to deal with different cases differently.

Because it is easiest, we should start with post-secondary, formal educational institutions of various sizes such as colleges, universities, institutes, etc.—referred to henceforth simply as "universities". Universities are easiest because they are more like governments and businesses, populated by adults with developed interests and the maturity that allows them to promote and defend those interests. As such, we have models of how we might restructure these already. With that done, we can turn to the more difficult case of secondary and primary schools. Here we must discuss how best to ensure these schools, of various sizes, have democratic structures given their students, those over whom schools have authority, are children. We must also discuss how children can be made into good democratic citizens, citizens capable of competing in a democratic environment so that they serve their own ends and the ends of the community. We do not face this question of "molding" students in universities as these people are already molded. They are relatively fully-formed adults. We must assume they are able to handle themselves. In the case of children however, this is an all-important question. We must make clear which sort of young person we are going to consider worthy of praise and which worthy of censure. We must answer the question: what sort of individual is best suited to success in our society and which is not?

Making Universities Democratic

Our first topic, how to structure universities so that they are democratic, consent-based institutions providing an equal opportunity for education to all, can be helped greatly by looking at the origin of one university in the West.

One of, if not the, first secular university in the Western world was founded in Bologna, Italy in the 12th Century.[4] It was founded primarily for the study of law and medicine by students from mostly prominent northern-European families. These young noblemen decided that to ensure they received a high quality education they must subject professors to rigorous standards of performance. The reputation of a professor was important of course, but reputation alone does not a good professor make. Professors then as now, regardless of reputation, have to work to their fullest potential in order for their students to benefit. Not only must they work to their fullest potential, they must care about their students or their work will have little impact on their students. These young noblemen were well aware, as any student in a contemporary university is aware, that sometimes professors, regardless of their reputation and talent, perform poorly and care little for their students. To guarantee, as much as it can be guaranteed, that professors performed well, the students, those that paid the professors salaries to be plain about it, established the following rules:

> *Professors* had to swear obedience to the student rectors and to the student-made statutes... *A* professor was fined if he began his teaching one minute late or continued a minute longer than the fixed time, and should this happen the students who failed to leave the lecture-room immediately were themselves fined. In addition, *a* professor was fined if he shirked explaining a difficult passage, or if he failed to get through the syllabus; he was fined if he left the city for a day without the rector's permission, and if he married, was allowed only one day off for the purpose.[5]

What is important about these rules for our purposes is not their specific content, though that is interesting, but what these rules show about the thinking of these students in Bologna. They believed the professors were there to serve *them*, not *they* to serve the professors. They also believed the only way to ensure professors served them well was by controlling the university and professors through formal, quasi-legal machinery and procedure. There was an inherent distrust of professors because they were people in positions of power, a distrust that was assuaged only through enacting certain institutional means for the students to control the professors. They saw that professorial power must be consent-based to some degree.

Compare this 12th Century institution, this institution from the "dark ages," with the contemporary university in the United States. Instead of today's students having any formally recognized process for checking the power of professors and administrators, of giving their consent to those in authority, they have just the opposite. They, particularly those seeking admission to the most prestigious universities, beg for a chance to pay whatever rate is deemed correct by these institutions in order to have the privilege to walk their hallowed halls. Once admitted, there is no formal mechanism for the redress of any, except for the most immoral or illegal, action of professors or administrators. "Of course," you might respond, "they are always 'free' not to go to a university or to leave one university and go elsewhere." But this is an attenuated freedom at best. To say this is to say that they can either forget about a higher formal education entirely, or risk that they will land in the exact same situation, or maybe even one that is worse, in another university. This is like saying to Thomas Jefferson or George Washington that if they do not like the British King, they are "free" to relocate under the Spanish or French King. An idea that is both idiotic and insulting in political and economic matters, as we saw in Chapter 1; and it is no better here. Even the American military, often thought to be the very example of a paternalistic, autocratic institution, recognizes the need to inform its raw recruits of the way to ascend the "chain of command" if they have a problem with a superior (not that they will necessarily get much satisfaction, but at least the problem is recognized and the institution has a structure to handle it). In the contemporary university, problems between professors/administrators and students is not even officially recognized, and certainly there is no formal mechanism to handle these complaints—that's right, I'm suggesting the university is more paternalistic and autocratic than the military. For instance, there is no section of the average student handbook that tells students how to complain if they don't think a grade is fair or they don't like a professor or dean, let alone a section that tells them how to rectify the situation. The professors/administrators are mostly viewed with awe, as almost untouchable in their judgments, and universities respect that sense of awe; as a professor once put it to me: "In the realm of grades at least, professors are like Gods." Gods who no student is given any formal process of challenging during the term, or after grades are given. Students are not even given a say about what "god" gets to teach what classes and what classes get taught.   The selection of professors/administrators, as well as of course offerings and academic policy in general, comes down from on high and the students are left to do their imitations of pigeons in a park. Either you pick at the crumbs someone throws you or you are welcome to dine elsewhere.

About the only possible option a student has for challenging the present system, besides leaving the university, is to challenge it "informally." They can engage in protests, strikes, sit-ins, etc.—the academic equivalent of mutiny or revolution.   This is a rare occurrence however, because the reward for challenging this system is to be judged harshly by it, and thus have denied many of the benefits that a higher education affords.   Revolution is always risky. Universities play on this fact, play on the control they have over the futures of their students, in order to maintain their unchecked power.   The students themselves are often complicit in this control as well because they believe they are incapable of self-management.   Largely as a result of having conformed inside paternalistic, autocratic educational institutions their whole lives, many students do not believe they are capable of taking responsibility for their education.   They believe they need a surrogate parent. Either that, or they just don't care.   Many students see their university education as one more hurdle that must be jumped *en route* to the world of "success" and money. The university makes about as much sense to them as the other hurdles they must leap, thus looking to make sense of, or more stupid yet help run, this hurdle would just be a waste of time.   It is senseless autocracy all the way down in every institution where people learn and work, so why make a stand here? This institution is only a temporary one in their lives and it doesn't even result in any direct cash reward. All they want to do is jump the education hurdle so that they can get closer to the prize dangled in front of them by the powers that be.

Autocracy in the university is not just an issue for students of course. Certainly the relation between students and professors/administrators is the most visible case where power is wielded largely unchecked in universities, but it is hardly the only place where this occurs.   Autocratic control occurs as well between faculty members and between administrators and faculty.

Between faculty members, there are two main sources of autocratic control.   The first is the initial hiring process.   No different than the hiring process of most businesses nowadays, new faculty are hired by existing faculty in a private process, using whatever standards they deem fit, and with no input from anyone else except, on occasion, their "bosses" in the administration. Candidates for teaching jobs in universities have no rights in the process, and can thus be treated in a grossly unfair or immoral fashion.   Any variety of ideological or even political, racial, ethnic, gender or other bias can play a role in hiring as all hiring is done in secret, literally behind closed doors. And even if the decision is "merit" based, it is merit as determined by the small clique of existing faculty that may suffer from outrageous intellectual prejudice.

The second source of control comes through the granting of promotion, and most importantly, tenure. Tenure was originally established in order to ensure the openness of the university. So as not to allow firings for ideological, political and personal reasons certain faculty members were deemed important enough to be beyond firing—unless they did something illegal or grossly immoral. That is, they were put almost entirely outside the university's control, in this case not just control of the students but the other faculty and the administration as well. In creating this elite, in creating those who are largely above all censure, a group with near absolute power was established inside the university, particularly when it comes to hiring and tenuring non-tenured faculty—and we all know what happens to those with absolute power…something about corruption, isn't it? This tenured faculty determines who gets to join their ranks and who does not; a process that allows the same unchallenged ideological, political and personal cleansing that occurred prior to the advent of tenure. The ideological, political and personal cleansing has now been moved from the administration to the faculty—or some combination of faculty and administration—but a cleansing takes place nonetheless. In fact, this is an amazingly subtle way for tenured faculty to keep the faculty "their" sort of people—that is, people who share their views or other "attributes." It does not require any active purging of undesirables, merely a withholding of financial and other support. Support which, when withheld, results in the withering of those who need that support. The point is that the non-tenured faculty who need promotion—because in many universities today you are either granted tenure, marginalized financially and professionally, or actually fired—are forced to conform to the largely unchecked standards of the tenured faculty who control jobs. Non-tenured faculty are forced to conform to the unchecked authority of tenured faculty the same way students are forced to conform to the unchecked standards of the faculty and administration—of course, like the students they can always leave, but hopefully this "love it or leave it" response has been addressed enough by now.

The effect of tenure in the university is like that of monopoly in the economy—an analogy we touched on in the previous chapter with the notion of "economic tenure." In the economy, we think that economic vibrancy depends upon competition. To ensure competition, we must actively work against the creation of monopolies. In fact, the major point in the previous chapter was that in order for our economy to be merit-based, it must be competitive; this means the elimination of all unearned, permanent privilege, as well as unchallenged control of businesses and markets. Tenure for faculty is like a monopoly. It gives one or a few faculty members exclusive, permanent "ownership" of certain academic positions and departments, and thus all the power and privilege that goes with that "ownership." And the effect in the university, especially when it comes to competition from "smaller" competitors—the junior faculty with differing views in particular, but students as well—is the same. It eliminates competition and leads to complacency, stagnation and ultimately abuse. In this way, authority is held over junior faculty and students without their consent. They are like small businesses trying to break into a market where a monopoly exists. They are let in only if those holding the monopoly *allow* them in.

Similar relations of unchecked, non-consent-based authority and control also exist between faculty and the administration—witness the growing union movement among part-time faculty on many university campuses. University presidents and deans control university policy, including standards of admission, requirements for graduation, pay scales, number of faculty appointments, etc. These people obtain their positions with little or no input from the faculty, certainly with no ultimate control by the faculty. These positions are almost always the appointments of those who control the money in the university. The financial backers of the university, in the forms of university "boards", express their will and it is done, normally without any member of the faculty having any formally recognized say in the matter. Those who control the money control the contemporary university.

Strangely enough, the money in question is not tuition but the "big" money given by benefactors, corporations or government. Those who pay tuition, oftentimes the students themselves or the parents of students who have worked their whole lives to pay increasingly exorbitant tuition, have *no* say in university management and hence policy. A situation that seems positively irrational when we consider the amount of money spent for an education nowadays. A contemporary university education for themselves or their children is the single biggest investment *in most people's lives*, next to their home, yet it is made with little or no formal control over what is being paid for. It is like someone picking a realtor because they have heard the realtor deals in "nice" homes, but not being able to control the actual home the realtor ultimately buys for them—and all the realtor's "competitors" function the same way. *Caveat emptor* is full-blown in contemporary university education. There are no consumer rights at all, let alone an actual say in how the university is run by those paying tuition. Ultimate control of the university is had by major contributors, and all faculty as well as students must bend to their will as that will is expressed through the administration they hire.

Go to any division of the contemporary university, or the university as a whole, and there is someone standing in a position of paternalistic, autocratic, nearly absolute authority over someone. How did this happen? How did we get away from the model of Bologna?

There are many reasons: The alteration of focus in universities from the social mission of "Christianizing young men" to preparing students for specific jobs in the economy—turning the university into so-called "white-collar vocational education"—hence placing education under "market forces." The need to give social guidance to the ever-increasing numbers of young people who go to school far from home and need *in loco parentis*. The increased concentration of intellectual activity inside universities and thus the increasing institutionalization of intellectual life. The increase in the specialization of intellectual tasks and the distribution of resources based on these specializations. The increasing expense of research. These factors, and many others, have increasingly contributed to making the contemporary university paternalistic and autocratic, moving it away from the Bolognese model. Regardless of the causes however, we can use the model of Bologna as our way out.

To eliminate paternalistic autocracy inside the university we should stop leaving, or other drastic acts equivalent to mutiny or revolution, from being the sole means to challenge authority. We should do exactly what was done in Bologna in formal education, in the American Revolution in parts of our politics and what I have suggested in politics and the economy in the previous two chapters. We should institutionalize "revolution" by basing all power on consent. We should put the power to decide which students get admitted, what programs get funded, what courses get taught, which professors get hired, which classes they teach and who administers the university, in the hands of *each* and *every* member of the university. Each and every member of the university must be made into a "university citizen" and given "educational rights and responsibilities," and this includes students. Students must have an equal voice in university decisions, equal to that of administrators and faculty. Each decision in the university must be made as the result of a vote, a vote made after open debate among every member of the institution—or some sub-set if the institution is too large for participatory democracy.[6]

To be specific, a democratic University should work like this. At the end of the semester—after grades have been submitted—there should be a meeting of all those students who took classes in each academic department—if the department is small enough, otherwise there should be "improved representation" (see Chapter 2). At that meeting, the students and professors from the department should debate and vote upon which professors should be hired for the following semester, what responsibilities those professors should have, what pay and privileges those professors should receive, which students should be granted degrees, which students should be admitted for the coming semester, etc. In general, we can see this as the process of deciding who gets, or continues to get, the status of "university citizen" in a department and hence "university educational rights and responsibilities". At the beginning of the next semester, all new and returning university citizens in each department should debate and vote on which courses should be offered and which faculty members should teach them. Faculty members should then establish, unchecked until the next vote, the responsibilities of the students in their classes—attendance policy, course requirements, etc. Administrators should also be able to attend any departmental meeting they chose. If they do not attend, they should be informed of the decisions made at each meeting. They should then distribute money based on those decisions. If there is competition among departments for resources to pay for the classes and professors they want, then the competing departments, including all citizens in each department, should convene a meeting to debate and vote on the distribution of resources—if that is unsuccessful, see below.

Once the course offerings and faculty assignments for each department are finally made, and the resources allotted to pay, registration should then take place and the semester begin. This process should repeat itself every semester or at least every academic year.

This is how each department should be run, and how inter-departmental competition for resources should be handled. As for the running of the university as a whole, at the end of the academic year, administrators for the coming year should be elected by all "university citizens" regardless of their departmental affiliation, and this includes current administrators—if the university is small enough, otherwise improved representation.[7]   These appointments should include agreed-upon pay and privileges allowed each administrator. These administrators should then have suzerainty over all the departments of the university, allowing them autonomy until they come into conflict with one another. When this occurs, the departments in conflict should work this out—as per the above procedure—or the administrator should arbitrate.

For the university to be structured in this way, all assumed privileges for administrators, faculty members and students should be removed. Tenure should be eliminated for faculty and administrators, upperclassman should be given no necessary preference in selecting or registering for classes, etc. All positions of authority should be granted after open debate in a public forum based on the merit decided by those being affected by the decision. The only privilege, in other words, is the one earned democratically. And as in the case of government or business, per the reform suggested in previous chapters, this privilege should be earned on an on-going basis. There should be no granting of permanent privilege.[8]

As for the role of big-money contributors in running the university, they should have the same role as purely charitable donors in any institution. This is to say charitable contributions to the university should still be allowed, as long as the university citizens or their representative bodies permit it. But permitted or not, charitable contributions should amount to nothing more than charitable contributions. They should grant those giving the money no control over the institution receiving the money, and as in the election process in politics, such money must be matched by government funds granted to other universities of similar size and mission to ensure no university is able to gain unfair advantage over others—for more on the role of money, see below the discussion of funding primary and secondary education as I suggest the same funding strategy and measures should be applied for universities.

Ultimately, what I am suggesting is that universities should look very similar to the other institutions we have outlined in the two previous blueprint chapters. They should look similar because they are similar. Universities make crucial decisions regarding the merit of adults, just like institutions in politics and the economy, decisions that dramatically affect the opportunity and security of the individual being judged. Thus, it should come as no surprise that they should look the same. Being a university citizen should be a lot like being a citizen of the state or of a business.[9]

This is how to ensure that authority in the university is consent-based, and that judgments in universities are the result of an open, formal, democratic process. But how should we ensure that our other main concern is addressed, namely, that individuals have an equal opportunity for, in this case, a higher education? In order to ensure equal opportunity in higher education, the following two U.S "higher educational rights" should be granted all U.S. citizens—these are rights that should be given to all citizens and are independent of those discussed above granted to "university citizens". First, anyone with a secondary education should be allowed to take an admission test—designed by each democratically-run university itself and possibly modeled on an SAT or other standardized test format—for admittance to any university. Anyone who passes one or more tests should then have to be considered for admission by the appropriate democratic governing groups making admissions decisions inside each university where an exam was passed. This step should be just a first hurdle in the admissions process, but this first hurdle should be open to all those desiring to try. After that, the admissions process should be an open, formal process for all those who passed the initial entrance test and still seek admission. By open and formal I mean they should be allowed to speak, on public record, in front of the democratic body granting admission, and the actual decision making process should also be a matter of public record. To put this simply, applicants to universities should be granted the same rights as those applying for jobs. Second, those who demonstrate they are qualified for an education and cannot pay should be given the necessary tuition and other fees to allow them to attend the best university to which they could gain admittance—for funding this, again see the below discussion of funding primary and secondary education. To sum up, as a function of law every university should be open to any student as long as that student demonstrates the ability to succeed.[10]

Making Primary and Secondary Schools Democratic

We must now turn to the more difficult case of primary and secondary schools.

As for democratizing primary and secondary schools—basing them on the Consent Principle—the only way institutions populated by children can be made democratic is that someone must speak on behalf of each child. Someone must be there to ensure that the child's interests, interests of which the child is either unaware or only partially aware, are defended. This person must be afforded full democratic rights inside the primary or secondary school attended by the child—they must be made a "school citizen".

The obvious choice to play the role of the child's "mouthpiece" is the child's parent(s). Though not an ideal choice, as some parents do not have the best interests of their children in mind or are unable to speak on their children's behalf for various reasons, this is nonetheless a good choice. Most parents care for their children more than they care for themselves. Therefore, we can depend on them taking a strong interest in their children's education, and in their doing their best to make sure their children's interests are looked after. For those children whose parents either do not want, or cannot handle, the responsibility of speaking for their child, then some appropriate legal guardian can play that role—a guardian chosen in the same way they are currently chosen. But whether it is a biological parent or someone else responsible for the child outside of school, they can speak for the child.

Our current situation in primary and secondary education is not far from this democratic conception—we are far more democratic here than in universities. Through organizations like the PTA and PTO, as well as through the election of school boards, parents and guardians have a great deal of say over their children's education. They are almost "school citizens" already. What I am suggesting is that we simply expand and update what already exists. The following are my suggestions for exactly how things should be expanded and updated.

Schools should be run in a participatory fashion—just like government, most businesses and universities—as long as size permits. Much like the system outlined above for universities (except parents and guardians will speak for students) each parent and guardian, as well as each teacher and administrator, should be allowed to speak on any issue facing their schools.[11] This goes all the way from who will teach and administrate, to what subject matter will be taught. The vote taken at the end of such debate, debate that should occur at the beginning and end of every school year, will then decide the issues at hand. If a school or school system is too big, then "improved representation" should be used. In fact, educational institutions are often public, governmental institutions, and thus they would be covered by a democratization of the government—see also my discussion of government employees at the end of the previous chapter, as well as non-academic employee/citizens of universities in note 7 of this chapter. The amount of democracy allowed in a system such as this would be far greater than is presently allowed of course. But it is not out of line with what is currently allowed. Change here would be far less drastic than it would be in most businesses or universities.

So much for making schools democratic. How can we ensure that every student has an equal opportunity to obtain an education *and* how can we ensure that the education received is roughly equal in quality? Not only must opportunity to obtain an education be equal, as we have already seen, the education itself must be kept equal in quality for every student to have an equal opportunity to develop and show their merit. How can this be done?

Currently every student has the right to an education through secondary school. This should continue. Thus, we already provide an equal opportunity to obtain an education. No change is required here from our present system. This handles only the problem of equal opportunity to an education. As for making sure the education received is equal in quality, here we should alter our current system. First and foremost, no student in this country should have more money spent on their education than any other. All schools should be funded up to the level of the best-funded schools, with adjustments made for differences in economic region of course—as the value of money varies from region to region. If the most expensive school in an economic region spends $20,000 per student, then every school in that or a similar region should be required to spend the same. This is to say, $20,000 might be a lot more in rural Mississippi than it is in suburban Connecticut, so adjustments should be made to the raw figure spent. Nonetheless, equivalent monies should be spent on all students across the nation, equivalency meaning we spend up to the highest level. Of course, equality of money does not guarantee equality of education, but it sure helps.

Second, to try and further equality of quality, we should institute a nation wide set of exams. These should test each student to make sure that if they have studied a certain subject, they have learned the same basic content—these exams would be national versions of the current "Regents Exams" given in New York State. Without passing these tests, the student should not be allowed into other levels of the same subject, leave a grade or have a degree conferred.

Third, a set of exams should be instituted for teachers in each subject matter. Teachers should be required to score at a certain level on these exams, in the subject matter they teach, even to be considered by a given democratic governing body for the job of teaching in *any* democratic school. These exams should be administered to all teachers on an on-going basis—ever few years at least—and they should be added to the current degree and certification requirements for teachers.

Last, but certainly not least, teacher's salaries should be increased to match those of the "average" college-educated worker with a technical expertise, and with an equal quantity of experience, in a given economic region. Teachers should make as much as engineers, computer programmers and the like. Their jobs require as much detailed expertise plus they play a vital social role, so we should try and attract the best and brightest to teaching with increased pay and other privileges.[12]

Democracy and the Goal of Primary and Secondary Education

With some sense of how to democratize schools, as well as how to obtain equality in the quality of education, we must now turn to the difficult task of discussing, in general terms, the content of primary and secondary education. Though a morass of theoretical and practical issues run together when the content of education, designing a curriculum for lack of a better way of putting it, is at issue, we can start by saying that the most important choice in this regard made by parents, teachers and administrators in democratic schools would have to be the overall goal of education. It is in terms of this choice that all other specific decisions about education must be made. We must know our end before we can pick our means.[13]

To start, we can say that the goal of education must be the ultimate success and happiness of the children. No parent, guardian, teacher or administrator would suggest anything less I am sure. This goal has the advantage of universality only because it has the disadvantage of vagueness. Everyone can agree to this goal because it is so ill-defined. In order for this goal to truly help design curriculum, as well as teaching methods, school structure, etc., it must be more clearly defined.

A democratic society has a structure just like any other. This is what we have been laying out over the past few chapters. As such, we must ask: what type of education might promote an individual's success and happiness, in general, in a democratically structured community like the one we have been outlining? Militaristic communities must make good warriors. Trading communities must make good business people. How can we make good, successful, happy democrats? In order to answer this we need to answer a prior question: what does a democratic society demand of its members? We must answer the latter to answer the former because knowing what will make an individual happy and successful requires knowing what society needs. An individual's happiness and success largely depends upon their ability to fulfill some social need. Contrary to the opinions of many, individual happiness and social "happiness" are often intimately linked. The individual and society are not necessarily in conflict. Thus, we are left asking about the needs of a democratic society and then education can be designed to help students find happiness fulfilling that need—for those worried that this sounds fascistic, please keep reading.

What a democratic society needs is two-fold: first, individuals with diverse interests; second, individuals who can promote their interests in a democratic forum. Diversity of interests, or better yet perspectives, is needed by a democratic society because a democratic society depends upon this diversity to explore the many possible solutions to the problems it confronts. Diversity ensures that rigidity will not set in to society, a rigidity that would guarantee society's demise in the ever-changing world in which we live. Our society is always encountering new challenges, and it is only by maintaining our flexibility that we will be able to handle these challenges. This flexibility is ensured by promoting the development of diverse individuals. As the famous American educational theorist and philosopher John Dewey puts the point:

> Whether called culture or the complete development of the personality, the outcome is identical with the true meaning of social efficiency whenever attention is given [by those defining social efficiency] to what is unique in the individual...[14]

With democracy, Dewey is saying, we come closest to unifying the demands of individuality and society. What a democratic society demands to run "efficiently", as he puts it, are well-developed, unique individuals. Unlike other societies where the individual must be subsumed by society to be effective, a democratic society fails if it does not allow, in fact promote, the flourishing of individuality.[15]

The reason for the second need is more obvious. Diversity is only helpful if that diversity can be expressed in a way that allows differing views to play off of one another. If we cannot bring diverse and disparate perspectives into dialogue in a way that all are understood and then adjudicated, such perspectives will do no one any good. Democratic society needs people who can defend what they believe, and the individual's themselves will only benefit from their diverse views if they can articulate them well. A different perspective is going to do little, particularly for the person holding it, if it cannot be examined and assessed by everyone debating an issue.

These democratic social needs provide the goal for education in a democracy. What any parent or guardian, teacher or administrator ought to want is a student with a unique perspective, and an ability to promote that perspective when encountering other perspectives. Given this goal, the next issue is how a formal education might promote this goal, but before tackle we this question, we need to address a problem.

As difficult as it may be for some to swallow, though the goal defined above would seem the one needed to ensure the success and happiness of children in a democratic system, it seems we must accept the possibility that local communities might define success and happiness for their children in other ways. For instance, if the majority of school-citizens in a given school belong to a fundamentalist-Christian community, they might define happiness and success in terms of piety not the democratic goal we have outlined. No doubt provoking in some the response: "Force them to conform!" But to force a local community to conform would run counter to the democratic spirit championed throughout this book. However, were we too allow such a different goal it would result in radically divergent curriculum, school structure, etc., and might even make difficult to impossible the demand that students receive equal education as the meaning of "equal" would be unclear. What can be done about this in a democratic system such as the one outlined above?

The first thing to say is that though a possibility, this is not a likely possibility. As every community exists in a wider society, in this case it would be a wider democratic society, for a local community to have a radically different goal for their children's education would be to the detriment of both their children and their community as a whole.[16] Communities are not islands, and thus no community would want to isolate its children from the wider world, particularly as that wider world in this case would demand they interact with, and understand, those different from themselves. At some point in the democratic processes in which children from any local community would ultimately find themselves in a society like the one outlined in this book, they would be forced to encounter those different from themselves. If they were to excel in such an exchange, that is to say, if they were to make a good case for their viewpoint, then they need the training necessary to allow them to give a good account of themselves. And such training is exactly what we are talking about providing with a democratic education. In short, largely from the motive of self-interest there would be pressure placed on every community to bring its educational goal into line with the democratic goal.

Another way to respond to this possibility is to point out that the purpose of a democratic education is in part, as we have seen, the development of diverse perspectives. Thus, a democratic educational system—one pursuing the democratic goal—can accommodate the desire on the part of a community to inculcate different values in their students. The only thing a democratic educational system would demand is that in addition to the inculcation of such different values, they also train their students to encounter others from different perspectives so that they can work together and inform one another in democratic debate. To put this plainly, the community that desires their children to be educated differently is not giving up anything by accepting the democratic goal of education as that goal accommodates their different perspective. All they would do by accepting the democratic goal would be to add a part to their education, one that, to connect with the previous point, would be necessary for the success of their children in the wider democratic society. Democracy need not conflict with diversity, indeed it needs it and even thrives on it, and so a community that wants to define happiness differently for their children can certainly be accommodated inside the broader concerns of a democratic educational system and a democratic society. [17]

With the goal of a democratic educational system set out, and how that goal allows for other goals as a proper part of the educational process, the question is then how to achieve the over democratic goal. How can the formal educational process create a set of diverse individuals who, for all their diversity, are capable of debating with one another, resolving differences in a peaceful fashion, and in so doing designing a profitable course of action for themselves and the community? It is the means to the end to which we must turn now.

Making Good "Entertainers" Part One: Identifying With Others

First to diversity. Democratic schools can promote diversity by promoting two conditions for their students: identification with the interests of others and difference from the interests of others. [18] Identification with the interests of others is necessary because our sense of ourselves as individuals involves saying who we are and what we find important. Saying who we are and what is important comes from saying who we are like; we do not develop an identity in a vacuum. This is because saying who you are and what you find important, having an identity, involves the identification of yourself as a certain type of person with certain interests, or more commonly a combination of types with various interests, i.e., a fine artist, an actor, a doctor, etc. This identification of yourself as a type of person means you identify with others of the same type. To develop an identity is to develop an identification with the interests of others; you do not have one without the other.

Possessing interests different from others is necessary because diversity implies difference. If we are to encourage people to obtain their own voice, we must encourage them to resist conformity. This resistance need not be tumultuous, though for many who do resist conformity it can be the most upsetting episode of their lives—witness the difficulty between many parents and their teenagers. Regardless of how the establishment of difference occurs, there is no diversity without resisting conformity, without developing a sense of our interests in contrast with those of others.

Given the type of diverse individuality we should seek in our democracy, if democratic schools are to promote such individuality, they must promote these conditions. Can they do so?

Let's turn first to identification with others. Identification with others requires that we see little or no separation between our interests and the interests of those with whom we identify—these need not be people immediately around us in time and space of course. They are like another one of us, and we are like another one of them. Given this, how can a democratic school promote this sense of identification, if it can do so at all? How can a school help us connect with other people? Creating this identification or connection would appear particularly difficult for schools in a democratic society. A democratic school in a democratic society would seem to have almost nothing to say about how we relate to others, about who and what we find important, about who and what we connect with. The only effect democracy is taken to have by most people on how we relate to others is in the negative sense of preventing us from violating the rights of others. Short of this, democratic societies, and hence their schools, look unable, or at least unwilling, to intrude into the personal realm and help people develop the connections with others that forms the basis of our identities. If this connection does develop in a democracy, it would seem to be the result of some other factor than democracy itself. Democracy appears able to give the individual the chance to connect with whomever they want, but it cannot *promote* any connection.

This image is mistaken. A democratic society such as the one we are outlining can promote these connections, and in particular it can do so through its schools. [19] Democracy can promote these connections by teaching students our historical and contemporary artistic, scientific, philosophical and religious conceptions of the forces with which they interact, both natural and social. Identification requires a level of awareness about those things that shape our lives and development, because without such awareness the natural and social world will be an alien, and often hostile, place. For the world in general, or any part of it, to seem like home—something which is a part of us and with which we identify—it must seem familiar and not alien. We must see how our story connects with the story of the world around us. Without awareness and familiarity there is no identification, no connection. And what better place is there to make young people aware of our cultural conception of the world than in school?

Nothing would teach our conception of the world better than a traditional "liberal" education and curriculum. By a traditional liberal education and curriculum I mean one where basic skills are established en route to a thorough study of the arts and sciences. Education must concentrate on the development of a more than basic understanding of "our" system of beliefs—those most widely held in the U.S. such as democracy is the best form of social organization, freedom is better than oppression, science leads to truth, etc.—and when they are ready, this must lead students to an exploration of other belief systems. In particular, how these other belief systems differ from our own, and how various belief systems have influenced one another. Ultimately, education with the intent of producing identities and hence individuals needs to promote an understanding of as many different perspectives on human life as possible.

This sounds nice, but it is admittedly vague. In order to be useful, we need to say something more definitive about how a liberal education and curriculum will help individuals to achieve an identity, and how that education should be structured. After all, it could be protested that making people aware of our cultural conception of the natural and social forces which shape us is not something that will necessarily lead to a connection or feeling of identity with anyone or anything. The point being, establishing a connection with others is not something we can teach people how to do, at least in the formulaic fashion that is necessary to structure an educational system. It does not seem teachable in a formulaic fashion, because such connections are not something developed by the inculcation of certain information. Some basic knowledge might be necessary in order for a connection to be achieved, but this cannot result from the mere memorization of certain information. Possessing information is a necessary but not sufficient condition for the development of an identification. At a certain point, an identification, a connection, is either something you obtain or you do not, but it is not something guaranteed to result from knowing any particular facts. The achievement of a connection involves developing the habits in thought and action of others, and it is not clear that this is something we can teach, or at least place at the heart of an educational system.

To make clear on how a liberal education and curriculum might help individuals to develop an identification, I believe we should see the development of such identification as similar to the development of a skill. Developing a skill is learning the habits of thought and action of some group, and this is exactly what we do when we come to identify with others. The development of this identification is the development of ability to think as they think and act as they act. If we see the development of identification as similar to developing a skill, we will see just how a liberal education can help in this process. So what is involved in developing a skill?

The first step in developing a skill involves learning the goal of the skill. It is in terms of their goals that we define skills. The goals define the skills by giving us the purpose of the activity and clarifying success and failure. We define the skill that is medicine by its goal of curing illness. To have this skill is to be able to cure, if you cannot cure, then you do not have this skill. From the architect we want buildings that stand up, work well and suit our sense of aesthetics; from the lawyer we want protection from, and victory over, others regarding legal problems. If you are an architect or lawyer you can do these things, if you cannot do these things then you are neither an architect nor a lawyer.

Once we learn the goal of the skill, the next step in developing the skill is developing the ability to achieve that goal. This ability is developed mostly through the obtainment of "knowledge how", not "knowledge that". For instance, in order to learn *how* to swim, you need to know *that* you must get in the water, flap your arms while kicking your legs, turn your head to breathe, etc. With this "knowledge that" firmly in place, if you are pushed in the water for the first time without help, you will drown. The reason is that swimming is a skill; it is an example of knowledge *how* not knowledge *that*. To develop a skill, to learn *how* to do something, is not something that can just be taught in a classroom. It takes time and practice—and practice and practice—and even with this some people will never develop the skill.

This is what it takes to develop a skill. If we look at developing an identification with others as we look at developing a skill, then we must first define the goal of this "skill". This is a problem. It might seem there is no concrete goal and hence there is no "skill" here at all. The point of developing an identification with others seems not to *achieve* some specific goal, but to *create* some specific goal with which we identify. We seem to make up our goal as a part of the process, by developing a sense of who we are through interacting and identifying with others. This lack of a definitive goal also leaves it unclear just when someone is successful and when they are unsuccessful in using this skill. It is so unclear, that this might seem another reason to conclude that there is no skill here at all. To make our program of promoting individuality successful, we must overcome the impression that there is no goal here at all.

In order to develop identification with others, we must develop their habits of thought and action. We can say this is the goal of the "skill", but what does it mean to do this? This is too general to be of use. Is it that we mimic them? Is it that we understand them? Neither. It is that we can tell "stories" that they find interesting; it is that we can be "entertaining"—more on the meaning of these two words in the coming pages, but they have a much broader meaning for me in this context than they normally have hence the scare quotes. When we are able to tell such stories, when our lives become pieces of art in this way and we are entertaining, we are showing our identity with those around us. We are showing our identity because it is this identity that lets us know what will be interesting and entertaining to them.   Identification involves more than copying. If we copy others we are not identifying with them, we are merely seeing them as an object of study. Identification takes an internalization, an internalization that is shown when you can take their outlook one step further. To really *be* with others is to know not just what they like, but what they *will* like. It is not just to know what they have done, but what they will want to do. When this has been achieved, when you can interest others with your stories, when you can entertain, then identification has been achieved. And it is through such identification that we develop our identity because their stories become our stories. It is through a sense of community that we become most ourselves, and this sense of community is shown when we are able to make those around us interested in what we are doing. The goal of our skill is the ability to tell stories that others find interesting.[20]

If we accept this as the goal, our next question becomes: can we teach the ability to achieve this goal? This question actually has three separate components: One, what method must we use to teach this ability to tell good, entertaining stories? Two, is it possible to teach a skill of this sort on a very large scale? Three, as some never learn to swim, or ride a bike, or play tennis, etc. so some may never learn the skills necessary to develop an identity; does this mean that this educational system will fail many?

The second two questions can be dealt with quickly. We can and do teach people skills on a large scale with a great deal of success. Without this ability to teach a skill, almost any practice could not be passed on, and our continued existence as a society shows we have been successful at passing skills on. It is skills that are learned, mostly on the job, by those in many walks of life. From the carpenter to the lawyer, the artist to the medical doctor, the chef to the architect, these are all activities learned largely through the communication of certain practices, i.e. skills. We are very successful in teaching these to one another—though often not in the present-day classroom—so a skill is certainly something we can teach on a large scale. We may at times not succeed as much as we might like, but by and large, we do very well.

The first question is not so easily dispensed with. What method can be used to teach the ability to tell good, entertaining stories? Our classrooms are at present largely structured for the conveyance of "facts"—knowledge *that*, not knowledge *how*. Learning to tell good stories often has little to do with remembering facts. Thus to teach the skills necessary to achieve identification the present classroom would have to be altered. But how? How do we teach people to tell good stories? How can we teach people to be good entertainers— meaning this in the broadest sense of the term entertainer of course?

The answer is first and foremost that we give recognition to the fact that this is our goal. We must avoid the belief that the main focus of education is about doing something "right", about discovering the facts, about determining the proper story in the face of many improper stories. This is not to say that any story goes. It is to say that we should see education as about human communication and entertainment. Right or wrong in story telling depends only on success and failure in communication and entertainment, not on something more abstract like "Truth". Education is about communication and entertainment, so how do we develop this ability to communicate and entertain?

Through a progressive education in story telling, from the simplest stories, orally told, as children in the classroom, to the most advanced stories that comprise our cultural tradition in art, science and philosophy. It is here that we can see the use of a liberal education. A liberal education is just the introduction of various stories to a population of students. It is to show them what stories have been told so far, and what might be told in the future. By story telling, I mean of course something more than this term normally connotes. Physics, philosophy, literature, religion and fine art are stories as I use the term. They are activities where the point is to learn what has been said before, and to see if you can say something different that people find entertaining and interesting. Each activity will have its own norms regarding what must be known in order to become part of the story telling circle, and they will have different norms for identifying what is entertaining and interesting, but that does not tell against my basic point. Each activity in which we engage can be seen as story telling, as the creation of a narrative, the point of which is to add to that narrative.

The ability to tell a good story really has two components—components that are not necessarily distinct—and a liberal education can help us with both. The first is the ability to make us see more clearly what we already know. It is to let us see who we are. A major part of the liberal education is the history of the stories that you are studying. The second is not to help us appreciate the old but see something new. These stories let us go beyond who we are to who we can be. This is also part of the liberal education, normally taught through the study of those who have said something new in their time. By studying the "geniuses", the great entertainers of the past—those who took a story in a new direction that no one anticipated and many found interesting—we get a sense of how this might be accomplished. We not only get a sense of how this might be accomplished, but we often get a desire to accomplish it ourselves.

Both these abilities are necessary for the development of good story telling, and if both are accomplished, an individual will be a good story teller. When both of these are accomplished, the end result will often be the identification with others that is necessary for the development of an identity. The best way to ensure that these are both accomplished is through a familiarity with the great stories, and great story tellers of the past. This is all that a liberal education is, and it is a great way to allow us to accomplish the goal of telling good stories and achieving identification.

A liberal education is not guaranteed of success. It is not because the ability to tell good stories, to be a good entertainer, ultimately requires creativity, and creativity is not something we can teach. Why can't we teach creativity, or better yet, create creativity? Creativity, the ability to see something in a new way, cannot be directly taught because if we had a formula for its production, then what was produced would be predictable. Predictable is just what creativity is not though, so there is no way we can apply some formula to our educational system and be guaranteed to produce creativity. We will obtain no guarantee, but we can establish conditions that will promote the ability to see creativity in action, hence making its development more likely. We can do this by providing everyone with a liberal education. This education will communicate the various parts of our cultural tradition—introduce us to our story telling traditions—and give us examples of those who have made those stories more interesting. By so doing, we stand the best chance of producing interesting storytellers, good entertainers, and hence those who have an identity with others.

Making Good "Entertainers" Part Two: Differing From Others

This discussion of identity leads naturally to a discussion of the second necessary condition for the development of individuality: difference from the interests of others. Luckily for us, developing an identification with others as we conceive it, the ability to create interesting and entertaining stories, entails at the same time the development of a sense of difference from others. Developing the one entails developing the other because creativity is about being different. The very development of identifications, of connections, thus involves insight into what is different, and this forms the basis of an individual's difference from others. To say who you are and what you find important, involves saying who you are not and what you do not find important. Therefore, a liberal education does more than just promote identity. At the same time it promotes a sense of difference, a sense of difference which completes an individual. By educating people to be good storytellers through showing them other good storytellers, our educational system becomes a complete system for the production of individuality.

A liberal education with the goals and curriculum outlined above is thus the stone with which we kill two birds. We must admit however that this educational process will not always be a smooth and easy one. In fact, I can see two negative consequences that are likely to result from such a system at times. One is that by developing identifications and differences we are encouraging divisions among people, and such divisions can cause conflict. In particular, it can cause conflict between the products of the educational system, the students, and the institutions that educated them—students are often the most active subversives and revolutionaries. In such cases, what can we do?

When differences lead to divisions and ultimately to conflict we can only appeal to democratic decision making to settle these conflicts. Those who are in conflict must be brought into open competition, and that competition must decide what ever might be at issue. Everyone should be given a maximal chance to win the day, but even with that, we are practically guaranteed that some individuals or groups are going to walk away from this process unhappy. All that we can say is that democracy is not utopian.

The second negative consequence of this system is that the process of achieving an identification and difference may go too far. Someone may come to feel almost no identification, complete alienation in fact. No one may want to listen to their stories. This person may then become resentful and give up on the community or even develop hostility towards it—I think something like this must have gone on with the two young men who killed those people in Columbine, Co. This is a more threatening situation to a democracy, in which case what can be done? What are we as good democrats supposed to do with the individual who identifies little with the social forces that shape them, one who feels nothing but difference from them—they do not seek to add creatively to their own community but hate that community in its entirety? How can our system handle the anti-social tendencies that might result when this system fails some entirely?

Again, our only recourse is to allow them access to the democratic institutions of which they are a part, yet which they hate. At times they may convince these institutions to change, or just leave them alone. At times they may fail, and there will be complete conflict and alienation. There is nothing in our system to remove this possibility. As we have just suggested, this system is not a utopian. One thing is for sure, those who attempt to overthrow this democratic system instead of working within it, must be resisted with the full power that we can muster.

We should keep in mind however, though there will be chances for failure, the successes that such an educational system might achieve could be fantastic. Beyond the potential increase in general happiness, the increase in creativity could result in more socially beneficial ideas and activities. What we are talking about is nothing less than a large increase in the quantity of creative brain power brought to bear on various aspects of our lives. Such an increase could bring about untold riches in both the lives of the community and of the individual.

A Critique of Our Current System

Before we continue, I want to address a question that some of you may be asking at this point: Don't we do this already? Aren't we currently giving students a liberal education, and thus mustn't we already promote the development of diverse individuals right now?

I can respond by saying our record speaks for itself. Many students leave the current U.S. educational system with little sense of commitment to anything or anyone. I see this all the time in my new students in the university where I teach. Students who are bored, without direction, without the identifications and sense of difference that makes them individuals are a common phenomenon. As such, our schools cannot be doing what I suggest they should be doing. But why?

The reason is our schools are not really providing a liberal education. Schools are little more than job training centers where we tip our hats to the vast story-telling traditions that make up our culture. The economy rules in our schools.[21] Education is dominated by the demand to develop job skills, not identities. Of course by getting job skills some students develop an identity. They like what they are learning to do. Most students are not so lucky. They learn the job skills that will make them money, believing that through money, they will be able to buy an identity. They are wrong, and our schools are fostering this attitude. We focus on making money makers, with the production of individuals a residual effect at best. We need to reverse this.

We need to focus on producing passionate committed individuals, and then see job skills as a residual effect. We need to blur the line between education and entertainment, making school fun, and thus making the students feel a part of what they are doing. We need to make them passionate about the traditions they are being introduced to, not simply trained to play a role in the economy. Just how this can be done is something that we have touched on, but we cannot go any further here because I believe there are no real general answers. We must rely on our teachers to produce creative strategies for developing identities by blurring the line between education and entertainment. What we can say is that we democrats must recognize a change in priorities in our schools if we are to produce the sort of individuals we need. We must make the development of individuality our focus, and we must do this by seeing the point of education as introducing students to story telling traditions. We must give up on education as a dry transference of facts that can be used when working jobs and see education as becoming part of a story-telling tradition and taking that tradition one step further. We must come to see that education is about making good entertainers.

Defending Your (Our) Differences

A democracy needs people with diverse interests. We have now discussed how this need might be fulfilled. Democracy needs more than this however. As we pointed out earlier, diverse interests are of good to no one, particularly the individual with the interests, if they cannot be articulated and defended to a population at large. Can we teach people to articulate and defend their interests in the democratic forums we have been designing?

It would seem, given the education we elaborated above, becoming a part of a story telling community would involve learning to articulate our interests. What else is it to tell a story, to be an entertainer, other than to articulate a vision of the way you think things are, could or should be? True enough. But what about the ability to defend one's interests, and defend them to people whom might not share your interest in your stories? Articulating presumes the ability to make oneself understood, regardless of the attitude of the audience. Defending presumes an ability to maintain one's position in the face of an indifferent or possibly hostile audience. The tasks are very different and the education we have designed so far is going to promote an ability to articulate but not necessarily an ability to defend. What does it take to defend one's interests in a democratic forum? What can an entertainer do when the audience is hostile?

What it takes is rhetorical and polemical skill. In a word: marketing. Our interests, to have any chance of success, must be packaged in a way that is compelling. After hearing the case for our side, people must want to join our side. That is what is required for the defense of our interests. And this is nothing more than what is taught in contemporary courses on marketing, advertising, political consulting, legal litigation, public speaking and even informal logic. What every person must receive, therefore, as part of their education is a thorough grounding in these subjects. We must mandate that every student, starting as early as possible in the education process, must receive a complete course of instruction in what we can call rhetoric—a combination of both the art and science of being convincing.

We can look at this as an extension of the contemporary civics education that almost every student in America already receives. Instead of just concentrating on democratic structure and procedure, we could also introduce students to actual democratic practice.[22] This already occurs in schools through the holding of mock elections for official government office, as well as through the actual election of student body president, student council, etc. We would merely have to extend this to a more theoretical study of what is behind such practice. To put it simply: why are some people successful at convincing others and some people not? This can go all the way from the study of actual votes held in and out of school, to an examination of the general principles of the fields concerned with being "convincing".

There would be at least two benefits to this expanded education. First, it would help each individual citizen in the various types of citizen roles they may play. The citizen would be benefited because they would now stand a better chance at making their case for their interests in a democratic forum. They would at least stand an equal chance of success with others in most cases. Of course, some people are going to be better at rhetoric than others. This cannot be avoided. But what is preferable, to give everyone a chance to make their case in an open forum, or to allow closed processes, which are not skill based but power based, decide issues without most people having a say? I know what I would prefer.

Second, the community would benefit in that the quality of the debate would rise. As each citizen would be more skilled in the art and science of debate, the debate would take place at a higher level. Everyone would be aware of the tricks and fallacies that could be used by an opponent and hence those tricks and fallacies would be less useful. The case for each side would be decided more on the actual merits of the case, and less on the pure "presentation quality" of a case. The result of which would be that the decisions made by the community would be more likely to lead in the direction of success for everyone. Again, we must continue to remember that there is nothing utopian about this system. Will it be the case that some will be less successful simple because they were less able to make their case in a democratic forum? Yes. But again, which a the non-utopian systems we have before us would you prefer? Which, if not completely fair, if fairest?

Going from Here to There

As with every other chapter, we must connect the system just elaborated with our current system. How do we go from what we've got to what we want? The following steps will allow this to occur, I believe.

1. The following recommendations should be made a part of the party program discussed at the end of Chapter 2.

2. An "Educational Rights Amendment" mandating equal education for all from kindergarten through the highest level of education an individual can achieve.

3. Passage of a law establishing that in order to receive government money, tax-exempt status or accreditation—to grant degrees respected by the necessary government regulatory agencies—any university, secondary or primary school must become democratic. They must create the role of citizen, as outlined above, in their respective universities and schools.

4. Congress must create national standards for spending per student, as well as student and teacher performance.

    a. A formula should be derived through which spending per student is calculated and raised to meet the highest funded districts. This formula should allow for differences in costs experienced across districts.
    b. All standards for performance must explicitly state the criteria for receiving degrees and for being considered eligible to teach, as well as some way of judging whether individuals pass the designated criteria.

    c.   Exams should be employed where possible to maintain uniformity, that is equality.

5.   Congress should make salary recommendations for teachers and professors at all levels.
    a.   These are just recommendations, as all salaries and other privileges are to be established by the local democratic institutions responsible for such decisions. They are intended only to help in this process by providing guidelines.
    b.   All increased expenses incurred by raising salaries as well as other capital improvements in our schools should be paid for by the reduction in prison projects that will be made possible as a result of the legalization of drugs. If this is not enough, then a larger sales tax should be added to traditional "sin" items such as alcohol and tobacco.
    c.   Additional funding could be attained by requiring a time of service from each individual receiving an education.

6.   A national conference of educators should be organized by the President to discuss curriculum alterations and suggest changes. These should focus on how best to blur the line between education and entertainment with the goal of making members of story-telling traditions.

Notes

[1] I call this chapter "Democracy and Formal Education" rather than simply "Democracy and Education" because we are concerned in this book with restructuring institutions, and informal education, for instance, what happens in the home, is beyond the scope of this essay. I would also like to mention this entire chapter has been greatly influenced by Frithjof Bergmann's *On Being Free*, and John Dewey's *Democracy and Education*.

[2] Equality of quality must always remain, though students may start to receive different types of education, specializing in different areas, as students show they have more ability in certain specialized areas or grow up in different school districts with different requirements. However, go to any two districts and students on the same level, in the same subject matter, must be receiving an education of equal quality.

[3] It is a longstanding myth, but one that was mortally wounded by the experience of the 1960's in America and elsewhere. Let's hope this myth finally dies soon and is put out of its misery. Though with the advent of "political correctness" the myth seems to be stabilizing and even making a recovery. This is because the essence of political correctness seems to be that no one should judge anyone else, especially those from a different background.

[4] David Knowles, *The Evolution of Medieval Thought*, (New York: Vintage Books, 1962), pg. 153.

[5] Ibid., pp. 161-162. My addition in italics.

[6] The issue of size can be handled here exactly as it has been in the previous two chapters. Participatory democracies will run departments and other sections of the university, and the entire university if the school is small enough. As sizes increase however, the system of improved representation outlined in Chapter 2 should be employed.

[7] Employees of the university who do not have academic responsibilities, i.e. maintenance personnel, security, administrative assistants, etc., should not be "university citizens", but rather should be "employee citizens" and thus should be allowed to give consent as per the method for employee citizens set down in the previous chapter. This should include who administers the university overall, as well as whom they work for in their chain of command—though some of these decisions will have to be made jointly with university citizens.

[8] Some of you are asking at this point: "Won't this amount to universities being run by the less qualified?" If you are asking this question, I suggest you return to the sections of previous Chapters where this fear is addressed, as what is said there applies here.

[9] The only universities that should be excused from such mandatory re-structuring are those that receive *no* government money, tax-exempt status or government accreditation. Such universities should be allowed to structure themselves however they choose.

[10] More on funding at the end of the chapter.

[11] Any school that receives no government money, no tax-exempt status and seeks no government accreditation, should be allowed to structure as they choose.   As for democratized schools, what school you are a citizen of as a parent or guardian is determined by where you live, just as currently the school a child attends is determined by where he lives. Though students should be allowed to seek admittance to any school they desire, subject to approval by the democratic bodies running the school they would like to depart and enter. This should be regardless of whether the school is public or private, with the exception of those non-democratic schools that receive no government money, tax-exempt status and seeks no government accreditation. If a child wants to attend a private school, and they can pass the schools voted on test of admission, then the government should pay for it.   Admissions to primary and secondary schools should work the same as in universities.

[12] Concerned about funding these changes?   See the end of this Chapter as well as Chapter 3.

[13]See John Dewey's *Democracy and Education*, pp. 81-99 for a discussion of various historical views on the ultimate purpose of education.

[14] Ibid., pg. 121. My addition in brackets.

[15] This fact should also help mitigate the concern that the previous paragraph may have raised in you that we will define individual happiness in terms of an ability to fit in.

[16] Such a community would most likely opt out of the whole system we are outlining, but they could only do so if they abandon funding, tax-exemption and accreditation from the government. Of course, if they choose to stay a part of this system, they must be subject to the demand that their teachers and students pass national exams for any subject matter in which they give instruction. As well, they must also accept any students who desire to attend their institution as long as they pass their academic admissions requirements.

[17] Though practically successful, this does not entirely settle the issue. For those who see this as a fundamental conflict between rights and the democratic process, between privacy and majority rule, see my discussion of human rights in Chapter 5.

[18] See Chapter One of Frithjof Bergmann's *On Being Free* for the source of this claim, though it is also quite common-sensical. His discussion is more lucid and detailed than I could hope to recreate, or have space for, here.

[19] There is a second way that such identification can be promoted by a democratic community, one that goes beyond anything taught in schools. By the mere fact of being democratic, of allowing citizens to jointly structure the institutions in which we learn, work and govern, we help create a sense of identity, of connection between citizens. A society structured by the input of everyone—where people are forced to listen to others ideas all the time—is a community likely to give birth to the sense of identification we are seeking. This would have little to do specifically with education however; it would be a natural outgrowth of democracy in general, and so it does not merit discussion here. As well, considering it would be a natural outgrowth of democracy, we need not really make explicit how we could help bring it about. All we have to do is increase democracy and it *will* come about.

[20] Notice how very different this goal is from the current goal of education which is simply remembering information to be accessed when needed. Education currently is not about making people interesting, it is about making them useful. What is great about our more thorough-going democracy, of course, is that being interesting is being useful.

[21] Don't believe me? Well, explain to me why there is a fight currently underway to preserve music education in our schools, but no fight to preserve classes on computer skills.

[22] For an interesting discussion of civics education, see Paul Gagnon, *Democracy's Untold Story* (The American Federation of Teachers, 1987).

Chapter 5
Why Complete the American Revolution?
Part II:
A Philosophical Justification

In this chapter I want to return to the topic from the first: *why* complete the American Revolution? Now that you know what completing the American Revolution might mean, justifying its completion should have a new significance.

Shopping and the "Logic" of Choice Making

Imagine you are shopping for something. A sports car let's say. You are immediately confronted with the question: which sports car should I buy? You decide first on a type. Given you are imagining this, make money no object and say the type you choose is a Ferrari. Having decided on the type, you must then chose the particular Ferrari you want. You go to the nearest Ferrari dealer and walk through their showroom to see if you find an acceptable candidate—good design, proper color, appropriate engine size, etc. If you do, you may buy that one immediately. If you don't, you may settle for one that is less than optimal—black rather than classic Ferrari red. If you don't find an acceptable candidate at all, given what you are looking for in a Ferrari, you will probably go to another Ferrari dealer to buy your car. Either that, or you may choose another type of sports car—the new Porsches look awfully good. You may also abandon your quest altogether. Your desire for a sports car will simply have to go unsatisfied for now because no acceptable candidate can be found.

Shopping requires making choices between competing or conflicting options—the options must be in conflict because if they were capable of mutual satisfaction, you would not have to make a choice. You make these choices, settle these conflicts, by assessing the *value* or *quality*—what we have been calling "merit" so far in the book—of the many options available. On the most basic level, when you buy something, a sports car in our fantasy scenario, you choose one or another particular sports car because it is the *best* sports car you can find. This means it exhibits a *superior quality* to all its competitors. It is *worthy* of your purchase; it *merits* your spending your hard-earned money. On a bit more abstract level, you choose based not simply on the fact that you judge this or that particular sports car to be *best*, you choose based on your judgment that any quality sports car has certain attributes. For a sports car to be a *good type* of sports car it must be beautiful, fast, dependable or what have you. You decide this about sports cars, not on the spot of course as you most likely came with this judgment already made—either consciously made or inculcated through personal experience and habit—but it is another value judgment. And this value judgment serves as the basis of your choice about the specific sports car you *should* buy. Without your general view about what makes a sports car a quality sports car, one that merits purchase, you would not, and should not, choose the particular sports car you choose.

On yet a more abstract level, your choice to purchase a sports car involves other choices, choices about how to spend money for instance. Choices again made based on value judgments. You chose to buy a sports car at this point because you believe it is *better* to use your money now, for this purpose, than it is to save your money to buy something else later on. You judge that immediate satisfaction of your desire for a sports car *merits* action in a way that holding off does not. Or, maybe you chose to buy a sports car instead of save for retirement because you judge that you should have fun now and let the future take care of itself. The desire that *deserves* satisfaction at this point is thus the one that contributes to your current good time. Even more abstract still, you choose, or have chosen in the past, that your purchase of a sports car is *better* than sending your money to relieve famine overseas. Not that relieving famine isn't important to you let's say, but you think there is no point to sending the price of one sports car because it will have so little impact given the vast nature of the problem...or the problem of famine cannot be helped by individual contributions, no matter how large, but only by systematic change...or the pleasure you will derive from your sport's car is more important to you than the pleasure that you and others will derive from your giving the money away...or...

This is only the tip of the iceberg. There are many more value judgments involved in your choice to purchase a sports car, or spend money on anything else for that matter. And, value judgments are not restricted to choices regarding the world of shopping and spending money of course. When we choose to get married we make a value judgment about our particular spouse, about spouses in general and about the institution of marriage. Our particular spouse is the *best* available candidate given we believe any spouse should be intelligent, beautiful, loyal, in love with us, etc. Our mate has the attributes we judge to be the *best* attributes in any mate, and we judge the institution of marriage to be *better than* living together or remaining single. Anytime we make *any* choice in fact, we are explicitly or implicitly making a number of value judgments, or employing value judgments made or inculcated in the past. *Choices are judgments*, and judgments imply our possession of standards of good or bad, or at least better or worse—measures of value, quality, merit, call it what you will—and it is in terms of these standards or measures that we make choices between competing options.

The American Revolution and Value Judgments

This discussion of shopping, and the logic of choice making in general, may be very interesting but you are probably asking: *What connection does this have with a "philosophical" justification for completing the American Revolution?!*

The connection is as follows. Groups also make choices, choices between competing options, by making value judgments. As individuals must decide which actions to take by making value judgments, so must groups. When it comes to group value judgments, right now we accept that if these value judgments are of a certain political sort—who is the *best* person to represent us in Congress for instance—they should be made in a democratic fashion. "Contemporary America" from our earlier diagram expresses this basic idea about making group value judgments:

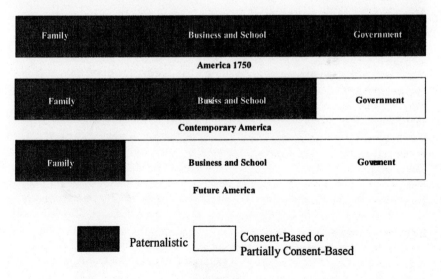

Figure 2

What I am arguing in this essay is for the American Revolution to be complete we need to go from "Contemporary America" to "Future America." We need to make our group value judgments throughout politics and our economy and educational system as we do now in part of our politics. Our discussion of choice-making connects with a philosophical justification for completing the American revolution therefore, by allowing us to see that the American Revolution is about a method of making value judgments, a method of deciding "merit", a way of "shopping". And, if we are to justify completing the American Revolution, we must justify a way of making value judgments, something done best by appeal to philosophy. It is done best by appeal to philosophy because it is philosophers who focus their energies on questions concerning how things *should* be, not how they *are*, how the world *ought* to be, not how it *is*, the issues behind all value judgments. How does our discussion of choice making connect with a philosophical justification for completing the American Revolution? It puts the revolution in a different context than it is normally seen, one that shows we can use philosophy to justify the Revolution, and to justify taking it further.

Like the other chapters in this book, we can sum up our topic in terms of several questions: First, why accept the method of making group value judgments outlined in the middle line of the Figure 2? In other words, how can we justify what has so far taken place in the American Revolution? How can we justify moving from "America 1750" to "Contemporary America?" Second, even if we accept the method outlined in the middle line—if we accept what has happened so far—why go from the middle to the bottom—why complete the American Revolution? Why go from "Contemporary America" to "Future America?"

Unlike other chapters in this book, I do not think either of these questions will worry anyone. They may even bore some of you. These questions will interest only those who were not convinced by my more current events and historical argument in Chapter 1. I include this discussion simply to bolster the case to those still in doubt; a bolstering that even some who liked what I had to say in Chapter 1 might demand given the sweeping changes I am suggesting. For many of you however, no such bolstering is necessary. The points made in Chapter 1 are sufficient to convince you of the sense of what I am saying. You accept that history, combined with a good dose of common sense, shows that the Consent Principle is *the* principle for the distribution of power, and given this, we need to extend democracy into other arenas of power. If you have been convinced by Chapter 1, you need not read on. If you have not been convinced, or if you are simply interested in a further discussion of these issues, please continue reading.

Why, then, should we accept the middle line of the diagram, a democratic method of making at least some of our group value judgments? And if we accept the middle line, why not accept the bottom line, making almost all of our group value judgments democratically?

Methods for Making Value Judgments

Imagine you have now bought your Ferrari. You proudly drive it around for a day or two, you drive it so much you need to get gas in fact. You pull into a gas station and while pumping gas you start looking at the car and wondering: "Did I choose the right color?" You're wondering this because even though red is the classic color for Ferraris you did always want a black car. "Maybe," you think to yourself, "I should have gotten black." While this thought is running through your mind you happen to glance over at the left front tire and notice it looks a little flat. Leaving off the thought of the car's color for a moment you are now confronted with the question: what is the right pressure for the left front tire of my Ferrari? You didn't ask this question before your drove off the dealer's lot, so now what are you going to do? This is the first Ferrari you've ever owned, and you have little idea how much pressure the tires might require.

Standing in the gas station you realize you have more choices to make. Buying your Ferrari was one choice but a choice that has led you to others. Should I keep the car red or paint it black? Should I put 30 or 40 pounds of air pressure in the tire? And this means you have value judgments to make. Which color is *better*? Which pressure is *right*?

You are confronted with these further choices, but you probably think there is something fundamentally different about choosing the color of a car and choosing a pressure for one of its tires. If you are choosing a color, if *you* are making a value judgment about car colors, it would seem that *you* should make the value judgment and that *you* should make it however *you* want. Judging the value of a car's color is a *subjective* judgment. All you are doing when judging in such cases is expressing a personal preference. All you are doing is reporting your own attitude about the color not making a claim about the color itself. To say a color is the *right* color is to say nothing about the color *itself*, or about how someone else should judge the color. It is only to say that you enjoy the one color more than other colors. The only way your value judgment could be wrong is if you ultimately don't like the result of the judgment. In other words, your value judgment about the color of the car does not mesh well with the rest of your preferences—for instance, red cars get noticed more by the police and *you* don't want that kind of attention.

Change from color to tire pressure and the situation seems very different to you I bet. You believe if you are judging the *right* amount of air to be put in the tires of your Ferrari, the choice should no longer be up to you exclusively but rather you should follow what the car manual dictates. You should, as it were, let the engineers who designed the tires make this choice for you. And regardless of who makes the choice—who makes the value judgment regarding which pressure is *right*—they cannot make it however they want.

There is a *fact* of the matter about the amount of air a tire should take in order to perform properly. In this case the value judgment is **objective**. The individual making the judgment has now entered the realm where it is possible to make a **wrong** judgment. Wrong in the traditional sense. It is not that the judgment might fail to satisfy them, it is that it might fail to be **true** and **should** satisfy no one. Regardless of how much they might like or dislike the result of their judgment that is unimportant to the correctness of their judgment. And the way to guarantee that the right judgment is made is by allowing the **proper** people— experts—to make the judgment because they know the **proper** basis of judgment. Here there is talk of expertise, proof, evidence, justification, etc., and here the judgment is supposed to hold for everyone.

This characterization of the judgments about your Ferrari's color and tire pressure, a characterization I believe most of you would accept, is based on two beliefs about making value judgments and hence choices. First, who should make a value judgment and the basis of their value judgment depends on **what** is being judged. That is, the "method" of judging the value of something depends upon the subject matter being judged. Second, there are fundamentally different types of subject matter requiring differing methods of judging value.

We can call this view, that subject matter determines method of judgment and that there are fundamentally different subject matters that require different methods, the Common View. Of course, for this to be a "view" it needs to be more comprehensive. There are simply more value judgments being made than those concerning car colors and tire pressures—thank god. If the Common View is to be comprehensive, then every subject matter must be identified as something that can be judged subjectively or objectively. If we must first ask about what is being judged before we can determine what method of judgment should be employed, then every possible subject matter is going to have to be classified according to its "proper" method. This need not be done one by one with each individual subject matter however, as that would be an impossible task. There are simply too many subjects for us to go one by one and classify them all. We can group subject matters though, as many people already do, and then say what method is to be employed for subjects in each group—who is to make judgments in each group and how.

Most supporters of the Common View, again this is just about everyone today and most likely includes yourself, tend to make the following groupings. First, there are those subject matters that deal with our tastes such as the color of cars, our favorite ice cream flavors, and most would include music, fine art and anything else traditionally labeled "aesthetic". This group requires a subjective method—judgments here are all up to the individual ultimately and there is no right or wrong basis of judgment. Beauty is in the eye of the beholder, right? Second, there are those subject matters typically called "moral" which can range all the way from table manners to romantic relationships, international relations and beyond. This group is the most complex to classify. Some suggest this requires a purely subjective method, others purely objective. For yet others, a line between the subjective and the objective needs to be drawn somewhere in the middle of this group. For instance, our most fundamental moral principles might be said to be objective. That Nazis, serial killers and recreational torturers are bad is not an issue for the individual to decide and there is a proper basis of judgment. This is because Nazis, serial killers and recreational torturers are *really* bad. There is a fact of the matter. Table etiquette and sexual morality might seem a different story however. Whether one should or should not make noise while eating, have sex before marriage, have sex with members of the same sex, etc., might seem to be the provenance of the individual or their culture. No one can dictate to another the rightness or wrongness of such decisions, particularly if they come from a different background. Table manners and sexual morality are merely the expression of individual or cultural preference. Hence, many believe a line divides this category between the subjective and objective. Third is a group of subject matters we can call "scientific". The subject matters here concern views about the natural or possibly supernatural world—some like Pythagoras, Plato and a number of contemporary philosophers think mathematics concerns a supernatural world.   About "scientific" subject matters there is general agreement that a purely objective method is required. Whether a tire should have 30 or 40 pounds of air pressure, the interior angles of a plane triangle equal 180 degrees, we are descended from apes or matter is ultimately composed of particles, these are not something the individual decides. There is some *fact* of the matter about these. The individual's judgment is only as good as *the fact* it claims to represent, and there is a basis for judging if they have gotten the fact *right*.

This classification leaves out some important subjects. The most glaring is religion. The problem is that most supporters of the Common View, and again I believe this is most people and probably includes you, get very nervous when religion comes up. Everyone knows that if they believe in a religion they believe it is the *right* religion. To be religious is to believe there is a fact of the matter about god's existence and nature, making the religious judgment objective, and hence *your* religious judgment *true*. To say this, though, is to say that everyone who disagrees with you has gotten it *wrong* and thus their view is *false*. To say that others are wrong is to say that many people who are your friends, colleagues or countrymen are wrong. To claim religion is objective is to bring the religious person into the most fundamental kind of conflict with many people with whom they do not want to conflict therefore. It is for this reason that the subject of religion makes many religious people very nervous. They seem forced into conflict they do not want, or forced to claim that religion is subjective and hence not much different in nature than choices regarding the color of cars, ice cream flavors or table manners. Most of those who are religious end up opting for objectivity, but they opt for it *quietly*.

The Common View is the most widely accepted view about making value judgments—particularly in the U.S. and Western world in general—but it is not the only view out there. Some oppose the Common View with what we can call the Traditional View. Supporters of the Traditional view, a group that grows smaller all the time, agree with the first part of the Common View but reject the second. They agree that subject matter dictates method of judgment. They disagree that there are different subject matters requiring different methods. All subject matters are basically the same for supporters of the Traditional View and thus they believe only one type of value judgment is required.

The Traditional View itself comes in two varieties. One Traditional View we can term Objectivism. The Objectivist, as the name implies, believes that *every* subject matter requires an objective method for making value judgments. These judgments should thus be made by experts according to their views on the correct bases of judgment. The aesthetic moral and scientific may have different bases of judgment and different experts making those judgments, but each judgment is equally determined by the subject matter being judged. A painting may be judged based on the historical context of the painting by an expert who understands that context, whereas a scientific theory may be judged based on experiments conducted by a scientist with certain technical expertise. In either case however, the judgment is still determined by the subject matter at hand. Whether a painting or poem is good, whether it has positive value, is as objective as whether a tire needs 30 or 40 pounds of pressure, a triangle's interior angles equal 180 degrees, we evolved from apes or matter is ultimately composed of particles. All value judgments are capable of being wrong in the traditional sense.

The other Traditional View we can term, unsurprisingly, Subjectivism. The Subjectivist shares with the Objectivist their belief in the monolithic character of method. As the Objectivist thinks every value judgment employs the same method, so does the Subjectivist. How they differ is that the Objectivist tells us every value judgment is objective, whereas the Subjectivist tells us they are all subjective. According to the Subjectivist an unprejudiced view of any subject matter is simply not available to us. Our view of any subject matter is always *our view* and thus by definition skewed. Judgments of subject matter therefore ultimately express nothing but the attitude of the individual; they do not, nor could they ever hope to, report a fact. Every value judgment is "up to us", and thus the value judgments of every person become equally acceptable, meaning of course that each individual can make their judgments however they like. No value judgment, whether in mathematics, subatomic physics, sexual morality or poetry is "correct". Therefore, the "proper" method of all value judgments is subjective; which is to say, really, there is no method you have to use at all. You are free to make any judgment you like, in any way you like, on any subject. Subject matter still guides our judgments of course, only it guides us in a negative way. It is the failure of subject matter to guide us which acts as a guide in our knowing how to make judgments. It is the failure of subject matter to guide us which tells us we have no guide at all.

We can sum up these three views by use of the following spectra:

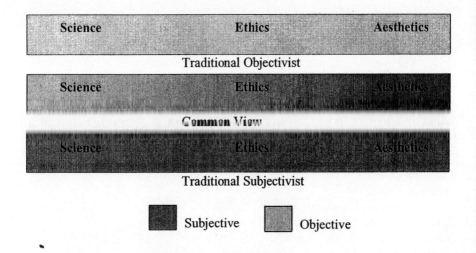

Figure 3

Though rarely discussed, there is one other view on making value judgments, one opposed to both the Common and the Traditional view. For ease, we can call it the democratic View—small d democratic so as not to suggest that this view has anything to do with any political Party. Supporters of the democratic View *disagree* with all the other views on making value judgments in the following ways.

First, they disagree with the fundamental assumption shared by both Commoners and Traditionalists that subject matter dictates method—the who and how of judgment making. Instead they believe method of judgment should be determined by who will be affected by the judgment. If the person affected by the value judgment will be only me, then I should be the one who makes that judgment, and it should be made according to my view on the correct basis of judgment. If the persons affected by the judgment are you and me, then we should both make the judgment together according to our views on the correct basis of judgment. If the persons affected by the judgment are all those who comprise a certain institution or society, then every member of that institution or society should make the judgment according to the majority's view on the correct basis of judgment; or barring that, some representative group which acts in the institution's name. To the democrat, there are right and a wrong methods of making value judgments, only right or wrong in method is determined by who is affected by the judgment not by what is being judged.

Second, unlike Traditionalists they do not think a single, uniform method is acceptable for making judgments, as my previous statements make obvious. democrats believe we cannot use the same method every time we judge. We must first ask about the impact of a judgment and then we can determine the method of judgment. However, there is a single principle guiding this idea, none other than the Consent Principle: choices should be made by those who will be affected by those choices, and according to their standards. So, the correct method varies given who is making the judgment, not what is being judged. The only important question here is the one made important by the Consent Principle.

To sum up, supporters of the democratic view believe that there are a diverse number of correct methods, but they do not believe this diversity results from the diversity of subject matter. Rather, this diversity of method results from the diversity of those who are going to be affected by the judgment(s) being made.

These are the main views on how to judge value and hence make choices. As should be obvious, the democratic View philosophically embodies the Consent Principle and hence philosophically embodies the American Revolution. Given this, our task of providing a philosophical justification of the middle line from Figure 2—"Contemporary America"—one made by appeal to a discussion of value judgments, has now become clearer. If we are to show that the Consent Principle and hence the American Revolution is "right, all we need do is show the superiority of the democratic View over its competitors. If we can show it superior, we will have a "philosophical" reason for our living by the Consent Principle and not some other choice-making, and hence value-judging, procedure. And as such, we will have our philosophical justification for the American Revolution, for "Contemporary America" vs. "America 1750." So why might we consider the democratic View superior?

Defending the democratic Method Part One: Separating "Truth" and State

When we were children and our parent(s) would go out for the night leaving us at home with our brothers and sisters, they felt a strong need to have some adult, some surrogate parent in the form a grandparent, aunt, uncle, babysitter, etc. stay with us while they were gone. Why? Because they knew that if no adult was present, no force that stood above the children and which the children had to heed, then there would be trouble. Inevitably conflicts would start between the children over some toys, television programs or what have you. Without some surrogate parent on the spot, these conflicts could then escalate to a dangerous height. In this situation they saw only two possibilities, either some force independent of the children was put in place over the children, or the children were left to their own devices which meant anarchy in the pejorative sense.

Not just our parents saw things this way. We ourselves, as children, accepted the need for the presence of adults as judges. When we were playing and we found ourselves in conflict with another child, what would we do? In most cases we would go to the parent or surrogate parent on the spot as we figured that they were neutral in our dispute, as well as smart, and could thus ensure a fair and wise settlement. Sometimes we did not seek the consultation of a parent or surrogate however; we tried to settle the dispute on our own. But this was rarely successful. It was rarely successful because without a neutral party making a value judgment *for us* to settle the dispute—Mommy says little Sally is *right* and little Bobby is *wrong*—we often just resorted to psychological or physical coercion. We ended up fighting. Hence, parents became a necessity, if not at the beginning in order to prevent a fight, then in the end in order to stop one. We seemed ultimately to have only two options in the face of competition and conflict: seek guidance from some higher power, or live unguided and possibly under the reign of bullies operating according to the principle that might makes right.

My point? Commoners and Traditionalists—at least of the Objectivist variety—believe we are no better off as adults than we were as children. They believe as adults we face the same dangers as children and to avoid these dangers we need to appeal to the same solution that works for children. Either we appeal to something outside ourselves to settle the conflicts involved in making choices—competition and conflict are a part of any choice, particularly any social choice, as we have seen—or we face anarchy in our judgments and choices. Either we allow subject matter to play the higher authority in our lives and make our value judgments *for us*, or admit that judgment making is a free for all. Either we take the power to make a value judgment, and hence a choice, out of the hands of those who are in conflict, or we place it firmly in their hands and yield to the reign of bullies, to those who can muster superior power.

Unfortunately, the problems with appealing to something outside our control, appealing to some absolutely neutral judge to make value judgments *for us*, was evident to us back in our childhood. We knew even then that an appeal to a parent or surrogate parent was no guarantee of fairness or wisdom. Parents and their surrogates are always subject to prejudices, favoritism, ignorance, etc., and thus their decisions can always be contested—how many of us didn't hear a parental verdict and then respond: "Mom always likes you best!" This is not to say that parental and other surrogate decisions did not often work. They were very successful at times. But their success had to do more with the fact that there really didn't seem a better method available—as children we had very little experience in these matters—and we were very used to allowing parents and their surrogates decide things for us. Not to mention, there was a concrete system of rewards and punishments for adhering to decisions made by those in charge whether we believed them fair or not.

As adults we are equally aware of the problem with appealing to something outside our control to make decisions *for us*. To appeal to something outside our control, to appeal to some *claimed truth about subject matter made by experts*, to be plain about it—hereafter just "experts and their truth claims"—places experts and their truth claims in a fundamentally political role. Settling conflict between competing sides in a dispute is a political action, and if experts and their truth claims are supposed to do this then they have now become political as well. As a result, neither experts nor their truth claims will be able to play the role that both Commoners and Traditionalists hoped they would play— though Traditional Subjectivists gave up on this hope and thus suggested there is no hope. They will not have the perceived neutrality that is essential for settling disputes. We can see this problem for experts and their truth claims in many places, but nowhere as clearly as in a court of law.

When a case is brought before a court it is common for expert and eyewitness testimony to be employed—and really an eyewitness is just a particular type of expert. This testimony is used to show what "really" happened, to lay bare the truth about the subject at hand, and hence end the dispute. The testimony of one side's experts and eyewitnesses is often contradicted by the testimony of the other side's experts and eyewitnesses however. If such testimony had guaranteed, built-in objectivity and hence fairness, if we did not have to worry about the effects of human bias, self-interest and simple inadequacy on expert's truth claims, this procedure of bringing multiple experts and witnesses would be unnecessary. But, as is often said, if you want to understand a particular expert's or eyewitnesses' testimony, find out who pays him or her. This is not to say that every expert or eyewitness is corrupt, far from it; most of the time such testimony is given with the utmost feeling of certainty and an unfailing belief in its accuracy. Even so, such testimony is still *human* testimony, and is thus subject to some level of distrust. Even if self-interest is eliminated as a motive—which can never really be done— humans make mistakes, and there is no way to ensure that any eyewitness or expert has not made a mistake about the subject at hand.

Extend these points beyond the courtroom to any competitive environment—which means, as we have seen, any environment where a choice, particularly a social choice, is necessary. No competing side is going to be forced to accept the victory of the other side simply because someone tells them the other side's view is true. The very claim to possess the truth is always made by a person or persons subject to various influences, and hence that appeal will not guarantee the fairness of a decision. Any time someone decides that a certain side in a dispute should win because truth dictates it should, someone will always be able to ask: "True according to whom?" or "Was the claim made by someone with a bias against one side and in favor of the other?" To put the point bluntly, Commoners and Traditionalists from the Objectivist camp appeal to experts making truth claims to play a political role, yet they do so because they believe them to be "above" politics. They cannot have it both ways. *Experts and their truth claims cannot play a political role and remain above politics*.

If the appeal to experts and their truth claims does not help, does this leave us with the Subjectivist view that our choice making is a free for all? Are we nothing but children left home alone without adult supervision? This is more unpalatable than appealing to some neutral judge, some surrogate parent, to make decisions for us. It is more unpalatable because this means that all judgments of value, particularly on a social scale, will be little better than civil wars decided by the side that musters the most force, as we have already hinted. Value judgments will simply be the result of someone who is strong enforcing their will on those who are less than strong. They will be nothing more than the adult version of the oldest sibling pushing around their younger brothers and sisters. Can we avoid this consequence however? Can we avoid the conclusion that without some parent or parental substitute dictating our value judgments that we are condemned to violence?

We can if we see ourselves as wiser than children, as capable of making our own decisions. We can if we fight a dominant trend in Western history that sees a childlike appeal to religious or scientific truth—as known and expressed by experts—as the only way to prevent the conclusion that "might makes right" and "anything goes." We can if we abandon the assumption that the only way to ensure fairness and protect ourselves from the dangers of bullies and unchecked power is by ultimately appealing to some superhuman, surrogate parent to guide us. We can if we abandon the assumption that subject matter dictates method of judgment and replace it with the democratic View that method of judgment is dictated by who will be affected by the judgment. By changing assumptions, we are relieved of having to say either judgments are made *for us* by experts and their truth claims, or judgments are a free-for-all won by the strongest side enforcing its will. We can use *ourselves* as the guide for making judgments, and when I say ourselves, I only mean the quantity of people affected by any judgment. We can allow all of those affected by a judgment to make the judgment *for themselves*. In other words, when we abandon the assumption that subject matter dictates method of judgment and replace it with the idea that the number of judges is the key to choosing method, we can see a way out of our dilemma. We can see a way to avoid the conclusion that comes so naturally from childhood, that if there is no parent to make judgments for us, then we are condemned to a free for all and the reign of bullies or demagogues. We can do what we *actually* did on rare occasions as children: we can allow those of us who are "playing" together to make up the rules of our game, to make the judgments of value that guide our choices, as a group as we go along.

We have come by another route to a point central in Chapter 1. Why is the democratic View superior? Why is "Contemporary America" better than "America 1750?" It is superior because it allows us to grow up. Democracy is the choice of adults. All varieties of the Common and Traditional View infantilize us. They attempt to appeal to subject matter to make choices *for us* as that seems the only way to ensure fairness, or they suggest we can't control ourselves at all and thus there is no fairness. They seek to put us in the position where all we need to do is follow what something outside our control has to say about what is inside our control, or accept that we have no control. They seek to place us in relation to the world the way we were in relation to our parents, and if the world can't do this, then we are without guidance. When we attempt to use subject matter to dictate our value judgments we are only doing what we did when we were children. If we want to grow up, we have got to stop relying on outside sources to handle our problems and instead take responsibility for ourselves. That is what the democratic View does, and that is why it is superior.

The democratic View is not only the view of adults, it is also the logical conclusion of something we in the United States hold near and dear to our hearts: the separation of church and state. As we now accept a separation of church and state, all the democratic View amounts to is the claim that we should also accept a separation of science and state, ideology and state, if you like, Truth (with a capital T) and state.[1]

In the 18th Century, in the first phase of the American Revolution, Americans saw the sense of separating our method of deciding value in politics from the truth claims of specific religions. To see the sense in this, 18th Century Americans did not have to look very far. Religious wars and intolerance had been a part of their recent past, and still reared its ugly head in their time—as it still does in ours—and the result was often great violence—and still is. The lesson they learned is that democracy must be made more fundamental to settling disputes in the community, to making value judgements, than religion. This is not to say that religion was not to remain important, but it was to remain important as a part of the conscience of individuals.

What I am saying is that we carry this separation of church and state to its logical conclusion. What is really going on in the separation of church and state is a separation of experts and their truth claims from democracy. We should continue this to include all experts and their truth claims, be they scientists, philosophers, clergy, etc. Again, not that I am saying experts and their views on certain subject matter will not play a role in democracy, their role will simply be seen in light of a more fundamental democratic procedure. To accept the democratic View, as opposed to the Common or Traditional View, is to do nothing more than accept the separation of church, science, philosophy, etc., and state, that is, to see democracy as the ultimate, fundamental method of making value judgments.

Democratic process will help us ensure fairness, prevent abuse of power and hence promote the happiness of the individuals involved in making judgments because it is a rule-governed, open process. The Commoner's or Traditionalist's longed for neutrality will be replaced by openness. When a decision is opened up to the widest audience possible in a systematic way, it makes increasingly difficult secret, conspiratorial activity of any variety, the very type of activity which people fear most as a limitation on fairness. Openness ensures that if someone is behaving in a way that the group does not like then everyone in the group will know about it and thus can throw their collective weight against that someone in a prescribed fashion. In other words, if the group confronts a bully or demagogue, the bully or demagogue can be reigned in by the community in some rule-governed fashion. A rule-governed fashion preapproved by the community. In this way, democracy can allow us to achieve what the appeal to experts and their truth claims was supposed to achieve: fairness and protection from abuse. Democracy can allow us to rely upon collective security to check force and ensure fairness instead of depending upon some superhuman judge in the form of subject matter, or worse yet, facing the unfortunate state of having no check at all to ensure fairness. Democracy does not rely on any parental substitute to settle things but instead allows us to work things out on our own in a way that is not a free for all. This ensures that no one feels left out and that the decision is made in front of everyone. A situation which will still leave some people unhappy, as no one likes to lose, but which will approximate fairness more than any appeal to the truth claims about subject matter.

Though this may sound very strange—what are we gonna vote to see what your tire pressure should be?—we should notice that we already live this way in many areas of life. For instance, the courtroom functions as a model yet again. The reason we have trial by jury is because we believe that the best way to ensure fair judgments is by having a rule-governed, open process of debate, one where experts and their truth claims as well as "the mob" are subordinate to systematic, open, democratic interchange. We do not allow experts and their truth claims to rule, we rule them, and we do not allow emotional crowds to have their way either; experts and crowds are subordinate to democracy, democracy is not subordinate to experts and crowds. Experts and their truth claims as well as the wider community continue to play a role in choice making and hence judging value, but ultimate responsibility for judgments rests on democratic decisions made after rule-governed yet open debate.

More needs to be said about this rule-governed process, and I will do so in several sections. Let me end for now by asking that you please notice this argument for the democratic View does not depend upon the claim the Commoners or Traditionalists are wrong about how to make value judgments. All it depends upon is that neither the Commoner nor Traditionalist is particularly helpful in handling a certain problem. I am not saying I agree or disagree with any of their views about making judgments, truth, etc; I do not want to get into a debate about whether truth is ultimately objective, subjective or some combination thereof—the history of philosophy is littered with the ashes of those burned up by that issue. All I am saying is that none of them really helps us achieve what we want to achieve when making value judgments, or more accurately, the democratic View would help us achieve this better. I am not saying the democratic View is *right* and every other view is *wrong*, only that the democratic View *bests* its competition.

Defending the democratic Method Part Two: Beyond Contradictions?

These points in favor of the democrat and against the Commoner and Traditionalist are all practical in nature. They stem from a concern with "getting on" with our group choices, with not getting mired in abstraction and theory. The democratic View is superior for other reasons, reasons of a more abstract, "philosophical" nature as well. We have seen that both Commoners and Traditionalists share the assumption that subject matter determines who should make value judgments and how they should make them. As I put it above, subject matter dictates method of judgment; an idea that it is quite intuitive at first blush. Common sense suggests that our efforts to make value judgments about things should be guided by the things being judged. And if the things can't do this at all or at least in part, as Subjectivists and Commoners believe, then all or at least some of our value judgments are going to be made however we want.

Though quite intuitive, when we think about what is really said here the sense it has at first disappears. Let's return to the fictitious Ferrari. Most people would want to claim your color judgment is subjective while your tire pressure judgment is objective. However, anyone who makes such a claim would be immediately confronted with a question: Why did they *judge* that your color judgment is subjective while your pressure judgment is objective? Maybe they decided based on their past experience with cars. They learned this back when they bought their first Chevy and found that they could pick any color they wanted but had to consult a manual to get the right tire pressure. Hence, they think the same applies to you and your Ferrari. But this just pushes the question one step further back: Why did they make their judgment in the past about the Chevy? Anyone who wants to claim that judging the value of colors is subjective while judging the value of pressures is objective is ultimately going to have to claim that this is so because of the nature of color and the nature of pressure. They will have to claim that colors are a certain way and pressures are a different way, and that is why they must be judged differently. Isn't the very method proper for judging the nature of color and tire pressure what is at issue though? They cannot appeal to the nature of what is being judged because how to judge that very nature is in question.

This point becomes more obvious, and more general—it applies to all forms of the Common and Traditional View because we are attacking their shared assumption—if we return to Figure 3. When looking at the spectra of each variety of the Common or Traditional View, we are confronted with the question: how did they know how to classify subject matters in order to make up their respective spectra? The only way they could do this would be by making value judgments about each subject matter so they know where to place it on their spectra. For instance, the *best* or *right* place to put value judgments about tire pressure is on the objective side for the Commoner or Objectivist, the subjective side for the Subjectivist. *But isn't the very point of each spectra to show how to make value judgments about each subject matter?!* You cannot presume to know how to make these value judgments in order to set out how to make these judgments. Commoners and Traditionalists alike are begging the question. If they can set up these spectra then the spectra are useless. And the only way to make their spectra useful is to make them impossible to set up.

To say "subject matter dictates method of judgment" assumes we have already judged the subject matter which in turn we are using to tell us how we should judge subject matter. But, if this is so, then subject matter cannot dictate our method of judgment. If we are to let the subject matter of our investigation determine our method of judging subject matter that means we have already made judgments about the subject matter—namely that it should be judged in a certain way. This is contradictory. Commoners and Traditionalists at one and the same time are assuming that we do not know how to make judgments about subject matter—that's why we are looking to subject matter to guide us. And that we do know how to make judgments about subject matter—otherwise looking at subject matter would not guide us at all. Surely we cannot have it both ways! Either, we do not know how to judge subject matter and thus subject matter cannot dictate our method of judgment. Or, we already know how to judge subject matter and that's how it can dictate our method of judgment, but our judgment about how to judge subject matter is now superfluous.

This is an abstract point. It might help if I use an image. All Commoners and Traditionalists assume that somehow we are cut off from the world. It is as if we judges stand on one side of a great wall and what we are judging stands on the other. That is why we do not know how to judge what is on the other side. They also assume that we have judged what is on the other side of the wall because that is how we know what method of judgment to use to figure out what is on the other side of the wall—in fact, that there is another side at all. Remember, subject matter dictates method of judgment. The question is though: how did we make the judgment that there are or are not certain things on the other side of the wall that can or cannot dictate our method of judgment? Where did we get the initial method of judgment we employed that allowed us our first glimpse across the wall such that we judged that there is another side and how to proceed further to understand it? Whatever method we employed certainly did not result from our judging about the other side as we are assuming that we did not know how to make such a judgment. This means the method must have resulted from something else. But this now violates the assumption that subject matter dictates method of judgment.

To make this point even more clear, let's use another image. Commoners and Traditionalists are trying to build a bridge across a canyon so vast and deep its opposite edge and bottom cannot be seen. They are doing this in order to determine what is on the other side. They stand on one side, and they are unsure what stands on the bottom and the opposite side, if anything, that is why they want to make the journey. In order even to begin constructing the bridge however, they need to judge what is on the bottom and other side, otherwise they will have no idea what type of bridge will work to get them across the canyon. In fact, they will have no idea whether any bridge at all will do the job. It seems they must start building blindly therefore, otherwise, they will never be able to begin their trip. So they must start without judging what is on the bottom and other side. Something that violates the very assumption of both Commoners and Traditionalists alike, that subject matter dictates method of judgment. What both the Commoners and Traditionalists seem to be assuming is that they have already judged what is on the bottom and other side before starting their journey.

I suggest this second image only to attempt to make more intuitive the criticism I am offering. It does not work completely, unfortunately, as few images ever do. It does not, mainly because Commoners and Traditionalists are in a much worse position than our fictitious bridge builders. They are in a worse position because the bridge builders have judged what is on *their* side of the canyon, and this judgment can serve as the basis for their judgments about what is on the bottom and other side. Those seeking their methods of judgment entirely from subject matter do not have such a secure toehold however. For them, *everything* would seem to be in doubt, not just what is on the other side, but what is on *their* side as well. In fact, the entire notion that there are sides would seem to be in question, making the entire nature of the journey unclear. Those seeking to make judgments about the world have to prove that there is a journey to make at all, but this requires them to have already made the journey. Something they cannot have done given what they are assuming.

What about the democratic View? How does it fair given this problem facing Commoners and Traditionalists? It fairs well. It fairs well because it changes the assumptions of Commoners and Traditionalists. democrats believe we need not appeal to something outside of the value judgment making process to show us how to make value judgments. Rather, the value judgment making process itself can show us how to start making value judgments. Anytime we go to make a value judgment we are settling a conflict between two or more sides— as we have seen. Given this, the best method for making value judgments is going to be the one that allows us the best way to settle this conflict. And what is the *best* way? This definition of "best" is something that the conflicting parties need to decide, and the way they can decide this is by hearing one another's views. In other words, the way to decide how best to settle this conflict is to allow each side the opportunity to make their case for their view of what is best, and then a vote can be taken. The very nature of conflict gives rise to its own method of solution. As such, democrats avoid the problem that Commoners and Traditionalists face. They need not travel outside the judgment making process in order to learn how to make judgments and hence they avoid the question begging nature of both the Common and Traditional Views.

To put it in the terms of our images, Commoners and Traditionalists feel the need to make a journey to help them with a problem. democrats are content to stay where they are and simply worry about making people happy. democrats do not worry about any walls to climb or bridges to be built. There is no wall or canyon for them to cross, as they do not believe they need to judge subject matter in order to learn how to make judgments. Judging subject matter isn't the focus for them, making happy whoever is making the value judgment is important to them. As long as the judge or judges are happy, then the method is good. If they are not, then the method is bad. There is nothing beyond this. The only thing of concern in designing a method of judgment for a democrat, the only concern in settling a controversy, is making sure that everyone impacted by a judgment gets heard and that everyone is given an equal chance to have their views win the day. This is of concern because it is what will come closest to ensuring the happiness of those impacted by judgments. Designing a method of judgment should take place without giving thought, ultimately, to what is being judged, because democrats believe we should see the purpose of judgment as making the judges happy. Thought should only be given to who is making the value judgment; and judging is better thought of without reference to subject matter. democrats ask the question: who cares about subject matter if all, or most, of the judges are happy?

In changing assumptions about how to address the problem of making value judgments, in seeing the point of settling conflict differently, democrats thus avoid the contradiction that these other views face. As such, it seems a better view.

Why Extend Democracy?

We have now added a more theoretical justification to our practical justification of the democratic View, and hence for "Contemporary America" from Figure 2. Having provided these justifications for making at least some value judgments in a democratic fashion, we must now attend to the issue of extending this view beyond its partial use in politics. Given we now have reason for accepting "Contemporary America," why should we go from what we now have to "Future America?" Some may accept our justification for living by the Consent Principle in the political arena but not accept that other arenas of power should be governed by the same principle. What can we say to them?

There are two reasons someone would accept the democratic View in politics yet not accept it in the economy and education. One is if they believed that judgments in politics were fundamentally different than judgments in the economy and education. The second is if they believed that somehow extending democracy into other arenas of power would make people unhappy regardless of the nature of the judgments being made. In other words, either someone might believe that there is something unique about the subject matter of politics that makes it amenable to democracy or that extending democracy outside politics will create havoc whether subjects are similar or not.

We can respond to both of these positions quite easily. We can respond easily because we have already done so before. All I need do here is point out what has already been said. As for the view that politics is a different field than economics and education and hence requires a different method, we have just seen that appeals to subject matter are of questionable use when talking about the proper way to make value judgments. Certainly the focus of a business person, an educator and a politician are different in some ways, but this has no impact on how their judgments should be made ultimately. In each case we are now accepting the democratic View on making value judgments and choices: that subject matter does not dictate method. If we accept that subject matter is not the ultimate deciding factor in determining who should make judgments and how, then this objection is moot.

As for the second response, we are returning to the largely historical issues discussed in the first chapter and the discussion of elites in the second. Some might fear the advent of universal democracy because they believe that non-political decisions are too difficult for the "average" person to handle. Sure democracy might be OK for the "simple" world of politics, but not where "expert" knowledge is required in business and education. This, however, is just to make the same point against democracy in business, education, etc., that was made against democracy in politics, as we saw in Chapter 1. We saw reason not to accept the point there, so we need not change our mind now. It is also a resurrection of concerns about elites we addressed in Chapter 2. Again, about this enough has been said at this point.

Two "Theoretical" Problems for Democracy

Our argument for completing the American Revolution, both why to do it and how to do it, is at an end. To make it truly complete however, there are two problems inside democratic theory I must address. I have left them till now because these problems may not have been obvious earlier, and there is no point in addressing problems that are not obvious. They are most likely obvious now—particularly now that you have my philosophical justification for completing the Revolution—so I end with their discussion.

First, if our "philosophical" argument is accepted, what will be said to have value, at least on the social scale, will be what "passes" the test of democratic debate. We are going to accept a separation of both church and state as well as science, philosophy, etc. and state. Given we are accepting this separation, how will the actual mechanics of democratic debate work? If democracy does not rely on underlying religious, scientific, philosophical or other principles, on what basis will we decide who has won a debate between conflicting parties? In order to choose what has value, we must uphold certain standards of argumentation upon which our choices can be based. These are the "rules" that I referred to when I called democracy a rule-governed process, a rule-governed process that makes democracy different from mere mob rule. But where did these standards, these rules, come from—again, if not from religion, science, philosophy, etc.? Can we just assume certain standards or rules of argumentation? We started discussing these issues two sections ago but we need to return to this very important topic.[2]

Second, a complete democracy, one such as we have outlined where almost every group decision is subject to open debate and vote, makes possible the abuse of individuals by the majority. If a decision voted for by the majority after open debate is a decision that will be followed, then it would seem the enslavement of a minority, scapegoating, torture and a host of lesser abuses would become possible courses of action. As long as such policies are chosen as a result of open debate, it is not obvious that on the conception of democracy outlined so far there is a way to stop their implementation, no matter how detrimental they may be to certain innocent individuals or groups. To put it simply, complete democracy appears to have a difficult time ensuring that everyone in a given institution is treated fairly—and isn't fair treatment our central concern? The interests of the majority count more than the interests of anyone else, and when group interests are always given priority over those of minorities or individuals, fairness seems to become impossible. The basic question here is then: how do we stop minorities or individuals from being abused in a democratic system? How do we stop the majority from abusing minorities, particularly a minority of one?[3]

Let's take these problems in order.

The Mechanics of Democratic Debate

The mechanics of democratic debate in any group value judgment will work exactly as debate works in a contemporary American courtroom or political body right now. The competing sides on any issue will be brought into open, non-violent competition with one another. This competition will allow, in a public arena, the employment of rational argumentation, appeals to experts and their use of various experimental scientific methodologies, appeal to eyewitness testimony, if appropriate, etc. These are the methods we have now and they can continue to be used to help adjudicate disputes among parties in any democratic forum no matter how large or small. We can use the standards we have but of course these standards are not above reproach; luckily an essential part of any democratic system is that it allows for change even in the standards of democratic debate itself. Nonetheless this does not prevent us from debating in the same way we debate right now.

But why accept the appeal to non-violent, reasoned debate, scientific experiment, etc., as the model of democratic debate? Haven't we just debunked at least some of these as we said we are separating science, philosophy, etc., and state?

First, we should because they have "stood the test of time", a test that can be seen as largely democratic in nature. We can see history as a democratic "distillation" process by which less successful methods of debate have been taken out, and we are left with the methods refined by the debate between various methodologies that has made up a good deal of Western intellectual history. We may be accepting a separation of science, philosophy, etc, and state but not history and state. Second, no other viable options have been offered. Has anyone come up with a workable way to replace this model?[4] Third, and closely associated with the second, does anyone know what debate would look like if it was not modeled along contemporary lines? A case may be made for the abandonment of the techniques of rational argumentation or an appeal to scientific experts but what *really* can replace them? How would other techniques work? This is not to say that there might not be other, new techniques available for guiding debate, but they are not available now, so what other options do we have? As I argued several sections back, we must keep in mind that all decisions ultimately rest in the hand of some participatory or representative democratic body, and it is their responsibility to decide which side wins. Final responsibility rests with the democratic body in other words, not with any scientific, philosophical, religious or other expert. Experts, eyewitnesses, etc. may be consulted to assist in making judgments, but their views are subordinate to the democratic body seeking their counsel. We can accept their authority but not give them ultimate responsibility. Truth claims are always subordinate to the democratic process. With this in mind, this still allows us to use reasoned argument, science, etc. as an essential part of our democratic interchange.

In giving these justifications, I am making no claim about why our contemporary model of political debate is necessary or right. All I am saying is that nothing better has yet come along and therefore we are best off accepting them for now. This justification avoids the issue of the truth of our standards of debate. It avoids philosophical, scientific and even religious questions about the ultimate "rightness" of logic, scientific experiment, faith, etc. All it depends on is that we have a certain set of beliefs that we accept because there are no competitors that have mounted any significant challenge to them. All other competitors, primarily dogmatic religious and totalitarian political practices have largely been cast off, and mount an inadequate challenge to what we accept—for those still having doubts, in all honesty would you choose to live in a fundamentalist society, one with a different model of "debate?"

The democratic debates that take place between supporters of certain beliefs will thus look very similar to debates as they occur now. Appeals will be made to rationality, common sense and "facts", challenges will be leveled due to inconsistency and impracticality. Debate will look very similar, but the justification for the rules of that debate will be different. Gone is the appeal to the ultimate truth or rightness of the standards of our debate—this is the price of separating state from religion, science, philosophy, etc. science—and in its place we appeal to what has worked given our historical experience, to what has passed the test of use over time.

Human Rights and Democracy

On to our second concern: how can we prevent democratic majorities from abusing individuals? This is an extremely important question to us as one of our central goals is promoting the development of the individual and ensuring fairness. This is also an extremely important question from a historical standpoint. It is of more than just idle philosophical interest. The dominant political struggles of the 20th Century pitted those who championed individual freedom against those who championed the "happiness" of the community. Anywhere where those championing community "happiness" over individual freedom have won—Communist Russia or China and Nazi Germany are but a few examples—large-scale horror resulted. How can this potential for abuse be eliminated in a completely democratic society? Given that the democratic society we have outlined seems to place such reliance on the community, and extends democracy into institutions where it has not existed before, how can we protect the individuals in these institutions?

To start, we should notice that we already have a model for how this can be done. Any institution that is democratic faces this problem; thus we, or more strictly speaking the Framers of the U.S. Constitution, already faced this in a political arena. Their solution, and the one to which we still adhere currently in the U.S., is to claim that each individual has certain rights which can never be overridden by the majority for any purpose. These rights, often called unalienable or inalienable human rights—the ones spoken about in the Declaration of Independence and added to in the Bill of Rights—are never to be taken from us unless we have taken another's—and even then some rights cannot be lost such as the right not to be cruelly and unusually punished. No matter how much the interests of the majority might be helped by taking these rights, they can never be taken. Even if it will save a million people, to use an extreme case of the sort philosophy professors love, we should not be able to take an innocent person's life, liberty, etc, that is, violate their rights. Saying someone has rights is in essence saying there is a private sphere into which no one can intrude for any purpose. In this sphere each individual is his own "sovereign" and is free to do exactly as he chooses.[5] To say we have these rights is to say that the public must butt-out; having no formal, coercive power over our actions. To return to the images from Chapter 1, our rights are part of the walls that protect our castle—along with our money—and these can never be breached for any reason, again, unless we have breached another's. The doctrine of inalienable rights is our attempt to protect the individual from abuses of power, both here in the United States and increasingly world wide, but it faces three major problems.

One is justifying that we have "inalienable human rights". It has not been obvious to most cultures historically, nor is it currently obvious, that there is a sphere over which you and I are our own sovereigns; a sphere that is our own private business and can never be rightly intruded upon. Very few cultures have held the Myth of the Castle. What then justifies the claim that we have these inalienable human rights? To put it in slightly different terms, what is the source of these rights? God? Human nature? Or might our possession of inalienable human rights simply be "self-evident"? If they are genuinely inalienable, they can't have any cultural source. That is, the community cannot grant them. It cannot, because that would mean our rights would be alienable, subject to removal by the community. They would be subject to such removal because if the community gives them, then the community can take them away. So what is the source of inalienable human rights?

A second problem with using inalienable human rights to protect the individual is enumerating what rights we have. To put this in the context of the Myth of the Castle, it is not clear just how much land we can build our walls around. Where must our castle walls end and public space begin? Where must our castle walls end, and someone else's castle walls begin? Do we have a right to life, liberty and the pursuit of happiness? Does this include a right to property in perpetuity? Does this include a right to use our property in whatever way we see fit, even if it pollutes? Does this include the right of a woman to determine the fate of a fetus? Does this include selling our bodies for sex? Does this include ending our own lives if we see fit? Do we have a right to an education, but not shelter? Do we have a right to support as a senior citizen but not as a young adult? The list of questions goes on and on. And this problem is exacerbated by the first problem: without knowledge of the source of our inalienable human rights, without justification for the claim that we have them at all, it is difficult to say what rights we have.

A third problem—the greatest problem—with using inalienable human rights to protect the individual is that historically this has been an ineffective tool at protecting individuals, particularly when individuals have needed it most. For instance, in this country the Bill of Rights was in full force during slavery, the systematic decimation of native peoples, the legal preservation of a second-class status for women and the internment of Japanese-Americans during the Second World War. No one could deny that these situations entailed gross violations of human rights, yet each occurred in a country itself sprung from the sanctity of inalienable human rights. And if you extend the scope of this examination outside the U.S., the failure of inalienable human rights to protect individuals becomes even more pronounced. The National Socialist movement in Germany came to power under the Weimar Constitution, a democratic constitution establishing a whole set of inalienable human rights, a constitution not much different from that of most democratic nations today in regards to rights.

Similarly, Stalinist crimes were committed in the name of a Soviet constitution establishing the rights of individuals to freedoms of all sorts, and minimally guaranteeing them a right to life. And if we are willing to go back in history we can add even more examples. Anyone remember a little thing called the "Reign of Terror", carried our under the influence of the then-recent doctrine of inalienable human rights?

Several solutions have been tried to the first of these problems, justifying the existence of rights, but I think they are all unsuccessful. God, Human Nature and self-evidence have all been offered at one time or another as the source of inalienable human rights as I suggested above—see the Declaration of Independence for examples of at least two of these. Unfortunately, none of these help very much. An appeal to God leaves us needing an appeal to a Deity, something that most supporters of democracy do not want at the heart of their system. Even if you are religious yourself, you probably feel squeamish demanding others believe in God. After all, aren't we accepting the separation of church and state? But without such a demand, what would become of using religion to justify the existence of inalienable human rights? We wouldn't want someone to claim that simply because he is an atheist he doesn't have to respect the rights of others—if you don't believe in God and God is the supposed source of rights, then you don't believe in rights either. But even if you believe in God, it is impossible to know what God thinks about any of this. Can anyone speak to God on this matter?

As for appeals to the self-evident nature of inalienable human rights, this seems little better than an appeal to God. If these rights are really self-evident, how do we explain the fact that most cultures throughout history have missed them? Have these cultures been, and many remain to this day, too ignorant to see what is self-evident? This cannot be the case. It is very difficult to call ignorant cultures as advanced as those of Ancient Greece, Rome, Egypt and China, as well as many very sophisticated cultures today. Yet that is what we must do if we are to call ignorant all those cultures failing to "see" inalienable human rights as self-evident. Few of us would want to do this however, but then the claim regarding self-evidence is in doubt. Something can't be self-evident to just a few people or a part of one culture.

As for using an appeal to Human Nature, what has been called "natural law theory", this seems worse than the previous two. It depends on philosophical or scientific accounts of Human Nature, accounts that are not universally accepted and always subject to change. Justifying inalienable human rights by appeal to an account of Human Nature is justifying the obscure by appeal to the ill defined. For inalienable human rights to be effective at protecting the individual, they must be based on something that is agreed on by most people, and certainly something that won't change with the publication of the next experiment or philosophical essay. They must be above such fluidity otherwise they will never be the impenetrable stone walls most want to surround their "castles". They will be more like chain-link fences, filled with a great deal of holes, easy to push over or move with just a little bit of equipment or a large enough number of bodies.

As for problem number two, that of enumerating our inalienable rights, no one has even made a half-hearted attempt to address it in any systematic fashion—you need only look at the "culture wars" debates about everything from abortion to gay marriage to see this. The closest we come appears in the philosophy of the 18th German philosopher Immanuel Kant. He argues that there is a test to determine whether we have a right or not, a test that follows from the nature of rationality and the analysis of what he calls "catergorical imperatives"—absolute injunctions against actions. Passing over the details, he believes we can determine if we have a right by determining that it is irrational to deny we have that right, but Kant's drawing a close connection between what is reasonable and what is moral smacks of a resurrection of the "self-evident" solution used to justify that we have rights, and about that we have already said enough.

As for problem number three, one "solution", or better yet excuse, that I have heard offered to address the historical impotence of inalienable human rights involves the claim that abuses of rights resulted from historically understandable cultural prejudice or the "tone" of "the time," and we are now "beyond" such barbarity. Hence, we need not worry about further abuses. Having lived through Pearl Harbor, to take one example, a number of people have said to me that I would understand better what happened to the Japanese in the U.S. during World War Two; to which is always added that we are now more open-minded so things would be different today. The Japanese attack on Pearl Harbor provoked such fear of the Japanese, so the story goes, that it was inevitable that people would fear the Japanese living in this country, particularly given we were a more prejudiced culture then. But now, Americans wouldn't be so simple minded. After the civil rights movement, as well as women's liberation, gay liberation and a host of other cries for equal treatment by traditionally oppressed groups, we are more culturally sensitive and hence rights would be respected. [6]

This response, as much as it is a response, is laughable. First, a look at any newspaper will show that we are not beyond such barbarity and prejudice. To suggest that we are is to ignore the obvious. With the passage of the Orwellian "Patriot Act" after 9/11, the frailty of inalienable rights in the face of majority bigotry and fear becomes all too clear. But regardless of this, when we need inalienable human rights to be their most effective is when times get tough and prejudices can get the better of people. We rarely need rights to protect us when times are good. We need them most when people are not at their best, and historically inalienable human rights have failed miserably at just such times. We only need rights in the face of strong prejudices, hatreds and the like, so if they do not work then, as they have rarely, what good are they?

The point of all this is that our current model for protecting the individual—and remember our current model only applies to the political sphere—is often inadequate or worse and seems difficult to justify. We have to do better. We have to do better not simply because of the problems facing our traditional model of protecting the individual, but because we want to extend democracy into the economy and education where obtaining a method for protecting individuals from majorities has never even been seen as a problem before. The way for us to do better is by altering our current model for protecting the individual in the three ways.

First, we should give up on inalienable human rights and see that the justification or source of rights, as well as what rights we can be said to have, results from the democratic community itself. Second, we should see that democracy requires granting a larger set of rights than are now recognized. Third, we should see that rights protecting individuals from majorities should result from membership not only in democratic government but also democratic institutions in the economy or education.

     The first alteration, replacing inalienable human rights with democratic-community-based rights, will handle the problem of justifying that we have rights. Traditionally, rights were taken to come first and then government, typically democratic government as democracy was taken to be the best governmental system at guaranteeing our set of pre-existing, inalienable human rights. As it says in the Declaration of Independence:

> We hold these truths to be self-evident, that all Men are created equal, that they are endowed by their Creator with certain unalienable Rights, that among these are Life, Liberty and the Pursuit of Happiness—*That to secure these Rights, Governments are instituted among Men...*[7]

We see here that rights are taken to come first, and then governments— *not even democracy, just governments*. Rights are inalienable, existing prior to governments and governments exists to protect them. However, this leaves us questioning the source of these inalienable human rights, as we have seen. What we need to do is claim instead that democracy comes first, and the origin of our rights can be derived from democracy itself. We must be said to have rights because that is what it takes for democracy to work—without protection the individual will be unable to perform as needed in a democratic system—not that we have democracy because that is what it takes to have rights work. We should abandon the notion that democracy rests on inalienable human rights. Instead, we should see that rights rest on democracy. Our rights should not be "inalienable human rights" but "democratic-citizen's rights".

By altering this order of priority, justifying the existence of our rights becomes basically the same task as justifying democracy. If democracy is justified, then so is our possession of rights. The way the Founders did it left us needing justifications for claiming we have rights, and for claiming democracy is the best form of government. By reversing the order, we have combined these two problems into one. And this one problem, justifying democracy, we have already handled in Chapter 1, and earlier parts of this chapter.

Changing the order of priority between rights and democracy, the first alteration of the traditional doctrine of inalienable rights, allows us to justify that we have rights and hence handles one of the major difficulties for the traditional view of rights. This first alteration in turn leads to the second alteration, namely the extension of the rights we are typically said to have, and in so doing handles the problem of enumerating our rights. The first alteration leads to the second by showing that the rights we can be said to have when democracy is made primary are those necessary to make democracy function well. We need to secure for each citizen the rights which will make them not just passable in a democratic environment, but maximally competent and competitive. This means we are not just going to have our life, liberty and pursuit of happiness guaranteed as these alone will not make each citizen maximally competent and competitive—you need more to perform well in a democracy. Added to this list of traditional rights must also be the economic, educational and overall increased civil rights that we outlined in previous chapters; rights necessary so that each individual has the greatest opportunity to develop their skills and hence compete to achieve success. And with this extension of our rights, we are also given a rather precise enumeration of our rights, as all we need to ask when we question whether we have a certain right is whether this claimed right furthers our ability to perform as a democratic citizen?

Alteration one of the traditional doctrine of rights, seeing democracy not rights as primary, leads to alteration two and hence a fairly complete enumeration of an extended set of rights. In so doing these two alterations work together to handle two central problems facing the traditional doctrine of inalienable human rights. These two alterations also lead to a solution to what I believe is the most pressing problem of the three facing the traditional doctrine of inalienable rights: the historical impotence of inalienable rights in the face of community encroachment. To see why this is so, I want to appeal to an analogy.

The defense of a nation, that is the defense of an individual nation from other nations acting individually or in concert, depends upon the possession of both a good defense *and* a good offense. Arms should be purchased, a military trained and treaties signed which attempt to prevent attack from outside, but this is not sufficient on its own. A nation must also purchase arms and train men so that they can attack if they are threatened. We may not like to admit it, but to rely purely on a defensive strategy with no offensive capability is very dangerous and a typically unsuccessful strategy for achieving national security. History has taught this lesson many times. From the Great Wall of China to the Maginot line, from the medieval fortress to the reliance upon natural boundaries such as the Alps, from the Treaty of Versailles to the Munich Accords, again and again defense alone has failed to gain security for nations. Neither nature nor man can construct an obstacle, nor make an agreement, so formidable that it cannot be breached or broken. What this means is that defense must be supplemented, and almost supplanted, by offense. What will keep the peace is not a wall or treaty alone, but these in combination with a guarantee that if you threaten my security then I will prosecute a war that will wreak havoc upon you and ultimately bring you defeat.

The situation is the same when it comes to protecting the individual in a democracy. For an individual to protect him or herself, they must have both a good defense *and* a good offense. An individual must be given two types of rights to gain real protection from the community in other words. Rights such as those in the Declaration of Independence and the first four Amendments to the Constitution, the first four rights listed in the Bill of Rights, are important of course. These rights are like a treaty we make with the community, or more properly the community's representative we call the Federal Government, such that they agree not to attack us in certain ways. The rights in the Declaration of Independence and Bill of Rights are like a non-aggression pact between nations. This is good as far as it goes, but it does not go far enough. [8] We must also give every individual a good offense as well as a good defense. We must ensure that when it comes to defending ourselves, each individual has the rights that provide them with a solid offense and thus makes them formidable opponents. They must not just have a guarantee from others that they will not be attacked, they must have the training and the resources to attack—attack in a democratic arena of course. They must have these offensive resources, and they must be provided with a forum in which those resources can be used. This is something we already do to a certain extent even in the Bill of Rights—Amendments 5, 6 and 7 guaranteeing such things as a right to jury trial are examples—but this should be greatly extended.

What I am saying is that the way to protect the individual is to multiply the rights that an individual is said to have, and to multiply them with certain types of rights. The problem with our current view of rights is that we neither give individuals enough rights nor enough rights of the proper kind. We must add to our existing rights the set of "democratic-citizens rights" I outlined in Chapter's 2, 3 and 4. We must create a 28th, 29th and 30th Amendment to the United States Constitution in which these democratic-citizen's rights are listed and guaranteed. The 28th Amendment should include the right to an equal education to the highest level your ability to learn permits. The 29th Amendment should guarantee the right to be kept competitive in the economy through mandated material support and retraining in the case of a loss in competition. And the 30th, the most important of them all, should guarantee the right to have almost any institution of which we are a part be consent-based—as per the discussion in previous Chapters. It is only by providing these more extensive rights that the individual will gain security. In short, what we need to do is not rely so much on establishing what the community should not do to you, and emphasize what the community must do for you, and allow you to do. We must not rely so much on setting up walls around ourselves which we call "inalienable human rights" or the "private sphere". Instead, we must make sure the public sphere is structured in a certain way, one that allows the individual to have as much opportunity to succeed in that sphere as possible, and as much impact as their talents will allow.

The point I am making here is really one I made earlier in Chapter 1. In Chapter 1 I spoke about the need as Americans to abandon the Myth of the Castle. The myth that our best opportunity for happiness and security is dependent upon escaping to a place where the world can not intrude, a place closed in behind the highest walls we can afford to build. Depending upon only the rights we have now, particularly those in the Declaration of Independence and Bill of Rights, is just part of this myth. We think that by achieving some sort of "legal" isolation in combination with some wealth, we will keep other people at bay. This is not so. History has shown us this again and again. To return to my military image, any barrier, be it material *or* legal, can be breached, and has been in history. What we must do instead is concentrate more on making a community where the individual has the maximum opportunity for impact, not one where the individual can "hide" away. We need to make individuals active in their own defense, not passively hoping that others will stick to agreements to leave them alone as long as they leave others alone.

To be secure we need more rights, the rights that make us formidable opponents in a democratic arena. These are just the sort of rights that follow when we alter the traditional view of inalienable rights in the two ways suggested above. When we invert the relationship between rights and democracy, as we have seen, this yields an extension of our rights, indeed, just the sorts of rights it takes for us to be better at our own defense. As such, when we alter the traditional doctrine of rights in these two ways, not only have we given a means of justifying we have rights and enumerating a larger set of rights, but we have also given rights "teeth." It is just these "teeth" that the traditional view of rights lacks, and so with these alterations in the traditional view of rights, every problem facing that view is given a solution.

These alterations in the traditional doctrine of rights help us solve the problems facing that doctrine, but we are left with the question of whether this new doctrine of rights works only for political institutions. Given I want to reform almost every major institution in our society by making it more democratic, how does this doctrine of democratic-citizen's rights work outside the political realm? We as economic or educational "citizens" would have to fear abuse from democratic majorities as well—everyone could, in theory, "gang-up" on someone in a democratic workplace and have them fired for example—and nothing we have said so far impacts this. It is here that the third alteration of the traditional model of inalienable human rights—seeing that rights extend well beyond their limits as proscribed by the traditional model—comes into play.

The third alteration in the traditional doctrine of rights, like the second, follows from the first. If democracy results in rights, not rights in democracy, then being a member of *any* democratic organization must result in the possession of rights in that organization. It makes no difference whether we are talking about democratic governments, businesses or schools: if they are democratic, then their members must have rights. What this means is that rights go far beyond the traditional boundaries that were set for them. On the traditional view, we were supposed to have rights only as citizens of the state because the state was that organization created to protect our pre-existing inalienable human rights. Now we are saying that democratic institutions are the source of rights and so we are going to have rights in other realms, not just that as a citizen of the state, as long as democracy extends outside of government—as we believe it should. The result is that individuals will have rights in every democratic institution of which they are a part, and in this way will gain protection for themselves from majorities in these institutions. Just what rights they should have in order to gain maximum protection in these institutions will depend on the type of institution they are in. We have seen what these rights might be like in Chapters 3 and 4 when we outlined the rights of the employee-citizen, university-citizen and school-citizen. But the list of specific rights is not important here. The point I am making is that in our new view of democracy, rights are had by any member of any democratic organization, in this way gaining for individual's protection from the majority in these organizations.[9]

By inverting the traditional relationship between democracy and rights, by seeing that democracy results in rights not the other way around, we can overcome the traditional problems facing rights and gain much more security for the individual than the individual has ever had before. We can do this, but some of you may have serious doubts about what I have just argued. I want to end this chapter by seeing why this might be so, and by addressing those in protest.

Addressing Protesters

First there is the question of expense. Every right we grant an individual is a responsibility for the community, and responsibilities of the sort I have outlined cost money. Second, we might not be able to guarantee all these rights at once because they conflict. If I am to have my education paid for, does that mean you are going to have to give up some of your hard-earned money to pay for it? Third, by inverting this relationship we seem to be saying that outside a democratic community, we have no rights. By saying we have "democratic-citizen's rights" not "inalienable human rights" we seem to be depriving all non-citizens of rights, an apparently dangerous thing to do.

As for the question of expense, we have addressed this already at the ends of previous chapters, but I will add this point here.[10] The system outlined in this book will not be as expensive as it might seem. It is my belief that there will be a great increase in the production and efficiency of the economy, and less expensive divisive conflict among citizens in general, as a result of increased democracy. A happier workforce and citizenry at large, happier because they are treated more fairly and feel more relevant, is a more productive and efficient workforce and a less needy citizenry. As such, the government will not have to give out too much more support than it does now. Or, to put this differently, most citizens will rely on the rights they have as employee-citizens, university-citizens or school-citizens, not those they have as citizens of democratic governments. Businesses and schools will bear the brunt of the expense in other words, as they do right now. And businesses and schools will be able to bear this weight better as I think they will be experiencing greater success.

As for those who do not see all of these rights as compatible, they are right. At times, rights are going to conflict with one another; they do now, and by adding to the list of rights we are adding fuel to the fire. In order to alleviate this problem—to overcome it completely is nearly impossible—we need to "rank" rights by order of importance. This may sound strange, but it is something we do already; all I am going to do is suggest we shuffle the ranking a bit.

At present we claim to consider the right to life more important than the right to liberty, the right to liberty more important than the right to the pursuit of happiness, the right to happiness more important than... We must change this now to see that the most basic rights are those that guarantee that we stay democratic as a society and that we keep individuals competitive in our democracy. The most fundamental right then is your right to consent-based arenas of power, and to have been trained to make impact in those arenas. These rights will be the most fundamental; they should trump other rights—of course a right to life, etc. would be a part of this as it is tough to make use of democratic access when you are dead. To be clear on what this means, let's use a specific example.

In a certain town it is determined that additional schools must be built in order to maintain class size at the allowed level, allowed in order to guarantee students an equal education. Upon consideration by engineers, town planners, etc., the only place where the school can be built is where your house now stands. This means your house will get torn down. As long as you were given a fair chance in your democratic government to make your case that it not get torn down, and as long as you will be given equivalent housing somewhere else, your house will get torn down. This would be an unfortunate state of affairs, but our first concern must remain keeping opportunity open, and this means defending certain of our democratic-citizen's rights before others. These rights are simply more valuable because it is only through the rights guaranteeing us access to power and opportunity that we will genuinely be able to defend our rights to liberty and the pursuit of happiness. As we have seen, without certain of our democratic-citizen's rights being made fundamental, the guarantee of a right to life, liberty and the pursuit of happiness is mostly empty. The right to life, liberty and the pursuit of happiness only gains genuine validity, teeth as I put it before, when they are placed in the context of a working democracy.

Giving priority to those rights that help us make a good offense is not all that different from how we live right now in some ways. We claim we have an inalienable right to life, liberty and the pursuit of happiness. We claim it, but we do not live it. Almost all our inalienable rights can all be alienated, but this can only be done as a result of due process—see the issue of eminent domain or watch what happens if you fail to pay the mandated tax of the property you "own." What I am adding to this is nothing more than an expansion of due process. Due process now, after these reforms are enacted, includes not simply a trial by jury, etc.—Amendments 5-8 on the Bill of Rights—but some assurance that you have been given an equal opportunity to develop your talents and show your merit in open competition. Your right to property, liberty, etc., cannot be taken from you unless you enjoyed *consent-based arenas of power and equal opportunity* as well as a trial by jury and the like. Any of us can have almost any of our rights taken away right now as well as under a more democratic system, but it will be harder under the democratic system because due process now means more. It makes you a more effective opponent. Nonetheless, we cannot deny that the most important rights we will have to guarantee are those that make democracy possible for all.

To be straightforward about it, we never live under the rule of law, we always live under the rule of man. People make law, interpret law and enforce law; law does none of this on its own. The only way we can make sure the law is fair then is to make sure that each person has the maximum opportunity to impact its creation, interpretation and enforcement. That will happen only when our democratic-citizen's rights are secure. Without their being secure, any law guaranteeing that our lives, liberty, etc., will be protected is mostly empty. Without guaranteeing our full democratic-citizen's rights we are simply hoping that those creating, interpreting and enforcing the law are doing so fairly. Something that history suggests we are foolish to hope. Thus, those rights most necessary for democracy are the ones that will have to be maintained before all others.

Ultimately, replacing inalienable human rights with democratic-citizen's rights, and slightly re-prioritizing those rights, best captures what most defenders of inalienable human rights want. Their desire to secure inalienable human rights is not so much because they believe those rights will never be violated, because they believe individuals really have some sort of moral position above and beyond the interests of their communities.[11] It is just that in making an absolute prohibition on the actions that are possible to take against an individual, stress is being placed on the fundamental importance of the individual. What our doctrine does, rather than making a mostly empty statement about the importance of the individual is actually make the individual important. Our democratic system makes its focal point the development of individuals. A strong, educated, developed individual is the highest priority of this system, and because of this, the supporter of the doctrine of inalienable human rights loses nothing in our conception. They actually gain something.

What they gain is a system whereby their individuality will not be assumed but will be promoted. This will make being an individual a more worthwhile prospect, because the favor will be placed on the side of the acting individual, the one who desires to promote their interests and defend their sense of value. This is a more open system than one which places absolute prohibitions on activity, and an open system will always be a benefit to the individual.

Of course, some might still worry that by depriving humans of rights and granting them only to citizens, I have lost us the moral toehold allowing us to claim that even those individuals who are not citizens of our community deserve protection. This is the last objection against inverting the traditional relationship between rights and democracy that I raised above. To which I respond: we as good democrats can certainly give all those who are not members of our community rights as "aliens", rights they can be said to have because of the nature of democracy. Aliens are potential members of our democratic community, and if they are ever to become members, they should be accorded full respect in our community. It will count as good training as democrats for them to obtain this treatment. We must also see that in denying people human rights, I am not really denying them much. Saying someone has rights just because they are human doesn't mean much in actual political, economic and social struggles, as we have seen. If we want to protect people from abuse, we must discard empty claims about human rights and instead concentrate on making as many people good democratic citizens as we can.

Conclusion

To conclude this justification of democracy and its extension, and this book overall, we must always keep in mind that the system outlined here is not utopian. I have appealed throughout only to a relative standard of value or merit. Complete democracy is *better than* any other system; I cannot claim it is the absolute best system, a perfect system, an ideal system or what have you. Certainly it presents problems, but it has the advantage over our existing system in that its problems are less numerous and less severe, and in that these problems can be addressed in the flexible manner that only the open forums of our expanded democracy can allow. To end on as simple a note as possible, this entire book is nothing more than an attempt to develop the belief that the solution for the ills of democracy is more democracy. Hopefully I have shown that "more democracy" can work to cure the ills of our current democracy, and how that more democracy might function in contemporary America, but only deeds not words can test what has been outlined here.

Notes

[1]Though he uses much different terminology, and does not make the point in such a general fashion, John Dewey does seem to agree with this basic idea. See his essay in Philip Green, ed. *Democracy* (New Jersey: Humanities Press, 1994).

[2] To see an example of someone concerned with this issue, see Seyla Benhabib's "Toward a Deliberative Model of Democratic Legitimacy" in her *Democracy and Difference* (Princeton University Press: Princeton, N.J., 1996). Her view, which she credits to Jurgen Habermas, and my view on this issue are ultimately very close. I would look to Dewey more than the turgid Habermas as my intellectual ancestor of this point however.

[3] This has been a concern of many since the American Revolution and the formation of the United States under the Constitution. See Pauline Maier's "Introduction" in *The Declaration of Independence and The Constitution of the United States* (New York: Bantam Books, 1998) for an account of how this worry impacted the thought and action of many, most importantly Madison, during the formation of the Constitution. More recently Charles Larmore expressed this worry in response to Jurgen Habermas in an exchange that took place in the *European Journal of Philosophy*, 3:1, 1995. These are just a few examples of an issue that many have, and still do, worry about.

[4] For examples of attempts to alter the nature of debate, see "feminists"—I use scare quotes because the meaning of this term has become increasingly unclear—such as Carol Gilligan and more specifically on this issue Iris Young in "Impartiality and the Civic Public," in Seyla Benhabib and Drucilla Cornell *Feminism and Critique* (Polity Press: London, 1998). Benhabib does an excellent job of arguing against these feminist attempts in her "Toward a Deliberative Model of Democratic Legitimacy" op. cit. I would add only this: many want to emphasize the importance of diversity in our society, even when it comes to the nature of debate in the public sphere—diversity must go all the way down in other words. Though a noble idea, there has got to be some *unity in diversity* otherwise the diversity will degenerate into chaos—a point I made in Chapter 4. And what is this unity? It is the unity provided by democracy and its method of reasoned deliberation.

[5] This way of looking at the private sphere is most famously expressed in the opening pages of John Stuart Mill's *On Liberty*.

[6] A similar story is often spun to excuse the support of slavery by founders such as Thomas Jefferson. We are simply told that his "time" made him incapable of arguing against slavery.

[7] The highlighting is mine of, course.

[8] By themselves, this "non-aggression pact" stands about as much chance of really protecting anyone from the government as the guarantee of Belgium's neutrality protected Belgium from the Germans in both World Wars. Not that anyone is

suggesting they can work on their own , but I want to make a point of this because too much emphasis is placed on these rights over what I believe are much more important rights for protecting individuals.

[9] Our rights as a democratic citizens will remain the most important as they are the most general, and subject to the least change. Government will also be the last "court of appeal" in cases of rights violations in other institutions thereby ensuring the importance of our rights as democratic citizens above all other rights. Nonetheless, it will be rights that are always used to safeguard individuals in the democratic institutions of which they are a part.

[10] See my case at the end of Chapter 3 for increasing public revenue to pay for increased public expense through the legalization of drugs, prostitution and streamlining the military. I don't think we can underestimate the "peace" dividend we will receive not only from altering our military strategy after the Cold War, but from ending the Drug and general Vice War.

[11] Of course some philosophers such as Kant and most Libertatians want to maintain the elevated moral status of individuals. But they are not concerned with practical issues at all and do so largely out of "theoretical" necessity. It is just this concern with theoretical necessity that has left philosophers *talking* a great deal about how individuals are important while individuals are abused all over the world. Philosophers should pay much more attention to what works and less to what theory demands.

APPENDIX

A Political Party Program

1. **Structural and other reforms in politics, the economy and education:**
    a. Government financing of all elections, either through the direct contribution of basic funding, or through matching funds that keep each candidate equal to the one receiving the most private contributions.
    b. Equal distribution of television, radio and other media advertising for all those candidates in any given district who qualify to be on the ballot.
    c. Direct election of all judges, combined with a review process by the legislature and executive of the appropriate jurisdiction.
    d. Convert all legislative bodies, at all levels of government, into participatory democracies where size permits. Where size does not permit, the lower houses of all legislative bodies should be composed of citizens chosen by lot.
    e. Mandatory democratization of corporations. For a corporation to be chartered ultimate power must rest in the hands of every employee "citizen" of the corporation regardless of their rank—on the model of the government.
    f. All employee citizens must have their healthcare paid for by the corporation of which they are an employee citizen.
    g. All employee citizens must have their family's healthcare, daycare and education through college paid for by the corporation of which they are an employee citizen.

h. All employee citizens whose employment is terminated must be offered retraining paid for by the corporation of which they have been an employee citizen.

i. All unions in corporations, schools and government should be disbanded.

j. All anti-trust regulation on corporations should be removed until such time as it may prove to be necessary again.

k. Convert all stock and other varieties of corporate ownership into non-ownership-granting lending agreements modeled on municipal or federal bonds.

l. Abolish all "luxury" inheritance—luxury defined as land, goods or capital had beyond the national average. All luxuries, upon the death of their owner, should be returned to the corporation, partnership or proprietorship from which they were made, or taken by the government.

m. Provide tax breaks and other benefits to corporations enacting the following measures:

   i. *Mandatory 36-hour week composed of four 9-hour, or three 12-hou, days.

   ii. *All employee/citizens should be paid at an hourly rate, ending the distinction between management and labor.

   iii. *Establishment of a "maximum" wage—no one earns more than 20 times the lowest hourly wage.

   iv. *Term limits imposed on the leadership of the corporation.

   v. *Where possible, the division of labor into brain work and brawn work should be minimized. Diversity of tasks for all employee/citizens should be sought.

n. Democratization of schools receiving government money, tax-exempt status or accreditation. Ultimate power should rest in the hands of every university or school "citizen" regardless of their status as student, faculty, administration or parent (parents where appropriate)—on the model of the reformed government

2. **Fundamental social legislation:**

a. Guaranteed government health insurance for all citizens of the United States not covered by other arrangements, i.e. they are not an employee citizen of a corporation or have not negotiated such coverage with the owners of the partnership or proprietorship where they work.

b. Guaranteed government housing for all citizens of the United States not covered by other arrangements.

c. Guaranteed government retraining for all citizens of the United States not covered by other arrangements.

d. Guaranteed government payment for education of any student, at any level, in any school, who demonstrates the ability to obtain entry to that school and who is not covered by other arrangements. Talent is to be defined by each school and all educational institutions that seek no money, tax-exempt status or accreditation from the government should be exempt.

e. Guaranteed government day care for all citizens of the United States not covered by other arrangements.

f. Guaranteed government unemployment insurance.

3. **Financing these government programs and other structural reforms and social legislation where necessary:**

a. Legalize all recreational drugs. A state monopoly should be created responsible for the manufacture, distribution, sale and regulation of these drugs. Once established, this monopoly should be dissolved and handed over to appropriate corporations.

b. Legalize prostitution on the model of the legalization of drugs.

c. Restructure the United States military from its current four-service model, to a unified command. The Army, Navy, Air Force and Marines should be renamed the "United States Defense Forces", and all redundant command and procurement should be eliminated.

d. Replace current federal income tax for private individuals and families by a federal sales tax of 15%. If this, in conjunction with the previous revenue producing measures suggested above, falls short of generating enough revenue to fund the current federal budget as well as other programs suggested here, a flat 10% income tax should be imposed.

INDEX